3⏻

DAY

ALCOHOL
REBOOT

Rethink Your Drinking,
Reset Your Life

KEVIN O'HARA

A UNIQUE, FREE, ONLINE QUIT-ALCOHOL RESOURCE
VISIT: ALCOHOLMASTERY.COM

First edition, 2017

ISBN-13: 978-1542886161

ISBN-10: 1542886163

Contents

INTRODUCTION 2

What is a 30 Day Alcohol Reboot? 2

Who is the 30 Day Alcohol Reboot for? 3

Why Quit Drinking Specifically for 30 Days? 5

Is the 30 Day Alcohol Reboot Healthy? 7

How is the *30 Day Alcohol Reboot* Designed and How
Should You Use It?...9

What Are You Waiting for?...10

SECTION 1: BEFORE 12

MOTIVATION 14

What Are My Reasons to Quit Drinking Alcohol?............14

Apart from Stopping Drinking, What Is Your Goal for the
30 Day Alcohol Reboot?...16

What Are the Benefits of Doing a 30 Day Reboot? 19

What Are the Health Benefits of the *30 Day Alcohol
Reboot*?..20

What Are the Mental Benefits of the *30 Day Alcohol
Reboot*?..27

What Are the Benefits of the *30 Day Alcohol Reboot* in
My Relationships? 33

What Are the Benefits of the *30 Day Alcohol Reboot* in
Your General Life? 38

What Are the Benefits of the *30 Day Alcohol Reboot* on
Your Alcohol Habit?...42

EXPECTATION 46

Is It Tough to Quit for 30 Days? 46

Can You Change a Habit in Just 30 Days? 48

Will Quitting Drinking for 30 Days Reset Your Tolerance?
.... 55

Will Quitting Drinking for 30 Days Reset Your Habit?..... 57

What Are Some of the Obstacles That Might Hamper Your
30 Day Alcohol Reboot?.. 58

How Can Your Fears Feed from Your Expectations?....... 68

How Long Will It Take for the Alcohol to Leave Your
System?... 72

Will You Experience DTs?.. 74

Can You Follow the 30 Day Alcohol Reboot for More Than
30 Days?.. 76

Can You Do This on Your Own?....................................... 77

Will I Get Alcohol Withdrawal?....................................... 80

PREPARATION 84

What Is Preparation? 84

Do You Need a Plan?... 85

How Should You Prepare Your Body and Mind for Your 30
Day Alcohol Reboot?... 88

How Should You Prepare Your Environment for the 30
Day Alcohol Reboot?... 96

How Should You Prepare the People in Your Life for Your
30 Day Alcohol Reboot?.. 99

When Should You Begin Your 30 Day Alcohol Reboot? 105

How to Find an Alcohol Reboot Buddy?.......................108

How Can You Measure Your 30 Day Alcohol Reboot
Progress? 110

Should You Visit Your Doctor before You Quit? 112

Should You Reduce Your Alcohol Consumption before You
Quit? 115

What Should You Do the Night before the Challenge?.117

How Will You Deal with Cravings?.................................121

How Can You Improve Your Chances of a Successful 30
Day Alcohol Reboot? 124

What Should You Replace the Alcohol with? 127

SECTION 2: THE 30 DAY ALCOHOL REBOOT 132

WEEK ONE 134

The 30 Day Alcohol Reboot - Week One 134

Believe That You Can Do It and You Are Halfway There137

Keep It Simple..141

Keep Talking Positive...142

Get Some Leverage on Yourself 146

Affirmations...150

How to Deal with Social Situations in Week One? 153

How to Say "No"!..157

How to Deal with the Criticism or Ostracism? 160

What Are Cravings and How to Deal with Them? 163

Celebrate Your Successes by Rewarding Yourself.........167

Good Nutrition for Long-Term Success 169

WEEK TWO 174

   The 30 Day Alcohol Reboot - Week Two........................ 174

   Going to a Party?.. 176

   Compare Your Alcohol Drinking with Others................ 180

   Are You Still Getting Cravings?..................................... 183

   How to Keep Yourself on Track in Week Two? 186

   What Do You Do If You Drink Again? 190

WEEK THREE... 196

   Half Way There... 196

   How Do You Think about Yourself As a Drinker?.......... 205

   Maintaining Your Motivation in Week Three 213

WEEK FOUR.. 220

   Almost There! 220

   Where Are You Right Now? 223

   Where Are You Going?.. 230

   Tolerance, Addiction, and Normalcy............................ 236

   Congratulations on Reaching Day 30 253

SECTION 3: AFTER 256

   Don't Go Yet... 256

   My Alcohol Story... 259

   After the 30 Day Reboot? 262

   How Can You Protect Yourself 264

   The Under Control Trap 273

   What Are the Benefits of Being Alcohol Free? 283

   Next? 289

Other Books by Kevin O'Hara 291

INTRODUCTION

What is a 30 Day Alcohol Reboot?

The *30 Day Alcohol Reboot* involves complete avoidance of alcohol for a period of 30 days. There are many reasons why removing alcohol from your life for 30 days works very well. We will look at this in much more detail as we progress through the material.

Why Complete Avoidance of Alcohol?

The *30 Day Alcohol Reboot* is aimed at people who habitually drink alcohol, whether that habit is confined to the weekend or spread throughout the week.

Having no alcohol for 30 days breaks the cycle and interrupts the drinking habit. If you just want to take a break from alcohol, 30 days alcohol free will help modify your drinking thinking. It will also lay the foundation for resetting your alcohol drinking habit.

Why Do Many People Find Difficulty with Moderation?

Moderation is very difficult because it relies on a personal interpretation of what moderation involves.

Everyone is different.

For some, moderation might be interpreted as cutting back on the amount of alcohol you consume during the week or only drinking at the weekend.

For others, it might mean reducing the amount you drink in any one session. For example, reducing your intake from four glasses down to two.

As we know, alcohol is a drug, and once you've taken that first drink, you're "under the influence". Once the alcohol is in your system, it lowers your inhibitions, reduces your willpower, and ultimately erodes your resolve to moderate.

So, although you might start out with the best of intentions, as your drinking session develops, and you consume more alcohol, it becomes much more difficult to stick to your plan.

Therefore, instead of the battle of constant moderation, you will see far more consistent and significant results if you can pull yourself through the relatively small amounts of discomfort needed for alcohol avoidance over 30 days.

Who is the 30 Day Alcohol Reboot for?

Taking a Break

The *30 Day Alcohol Reboot* is for anyone who wants to take a break from alcohol.

Do you feel you are drinking too much?

Do you feel too many ill-effects from drinking alcohol?

Maybe you just need a clear head while you get on with something important in of your life?

Perhaps you are just up for a challenge?

Taking a Longer Break

The *30 Day Alcohol Reboot* is also for anyone who wants to quit alcohol permanently but is not sure if they are ready. Maybe you have some fears about making the long-term commitment to being completely without alcohol.

Taking the *30 Day Alcohol Reboot* gives you the freedom to test the waters, to see how you feel after 30 days, and to determine if you are ready.

Change of Scenery

If you are a long-time alcohol drinker, you may not have taken a break from drinking alcohol for a long time. Perhaps you want to know what being alcohol free feels like.

Have you tried to moderate in the past?

Have you tried to stop drinking altogether?

Do you fear you may have a problem, be dependent, or be addicted?

Health and Wealth

You might also have fears about how your alcohol drinking is affecting other areas of your life, other people in your life, your career, your love life, your relationships, or your health.

If your aim is to be more health-conscious, taking the *30 Day Alcohol Reboot* challenge can be a good starting point.

Meetings and Ruts

The *30 Day Alcohol Reboot* is also for people who don't subscribe to the AA model of "alcoholism" or "alcoholic". Most drinkers don't see themselves as "alcoholic", nor do they feel they need to attend regular meetings with other "alcoholics".

Maybe you just feel stuck in a rut. Have been doing the same old same old, every weekend, or every night, and you want to expand your horizons a bit.

No matter, every alcohol drinker can learn something from this material.

Why Quit Drinking Specifically for 30 Days?

Why is this the *30 Day Alcohol Reboot* and not the *60 Day Alcohol Reboot*?

30 days to keep things very simple.

30 days is just a nice round number.

It is four weeks, a month.

It's easy for people to imagine 30 days into their future. It's a lot easier to go into a dark tunnel if you can see the light at the other end.

Just the idea of quitting drinking forever terrifies some people. That notion of never having an alcoholic drink again can often be the difference between doing something about your problem, or bottling it up and putting it off for a some distant day down the road.

In long-term goal setting, it is often more desirable to break big goals down into smaller chunks.

Projecting yourself 30 days into the future is not too difficult a task. Most people can easily plan for 30 days. You have a good idea about what might happen. You should know about any parties that are going to happen, or any stressful days, like filing your tax return, and so on.

Even though 30 days is short enough to be perceived as achievable, any 30 day challenge is still long enough to give you some very concrete results. It's these concrete results that can provide some great insights into your general behavior and the specific habit that you're trying to change, in this case alcohol drinking.

We'll take a further look at this towards the end of this material.

Taking a *30 Day Alcohol Reboot* probably won't change your life, but it will alter your view of how alcohol is interfering with your life.

The challenge will take you through four full work-weeks and four weekends. You will gain a different perspective on how you drink, how much you drink, when you drink, where you drink, and so on.

You'll experience what it feels like to go through your day-to-day life as a non-drinker. You will be able to appreciate how much damage alcohol has been causing in your life and you'll get first-hand experience of the benefits of an alcohol-free life.

30 day challenges allow you to test the waters, to see what works and what doesn't work, and to do so in a time frame that is relatively easy to achieve.

A 30 day challenge also helps you to remember more of that 30 days. Think about it. When you do something different for an extended period of time, it adds a dimension of memorability to it.

Exercise

As a quick exercise, ask yourself what you expect to achieve from your *30 Day Alcohol Reboot.*

Is the 30 Day Alcohol Reboot Healthy?

How will the *30 Day Alcohol Reboot* affect your health and your life? Will it cause you problems or health issues?

The short answer is no.

The human body responds to alcohol as if you've taken a very nasty poison.

Luckily, your body is tooled up to deal with alcohol, in small doses at least.

Any time you give your body a break from this poison, it can only be beneficial to your system in general.

That's not to say that you won't feel discomfort in the process, you probably will. But that discomfort is measly in comparison to the massive favor you are doing for yourself.

Do I Need to Go Visit My Doctor?

I am not a medical doctor. So any advice I give you has to be taken from that standpoint. This is not medical advice.

For the most part, quitting drinking alcohol is not a medical concern. The only medical issues from quitting drinking alcohol are in cases where the person has caused physical damage to themselves over the years through alcohol drinking. This damage is medical and will need to be treated by medical staff.

Most everything else about quitting drinking alcohol is psychological and beyond the scope of your typical medical practitioner. All they can do is refer you to outside programs such as the AA.

Having said that, if you are in any way nervous about how this challenge will affect you, don't be shy about visiting your doctor. There's no point in taking risks or being unduly worried.

If you drink a lot of alcohol daily and you haven't had a break in a while, it might also be wise to consult your doctor. For most people who want to take a break from alcohol, or quit for good, the problem is not that deep. Most drinkers don't drink alcohol every day. Most drinkers don't drink alcohol all day. Although this doesn't mean you are 100% safe, you are less likely to have any problems.

As I say, if in doubt visit your doctor.

If you do go to your doctor, please be honest with them. There's no point in making the trip and paying the fee if you're not going to tell them the truth.

Be honest about how much you drink and how often. That's it. If you're not honest, how can you expect appropriate advice or treatment? What you do with that advice is up to you.

Exercise

Think about how much alcohol you would normally consume in any one session?

How often do you consume alcohol in a week?

How early in the day do you start drinking?

How long is it since you've had a day off?

Do you think you need to visit your doctor?

If in doubt, give your doctor a shout.

How is the *30 Day Alcohol Reboot* Designed and How Should You Use It?

Work Your Way Through

You will get the most benefit from the *30 Day Alcohol Reboot* if you begin at the beginning and work your way through the sections, step-by-step, until you reach the end. Once you've worked your way through the material, feel free to dip in and out whenever you want.

Introduction and the Before Section

The introductory section starts with a run through what a *30 Day Alcohol Reboot* is all about, who it's for, and why 30 days is a good milestone to aim for. Next, we will move on to look at your motivations for the journey, what to expect, and finally how to best prepare yourself.

The During Section - Week 1 through 4

In the "During" section, we get into the *30 Day Alcohol Reboot* proper. The section is split into four chunks, weeks

1 through 4. Each week I'll be giving you a variety of tips and techniques to help you overcome your cravings, deal with any obstacles that might stand in your way, and to generally guide you through each week.

The After Section

To close, in our final section, we will look back over your successful journey. We'll look at you've achieved, what insights you have learned, and how you might use this knowledge in the future.

We'll also look at alcohol from a reality perspective. What does alcohol actually do to your body? How is your life affected by alcohol and our alcohol society? We'll look at moderation and alcohol control. We'll also take a look at the benefits of remaining alcohol free.

What Are You Waiting for?

So that's it for the introduction to the *30 Day Alcohol Reboot*. Now it's time to make your decision.

Is this right for you?

As we have seen, 30 days is not a long time. The time will pass whether you like it or not. Taking on this reboot challenge could be one of the best things you ever do for yourself, for your life, your relationships, your career, your health, and your family.

So what are you waiting for?

Are you ready to move forwards?

SECTION 1: BEFORE

MOTIVATION

What Are My Reasons to Quit Drinking Alcohol?

Motivation is a big factor in anything we do. What motivates you, drives you. It's the difference between the person who sits on the couch all day and the person who's pounding the streets on a cold and frosty morning.

Even though this challenge only encompasses 30 days, most people will still need a compelling reason to undertake it.

What's your compelling reason?

What's Your Why?

Nazi concentration camp survivor, Victor Frankl, in his ground-breaking psychology book *In Man's Search for Meaning*, said, "Those who have a 'why' to live, can bear with almost any 'how'."

He was drawing from his personal experiences in the Nazi death camps during the Second World War. He said that many of the people who survived did so because they had a strong and clear reason to survive.

What is your reason for quitting drinking alcohol?

What do you want to gain out of this process?

How can you put yourself into the position that achieving your goal is absolutely guaranteed?

Where is your motivation?

Motivation comes in many shapes and sizes.

For some people, motivation comes from the family. It could be your spouse, your children, or both.

For others motivation comes from money, career, or personal standing in the community.

Maybe you are insecure about your current health or you have fears about your future health.

Perhaps you are concerned about how your life is fast running out and you're looking for ways to change direction.

Exercise

Take out sheet of paper and write down your own reasons for quitting. If you need to encourage yourself to be a bit more honest, sign your name at the top of the page. Signing your name on any document can help you to live up to your ideals because it reminds you of who you are and who you want to be.

Apart from Stopping Drinking, What Is Your Goal for the *30 Day Alcohol Reboot*?

What is your goal for your *30 Day Alcohol Reboot*? Why are you doing this? Let's take a look at three areas, the physical, the mental, and the emotional.

Pain and Pleasure

Why do we do anything in life? One of the main evolutionary motivations is to move towards pleasure and away from pain. Many people want to quit drinking because they are feeling negative consequences, physically or mentally.

One glass of wine won't do you much physical damage. Even drinking a full bottle of wine won't do you much long-term damage. But if you drink a full bottle of wine every day, the likelihood of long-term physical and mental damage increases.

It's the toxic accumulation that does the damage, not the individual units of alcohol. Unfortunately, that's why it's so easy for us to rationalize our drinking. We only drink in the moment and it's easy to ignore what we drank yesterday or the day before.

Another physical reason for quitting drinking is our overall fitness levels. You might have noticed that the pounds have been piling on, you're not getting as much exercise as you would like, and you want to change all that.

Logical Goals

One logical reason for quitting drinking alcohol could be the realization that putting a toxin into your body might not be a good idea after all.

Maybe you just aren't being as productive as you could be. You see alcohol as being largely to blame and you want to see how your productivity alters without drinking.

You might feel that there is a permanent cloud hanging over your brain, a cloud that's affecting many areas of your life.

Maybe the hangovers are becoming too frequent, lasting that bit longer.

Ultimately, you would like to test the waters for a few weeks, see what life is like without alcohol.

Emotional Goals

There are many different emotional reasons for quitting drinking. Maybe alcohol is affecting your relationships. Maybe your marriage is suffering?

How do you feel alcohol is affecting your role within your family?

Are your relationships with your children suffering?

My Goals

Towards the end of my alcohol drinking life, the consequences of drinking alcohol were affecting me in many different ways.

My hangovers were lasting much longer. I was feeling tired most of the time. I had a persistent and very worrying dull ache in my right side. I thought the worst. I presumed it was liver damage.

My business was not faring too well either. Every time I tried to move my business forward, I felt I was taking one step forward and two or even three steps backwards, ultimately never making any progress.

I think the worst thing for me was a deep concern that I had about the lessons I was passing on to my son, not only about using this drug, but in how I was portraying myself in general.

- My goals in quitting drinking were:

- To be a good role model to my son

- To feel healthier and more capable

- Eliminate the pain in my side

- Eliminate the continuous and lengthening hangovers

- Have more energy

- Increase mental clarity

The fact is, I don't think there was a single area of my life which didn't need some care and attention. Above all, being a good role model to my son meant stopping acting like a drunken idiot, getting a grip on myself, growing up, and taking full responsibility for my life.

The only way I could do that was to quit drinking.

Exercise

Think about your goals for your *30 Day Alcohol Reboot*.

What do you want to achieve?

Where do you want to be after the 30 days?

Who do you want to be?

Do you want to alter people's opinions about you?

Do you want to change your opinions about yourself?

What Are the Benefits of Doing a 30 Day Reboot?

Before we delve deeper into the benefits of completing this challenge, let me say that there are many benefits to quitting alcohol, even for 30 days. This is only a small selection.

Take Notes

To get the most out of this section, think about and write down a list of your own benefits. Take a blank sheet of paper and draw vertical line down the center. On left hand side of the line, write your pros or advantages. On the right hand side, write your cons or disadvantages.

The Benefits of *Drinking* Alcohol

Before we delve into the many benefits of quitting drinking alcohol, let's not cover up the fact that there are benefits to *drinking* alcohol. If there were no benefits to drinking alcohol, nobody would do it. I drank alcohol for over 30 years, I wouldn't like to think that I did it for no reason at all.

The problem is that the benefits of consuming alcohol are far outweighed by the consequences.

The benefits of drinking alcohol are usually superficial, very short-term, and short lived. The consequences of drinking alcohol are usually much more profound, long-term, and sometimes permanent.

As a side note, any benefit that can be derived from putting this poison into your body can easily be replicated and exceeded, by far less harmful and more rewarding benefits.

But there's a catch. These benefits normally take a bit of work to achieve.

The Benefits of Quitting Drinking Alcohol

There is no doubt in my mind, from my own experience and the experiences of the many drinkers that I've worked with over the past few years, that the benefits of stopping drinking far outweigh the benefits of drinking. As we have seen, 30 days is more than enough time to start reaping some of the rewards of being alcohol free.

Over the next couple of sections we'll take some time to examine how quitting drinking alcohol can affect various aspects of your life.

Remember, these are only a few of the benefits that are on offer for anyone who decides to give themselves a break.

What Are the Health Benefits of the *30 Day Alcohol Reboot*?

One of the most obvious and life enhancing benefits of quitting drinking alcohol is an almost certain improvement to your health. How can your health not improve? Stop introducing this awful poisonous substance to any living organism and you are bound to see great improvements.

Where to start?

According to the World Health Organisation, "The harmful use of alcohol is a causal factor in more than 200 disease and injury conditions".

On this basis, anything you can do to stop this stuff getting into your body, or at least reduce the amounts that you consume, the better you are going to feel.

Your Skin

Let's start by looking at the benefits of quitting drinking alcohol for your body's largest organ, your skin.

You probably already know that alcohol is dehydrating. Part of your hangover is caused by dehydration. Alcohol decreases the body's production of anti-diuretic hormone (ADH), used by the body to reabsorb water. With less of this hormone available, your body eliminates more fluid than normal through urination.

This effect varies from person to person, but in general, the less a person weighs, the less alcohol it takes to bring on dehydration.

Chronic dehydration can adversely affect the color and texture of your skin.

Other effects of dehydration include:

- Fatigue

- Constipation

- High blood pressure

- Digestive disorders

- High cholesterol

- Weight gain

- Asthma

- Other allergies

Alcohol also prevents vitamin A from being fully absorbed.

Quitting alcohol, therefore, allows your body to absorb more vitamin A, which gives your skin enhanced vitality.

As a culture, we spend large amounts of money on skincare products to help moisturize our skin and give it a more youthful looking appearance. Yet, we regularly counteract these effects through what we put into our bodies, alcohol being one of the biggest culprits.

The Internal Effects of Alcohol

So, stopping drinking alcohol will help give you a more youthful looking outside appearance.

But what is happening on the inside?

We cannot see our internal organs. For the most part, what's out of sight is out of mind.

It's generally not until we feel physical pain that we take notice of the internal effects of alcohol. Apart from the drunkenness, the giddiness, the light-headedness, and so on, we don't usually think about how our bodies are reacting to the presence of alcohol. At least we try not to!

Increased Energy Levels

I'll say it again, alcohol is a nasty toxin. Your defense system treats this nasty toxin as a foreign substance which needs to be eliminated as soon as possible.

While your body is performing this life-saving service, it is burning nutrients and energy that are needed elsewhere.

When you eliminate the alcohol, these resources can be refocused where they are going to do the most good, where they are supposed to be.

One of the great benefits that you will get from your *30 Day Alcohol Reboot* is an increase in energy levels. Your body's filtration systems can climb down from emergency elimination mode and use its energy stores in more constructive ways.

Sleeping It off

Another area where your body will benefit from quitting drinking alcohol is your sleep.

Despite what you might think, even though alcohol might accelerate the onset of sleep, it does not improve the quality of that sleep.

Alcohol prevents your body from sinking into an essential part of sleep known as rapid eye movement sleep (REM). This is an essential part of your night's rest that you fall into after an hour and a half of being unconscious. REM sleep is where you dream.

REM sleep is also thought to be the area of your night's slumber which offers the most recuperative effects. When you don't get enough of this kind of sleep, your body and mind always suffer the next day.

When I quit drinking alcohol, my dreams were one of the first things to return. The silly thing was, I didn't even realize that they had left. Of course, I was still dreaming while I was drinking, but the dreams were garbled, hazy, and none of them made much sense.

After I quit, I started dreaming the most lucid and lifelike dreams. I had not dreamt in that way since I was young. It was then I knew how much I had been missing out on.

Irshaad Ebrahim, a researcher at the London Sleep Center says, "Alcohol may seem to be helping you to sleep, as it helps induce sleep, but overall it is more disruptive to sleep, particularly in the second half of the night."

A word of warning about quitting drinking alcohol and sleep. If you have been drinking alcohol as a medication to fall asleep, you'll find that it takes a while to get out of that cycle.

It took me almost a month after I quit drinking to get into a normal sleep cycle. I say I got into a normal sleep cycle, but I'm not sure how long it had been since I had slept "normally".

I had been drinking alcohol for over thirty years and I had been using alcohol as a self-administered sleep medication for at least the previous ten of those years. All I'm saying is that if you have problems sleeping without alcohol, don't be too disappointed if you don't sleep well on the first day.

200 Serious Diseases

The *30 Day Alcohol Reboot* also reduces your risk of serious disease. As we've seen at the top of this section, alcohol is responsible for over 200 medical conditions, some of them very serious.

3.5 million People die every year from alcohol-related reasons. That's more than the worldwide deaths from lung cancer and diabetes put together. Quitting drinking alcohol, even if it's only to give yourself a break, will go a long way in reducing some of this risk.

Fast Food and Vegging out

Another health reason for quitting drinking alcohol is that it can often encourage other good health choices.

How many times have you had a few drinks of alcohol and decided that it was a good idea to eat fast food or other unhealthy snacks during the drinking session or afterwards? That unwholesome frame of mind is also likely to follow you into the next day right when you are suffering from a hangover.

Hangover is also a real quick antidote to exercise. Who wants to go sweat it out in the gym when you're already sweating through alcohol poisoning you?

Again, it's not the isolated incident that does the damage, it's the accumulation of these unhealthy choices.

The occasional fast food meal won't do you any harm. Neither will vegging out on your couch, watching reruns of *A Game of Thrones*. Do this every weekend, or every other day, and the damage soon adds up.

Cornerstone Habits

Quitting drinking alcohol can become a cornerstone for a better health and a better life. A cornerstone habit is any habit which leads to a cascade of other changes.

Once you feel the benefits of not having alcohol flooding through your system, you can begin looking for other problem areas in your life, other places where you can make improvements.

Because alcohol causes such powerful internal effects, both physically and mentally, it can hide the symptoms of many other problems. Once the alcohol is gone, many of these problems will now reveal themselves, allowing you to do something about them.

Losing Weight

Will you lose weight with the *30 Day Alcohol Reboot*? That really depends on what else you do. Alcohol is packed full of calories. Removing alcohol for 30 days will reduce the overall calories entering your body.

Of course, if you switch from one high-calorie drink to another, or compensate with high-calorie foods, you won't see any significant weight loss benefits.

On the other hand, if you eliminate the calories from the alcoholic drinking, and don't replace them, you should lose weight.

Give Yourself a Break

At the end of the day, one of the simplest benefits of taking the *30 Day Alcohol Reboot* is that you just give your body a break. This can have tremendous general feel good effects on your physical, mental, and emotional well-being.

Exercise

As an exercise, take a look at the physical aspects of your drinking.

What long-term physical consequences have you been noticing because of your alcohol use?

What do you expect to achieve during this *30 Day Alcohol Reboot* in terms of improving your health?

What Are the Mental Benefits of the *30 Day Alcohol Reboot*?

It's common knowledge that quitting drinking alcohol, even in the short term, has significant physical health benefits, but did you know that quitting drinking is also a proven boost for your mental health?

Stress, Anxiety, Depression

People talk about alcohol helping them to deal with stress or anxiety or depression. Alcohol does none of these things. It merely masks the problem.

The alcohol camouflages the symptoms of the problem. But the underlying problem, or the issues that have caused the problem, are not resolved. In the long-term, alcohol makes these problems much, much worse.

Drinking alcohol to relieve the short-term symptoms of these problems deprives you of your ability to truly get a handle on them.

I'm not saying that relieving the pressure is not a good thing, it is. But there are much cleaner ways of relieving that pressure. Ways that will charge you up, instead of wearing you down.

Undesirable Emotions

Another problem area where many people use alcohol is in eliminating or reducing unwanted emotions.

Again, your emotions are there for a reason. They are your body's way of grabbing your attention.

Emotional repression is never good, regardless of how you achieve it. Using a drug to repress your emotions is even more problematic because you not only have an accumulation of suppressed emotions to deal with, you also then have the physical and mental consequences from ingesting this toxin.

Over time your emotional threshold becomes lower and lower.

What do I mean by this? As I said, human emotions, good or bad, are there for a reason. One way or another, they help us to deal with life.

Good emotions produce a stickiness that makes us want to repeat what gave us that good emotion.

Bad emotions create the opposite effect, repelling us from certain situations, people, thinking, et cetera. Bad emotions create an awareness that something needs to change.

Just with anxiety, stress, or depression, artificially covering up negative emotions means that the underlying causes become much more difficult to identify or deal with.

The consequences of this are that these same bad situations are likely to continue to develop in our lives whilst we never learn the skills for conquering them.

You then get caught up in a vicious circle. Your tolerance for negative emotional situations gets lower and lower. Over time, emotional situations that you used to be able to handle no longer seem manageable. You find ourselves turning to alcohol, or some other emotional suppressant, with more frequency.

It becomes a Catch-22 situation.

Alcohol is often consumed to reduce certain emotions. The minds capacity to think straight is reduced because of the alcohol consumed. This further reduces the ability to handle these emotions when they happen again.

If your default tool for handling your emotions is to drink alcohol, you can see where this can spiral out of control very quickly.

Medicating your emotions is never the answer because you strip out a very valuable and essential part of who you are as a human being. It's like gutting a building from the inside out. Eventually, the outside has no structure to hold it up and everything else collapses.

What's the solution? Simple, quit drinking and find more productive and healthful ways of addressing your emotions.

Even quitting drinking for 30 days will allow for a partial emotional resurgence.

Increased Self-Control

Another mental benefit of going through a *30 Day Alcohol Reboot* is an increase in mental discipline.

Alcohol plays a major part in almost every aspect of our culture, especially when it comes to socializing. It's easy to seek out relaxation by using alcohol or any other drug. Alcohol is culturally acceptable. It's widely used. It's easily accessible. It's cheap.

This cultural and personal acceptance is where a lot of dependency issues first manifest themselves. Alcohol reduces your inhibitions, allowing you to approach social situations with less anxiety and more "Dutch courage".

The reality is that it's the social situations themselves and the people within those social situations, which are the real cause for your relaxation.

It takes time to settle ourselves when we meet up with other people, even friends and family. These are the people we turn to for safety. When we are amongst people we trust, we can relax, have fun, laugh and joke. We are largely accepted and at ease.

Take the alcohol out of the situation and you will still have all the elements of fun, relaxation, calmness, and security. You just might have to take a bit more time to get used to being in the situation without the aid of this pernicious drug.

You might have to give the situation a bit more thought. What are you going to drink? How you going to explain why you're not drinking? Are you comfortable being in the same social situations or would you be more comfortable being somewhere else?

The 30 Day Challenge Accomplishment

The *30 Day Alcohol Reboot* gives you a sense of accomplishment. Undertaking any 30 day challenge is an achievement in and of itself. It's a great experience and can give you confidence in many other areas of your life.

The Blood Brain Barrier

As we saw in the last section, most people try not to think too much about the physical aspects of drinking alcohol, how your body will react in the long-term to this toxin.

There are also similar processes happening within your skull.

Alcohol is one of the few chemicals that can pass through the blood brain barrier.

This is a physiological, highly selective barrier, separating normal blood circulation from extracellular fluid. In allows the distribution of any molecules which are essential to brain function, among other things. In also prevents the entry of potential neurotoxins and infections.

Think about the blood brain barrier as similar to the amniotic sac which helps protect an unborn baby.

It turns out that alcohol is one of the few neurotoxins which can pass directly through this barrier, reaching the neurons directly.

Once the alcohol comes in direct contact with the cells, the cells themselves are altered, resulting in behavior change. This is alteration on a cellular level.

Not only does this have short-term effects, the behavior change of drunkenness, these neurons are also affected in the long-term. Long-term effects of alcohol on the brain include a restructuring of these neural pathways. This is where your addiction lies.

When you stop drinking for any length of time, your brain cells slowly revert back to their original structures. For most people, quitting drinking for a sustained period of time allows a complete recovery.

My Mental Post Alcohol Reformation

When I quit drinking, not only did I gain all that time that I would have otherwise been spending drinking or overcoming the alcohol withdrawal, my brain started to function a whole lot better and so I was able to perceive time in a different way.

Time seems longer. It took less time for me to think things through. My reaction times improved. My mental clarity improved. It became easier to solve problems and to see the relevant solutions.

This is an unbelievable advantage in a competitive world.

Gaining Mental Perspective

One of the biggest mental benefits of the *30 Day Alcohol Reboot* is that you will gain perspective of your habit and your life.

What does this mean?

30 days is not long, but it's enough time for you to begin understanding your habit. Without the mental fog that accompanies regular alcohol use, you will discover clearer perspectives throughout your life. You'll sleep better, think better, and feel physically better.

After 30 days, you should be able to feel that there's more to come, that there is more that you can extract out of this whole process. Hopefully, once the 30 days is over, you might consider continuing for another 30 days or longer.

30 days gives you enough time to start building the habit of not drinking. You might not have trashed your drinking habit entirely, but you will be well on your way. 30 days gives you enough time to make not drinking almost normal, almost automatic.

Exercise

Take a look at the mental aspects of your drinking.

What long-term mental consequences have you been noticing because of your alcohol use?

What do you expect to achieve during this *30 Day Alcohol Reboot* in terms of improving your mentality?

What Are the Benefits of the *30 Day Alcohol Reboot* in My Relationships?

We have looked at how the *30 Day Alcohol Reboot* can help you with the two of the most important aspects of your life, your health and your mental well-being. Another important area is your relationships.

The Personal Drunken Experience

There is a tendency for alcohol drinkers to legitimize alcohol consumption by calling alcohol a beverage instead of what it is, a drug. Our culture accepts alcohol drinking as "normal". In terms of harm caused to the individual and society as a whole, alcohol is the most harmful drug. However much we don't want to face the fact, as alcohol drinkers we are drug users.

Drug use, by its very nature, is a selfish act. The only person who gets the high from the drug, is the person who is using it.

Using drugs for personal enjoyment, to relax, to fit in, or to escape, alters us from the inside out. Nobody else can experience what we are experiencing in that moment while we are drunk. The only way another person can come close to your experience is if they are also drinking and getting drunk. Even then they will have their own version of the drunken experience.

What Determines Our Individual Alcohol Experience?

What makes up our individual alcohol using experiences depends on many different factors:

- What we are drinking

- How much we are drinking

- What we've eaten before we start drinking

- What we eat during our drinking session

- How tired we are

- Our present mood

- And so on

Our drinking experience also depends on some external factors:

- Who we are with

- The atmosphere

- The interaction between the people close by

- If there is music

- What type of music

The Meddled Brain

As we saw in the last section, alcohol is one of the few neurotoxins that gets total access to your brain. Once it's in your brain, alcohol can engineer a direct transforming effect on your neurons.

In other words, this drug tampers with everything you think and do.

Most drinkers insist that they drink for social reasons. The fact is, alcohol turns you inward, instead of outward.

If you don't believe me, try having a conversation with somebody who is drunk while you are sober. It's like talking to someone from a completely different planet. Their mind is drowning in a toxic cocktail, yours isn't. Their thoughts and actions are being influenced by this drug, yours aren't. They are drugged up, you aren't.

Neurotransmitters: Alcohol Interference

Human interaction plays such an expansive part in our lives. Our relationships are important.

Alcohol affects us on two different levels, the conscious and the subconscious.

The physical effects of alcohol last a lot longer than we consciously perceive.

We drink, we get drunk, and we go through the hangover. Once the hangover is over, we feel better and move on with our lives.

However, think about the complexity of the human brain. Think about the intricate processes that have to happen for you to speak, to decide which limb to move, or to add the totals at the end of your weekly budget.

All brain communication relies on the smooth and efficient release of neurotransmitters, a complex blend of cerebral chemicals. Every millisecond, billions of neurons transmit signals to each other. Alcohol gets through the blood brain barrier and interferes with several of these neurotransmitter systems. Your drunkenness is real-time evidence of this.

Neural Lag

The question is, how long does it take before those neurotransmitter systems are back to their original state?

Just because you don't feel physically drunk any more, does this mean that alcohol is not still having an influence? I think that's very optimistic and naive.

While the alcohol is being physically burnt off or metabolized, the alcohol is still present in your brain and these neurotransmitter systems are still in an altered state. This altered state continues even after the physical symptoms have worn off.

It is believed that it's once *all* the alcohol has left your body these systems return to their original state. But, how much lag do you experience? How much time passes between the end of your hangover and a return to 100% brain function?

How My Relationships Improved

Our relationships form the backbone of our lives. For me, the parent/child relationship is one of the most generous roles that you get to play in life.

Being a good parent involves more than just trying to advantageously direct your child's life, making sure that they have as good a life as possible. It's also about being a good example. As a parent, all children learn by following your lead.

One of the conclusions I came to, late in my drinking life, was that my drinking didn't fit into how I saw myself as a parent. How can I teach my son the importance of respecting his body and mind and staying away from drugs, when I was regularly using one of the most harmful drugs?

Children take much more notice of what you do rather than what you say. We are the early templates through which they form the basis of their lives.

So my primary reason for stopping using this drug was to deepen my bond with my son and become a better role model for him. Alcohol didn't just affect my relationship with him while I was drinking, it also had a knock-on effect for days afterwards. If your brain is not functioning 100%, it's impossible to give 100% to any relationship.

I'm pleased to say that I'm much closer to him since my Transformation-Day. As a drinker, I was very selfish. How *I* felt was the priority, not how anyone else felt, even my son.

Your Relationships

Living your life alcohol free will bring you closer to the people you really care about and those who care about you. You will become a better partner, a better parent, and a better friend. This will become crystal clear to you the longer you go without alcohol. You get to spend the time you are saving, from both drinking and the after effects, with the people you love. More importantly, you get more quality time.

Exercise

How has alcohol affected your relationships?

What long-term consequences do you notice?

Do you think the *30 Day Alcohol Reboot* can improve your relationships?

How so?

What Are the Benefits of the *30 Day Alcohol Reboot* in Your General Life?

Already we've touched on some of the major benefits of taking the *30 Day Alcohol Reboot*. I think you'll agree, our health is the most important benefit. Without our health we are screwed.

Time on Our Hands

One area of your life where you will notice an immediate change during your *30 Day Alcohol Reboot* is that you'll have a lot more time on your hands. We live busy lives, time being our most precious commodity. We each are restricted to 24 hours a day, 7 days a week, 365 days in a year.

Your Lifetime by the Day

If I asked you how many days you thought there were in an average human lifetime, what would you say? Most people completely overestimate the figure.

The average lifespan of a human being is about 27,000 days. And that's being generous for some people.

It's really not a lot when you think about it in those terms. When you quit drinking, you not only gain all the time you would have used up while drinking, you also gain the time wasted in thinking about drinking and overcoming the consequences of your drinking.

The day after a drinking session, even if you are not feeling the full-on hangover effects, your mind will still be sufficiently dulled to produce less mental efficiency in general. Less efficiency means it takes more time to do the things you want to do. It takes more time to think and more time to put those thoughts into action. That's if you ever do take the actions.

In the latter years of my drinking, I was losing multiple days to each hangover. I'm not sure I'd like to calculate my day loss through alcohol use.

Another benefit is the money you used to spend on alcohol. The amount you save will obviously depend on how much you are spending on alcohol. But for most people, this will add up to a nice tidy little sum.

I have saved about $15,000 per year since I stopped. That figure includes the direct purchases of alcohol from bars, restaurants, liquor stores, and so on. It also includes meals eaten out, usually junk food, bar snacks, both during and after the drinking session. Hangover day was always junk food day.

So far, it's been four years since T-Day. That adds up to a whopping $60,000.

And that figure doesn't count the opportunity cost, the money I've lost because of how alcohol affected my productivity.

Personal Productivity Boost

Whether you work for yourself or for somebody else, your productivity will increase because of the *30 Day Alcohol Reboot*.

As your brain clears up from the toxin, and no more toxins are being introduced, your brain will start to think more clearly and plan more effectively. This will have knock-on effects in many different areas of your life.

As we saw earlier, drinking doesn't just affect you during the time you are drinking, it also affects you before and after you drink. So the cumulative effect of quitting drinking is to increase your all-round efficiency.

Seeking the Divine

I found that quitting drinking alcohol really gave me a gateway into a spiritual aspect that I thought had long disappeared from my life. Don't get me wrong, I didn't suddenly find religion, but I did begin to think about the more metaphysical aspects of my life.

We've already looked at one of the most detrimental aspects of drinking alcohol, using it to hide from our emotions. Most spiritual awareness comes from taking a trip inside yourself, rather than outside. You can seek guidance from the outside, but most of your spiritual development needs to be undertaken on a very personal inner level. And it's quite an emotional journey.

As you go through this *30 Day Alcohol Reboot*, you can use all that extra brain juice, and the time advantage, to think about your life from a spiritual perspective.

Now, I'm not necessarily talking about spirituality from a religious perspective. I'm not a religious person. It's about trying to understand yourself on a deeper level. That's my form of divinity and spirituality.

Taking Back the Fun

Another benefit I have found from quitting drinking alcohol was having real fun again.

I always felt that alcohol gave me lots of fun and enjoyment. That was one of the excuses I used for not quitting drinking for so many years. How can I give up something which offers me so much fun?

The sad part is, while I was drinking, I was basically living a life of boring repetition. I would go to the same bars, hang out with the same people, talk about the same narrow range of topics, drink the same drinks, eat the same food, and my life in general seemed to be constricting in on itself, like a slowly deflating balloon.

I did have fun. Of course I did. But the moments of actual fun, where I felt alive and really enjoying myself, were few and far between. In fact, the more I drank, the further away from fun and enjoyment I got.

The fact is, I was drinking too much and I knew it. However, up until a month or so before I quit, I never really wanted to quit. I didn't think I needed to quit.

This was despite the fact that my life was getting out of control, spinning away on a vicious downward spiral. That was the reality. And I drank more to try and deflect that reality.

All the while I was slowly building an underlying tension and internal conflict that was strangling the life out of me.

I'll talk about my efforts at moderation later on, suffice to say here that they were a joke. I would always last a minimum amount of time, thinking I was doing well, and eventually I would fall right back into my old routines, into my old drinking patterns.

When I finally quit drinking, I felt like the world had just opened up to me once again. I felt like the possibilities were virtually endless.

A Taste of Your Future

Finally, I think one of the best reasons for taking on the challenge of a *30 Day Alcohol Reboot* is it will give you a peek into what life could be like without alcohol.

Many people have a fear of quitting drinking alcohol because forever is a long time. Saying you will quit forever is a scary concept.

It's a huge commitment to make. It's an intimidating commitment. How will you react? Will you be able to sleep? Will you have cravings and what will you do about those cravings? What will your life be like without alcohol? How will your friends and family react? These are all questions that we are going to cover in the *30 Day Alcohol Reboot*.

30 days is enough time to give you a taste of the action, a taste of the possibilities. And the best thing is that it will give you this taste without the anxiety of thinking about quitting alcohol forever. If you are considering quitting alcohol for good, this might just be the start that you need.

Exercise

Think about how alcohol affects your life in terms of time, money, and productivity?

How has alcohol affected your spirituality?

Do you really have fun while you drink?

Or are you just going through the motions, leading a boring existence?

What Are the Benefits of the *30 Day Alcohol Reboot* on Your Alcohol Habit?

As we saw in the last section, taking the *30 Day Alcohol Reboot* gives you a taste of what to expect if you were to quit drinking alcohol in the long-term. 30 days without alcohol is enough time for you to see the pros and cons first-hand.

In terms of your drinking habit, even if you return to drinking after the challenge, you can still take a few positives.

Reducing Tolerance

The first positive is that 30 days is enough time to reduce your tolerance to alcohol.

Alcohol tolerance builds up over years. Each time you take a drink, your physical tolerance increases ever so slightly. The longer you drink alcohol, the more alcohol you drink, the more alcohol you need to drink.

Once you go back to drinking after the 30 days, you will notice a reduction in the amount of alcohol that you need.

Having said that, this reduction will only be short lived.

Because our habits are so deeply ingrained, it won't take long before your previous levels of tolerance return.

But this will give you a glimpse into an aspect of your habit that you might not have previously thought about. It allows you to see just how much resistance to the effects of alcohol that you have developed over time.

We'll revisit this topic at a later stage.

Self-Confidence

A second positive is that going through any 30 day challenge, especially one dealing with a habit on this level, will increase your confidence in your abilities that you can break down any bad habit and replace it with something better.

Constructing or deconstructing habits is a skill. The skills you learn in tackling one habit can be used for tackling any other habit in your life.

Drinking Thinking

The third positive is that 30 days is enough time to stop you from thinking about drinking for a while.

Be honest and ask yourself how often you actually think about drinking?

You don't have to be consciously thinking about drinking to be actually thinking about drinking.

There's thinking about it when you buy it, when you drink it, and when have to suffer through the inevitable consequences of that consumption, the hangover.

Then you have the inevitable thinking about how many beers you've got left in the fridge, how much wine is left, is it enough to last the night, how you drank too much the night before, how much of the night you can remember, is it time for a hair of the dog, when will you be able to you drink again, can you control your drinking, can you moderate it, why are you so hungover, and so on.

When you don't drink alcohol, even for only 30 days, you don't have to ask these questions. It's difficult to understand how liberating this is until you do it.

Triggers, Behaviours, Habits

And finally, once you go through a whole month without drinking alcohol, you will experience and understand what life is like without alcohol, you learn about your alcohol habit, and a whole lot about yourself into the bargain.

You will learn about what triggers spark off your drinking, what rewards you get from drinking, and how bad the consequences are. Sometimes it's only when you step outside of the situation that you truly begin to understand it. There's nothing like being without something, even if it's the negative consequences, to give you a deeper understanding.

Exercise

Take a look at your own tolerance and self-confidence levels. How have these been affected over your drinking lifetime, especially the last few years?

How much time do you spend thinking about drinking?

Be honest with yourself. Remember that not all drinking thinking is conscious. Most of it happens just below the surface. This is the way with any habit. We'll be looking more at triggers a bit later on.

EXPECTATION

Is It Tough to Quit for 30 Days?

Four weeks really does pass very quickly. Four weeks and four weekends. Having said that, the toughest part of any alcohol quit is the first month.

How you think about the reboot will affect how you react. If you think four weeks is a long time, if you think you cannot quit alcohol for four weeks, then the likelihood is you will find it a lot tougher. The difficulty of any task is always measured inside the mind. Your perception can alter the difficulty one way or another.

In reality, to quit drinking successfully, you just don't drink it. Not doing something is really not that difficult, is it? You just don't do it.

Simplicity

Quitting alcohol for four weeks is very simple, you do not put any alcohol into your mouth for a month - simple!

Most obstacles or problems will be caused by you. Even if you don't cause them, you certainly have control over how you respond to them.

Take things slowly, moment by moment, day by day. Keep it as simple as possible. And keep your mind focused on your end goal.

Up for the Challenge?

Are you up for the challenge? Can you survive one month without alcohol?

Let's take a look at this from a different perspective. Let's say that you're not doing a challenge. Let's say that you have done something naughty, broken the law, and you've been locked up in a prison cell for 30 days.

During that 30 day stretch, you have absolutely no access to alcohol. Do you think you would have any problems quitting then? Could you go through 30 days without alcohol then? Of course you could! You would have no choice but to quit.

Take another scenario. Someone has offered you $1 million to quit drinking for 30 days. Could you do it then? Would you even think twice about not drinking for 30 days? Of course you wouldn't.

If you had a regular checkup with your doctor and he told you that your liver was going to explode if you didn't stop drinking for 30 days, again you'd have no problems quitting.

This just goes to prove that *your* level of fortitude is set by *your* brain. Put yourself in the right frame of mind, set your mind up right, and you can achieve anything.

Exercise

The ease or difficulty of quitting drinking alcohol will boil down to your frame of mind, the situations you put yourself in, the people you associate with, and so on.

Imagine that quitting drinking alcohol for 30 days is an absolute breeze.

How would you need to set up your environment?

Which people would you want to near you, who would you want to avoid?

Now think about the situations, environments, or people that would make it very difficult for you to quit drinking alcohol for a week, never mind 30 days.

Can you see how much control you have over your 30 day challenge?

Can You Change a Habit in Just 30 Days?

Because you are taking this course, you are a habitual drinker on one level or another (unless you are trying to help someone else). You might not like to hear that, but it's more than likely true.

However, habitual drinking is not as scary as it might sound. Habitual drinking is just a habit. It might be a habit which is causing you some problems, some difficulties. But it's a habit nonetheless.

Understanding Your Habit

We can learn a lot about our habits by understanding when we do them and when we don't do them. More appropriately, we can learn a lot about our habits by understanding why we don't do them, when we don't do them.

When Do You Drink?

Think about how and when you consume alcohol. When do you normally drink? At the weekends? After meals? With meals?

For me, I normally drank alcohol after I finished work in the evening. I'd also have one or two days over the weekend where I would drink a lot.

When Do You Not Drink?

When do you not drink alcohol? Most people will have days during the week where they don't drink, or at least they don't drink too much. Maybe you don't drink on a Sunday, not on a work night, not on a Monday or Wednesday, and so on.

I would normally choose a weekday not to drink or only have a couple of drinks. Weekends were my time for relaxation. Relaxation for me invariably involved some kind of drinking. So weekends were my time for drinking.

Why Do You Not Drink?

As I said, understanding your habits means you need to understand when you do the habit, when you don't do the habit, and why you don't do it. So why do you not drink?

For me, I didn't drink every day because of the way the after-effects of alcohol affected my life. I also thought it was a good idea to give my body regular breaks from drinking.

Another reason is because I didn't want to think of myself as an alcoholic. If I didn't drink every day, it meant I wasn't an alcoholic.

I tried not to drink on a Sunday because I had work the next day. There was no real rhyme or reason to this. I would often drink two or three days during the week, even though I also had work the next day. But, I generally would not go too overboard with alcohol on a work night.

The Morality of Habits

We perform hundreds of habits every single day. Without habits, we would find it very difficult to get through life.

Some habits are good and others not so good. Habits don't exactly have a morality compass. The habit works in exactly the same way if it's good habit or a bad habit. It's our interpretation of the habit which is either good or bad.

Going to the gym on a regular basis or getting out for regular walks is a good habit to get into. Smoking cigarettes, eating four cheese pizzas every night, or drinking alcohol, are not so good habits.

They're bad habits, not because of the habit itself, but because of the consequences of the habitual behavior. Lung cancer is a possible consequence of a smoking habit. Obesity is a possible consequence for eating four cheese pizzas. And cirrhosis of the liver is one possible consequence for drinking alcohol.

Is 30 Days Enough For Habit Change?

So, the question is can you change a habit in just 30 days? Habit is made up of many different actions, or behaviors. You can certainly alter many of the behaviors which make up a habit within 30 days, but most habits will take a lot longer to be completely eliminated.

This is especially true when you combine the power of the habit with an addictive drug like alcohol.

It only takes a couple of days before every trace of alcohol has disappeared from your body. The problem is that those cellular alterations that happen in your brain, every time the alcohol passes the blood brain barrier, start to have a long-term effect.

The neural pathways in your brain start to alter to accommodate the new habit. This is known as neuroplasticity. Neuroplasticity is how your brain changes according to what you do regularly and consistently. Again, this brain plasticity doesn't take into account good or bad, it only takes into account how often the behavior is repeated.

The same principles apply regardless of whether you are creating new habits and breaking old habits.

Replacing the Old with the New

Another point about habit change is it's very difficult to not do something, or at least to break the habit of not doing something, unless you are replacing the old habit with the new.

Think about quitting smoking and replacing the smoking with a quit smoking aid.

You get the urge to have a cigarette. But instead of picking up packet of cigarettes and smoking one, you now take some nicotine chewing gum or use an e-cigarette. Chewing on nicotine chewing gum or puffing on the e-cigarette become the active behavior.

This is why active methods of quitting smoking are a lot more effective than passive methods of quitting, such as a quit smoking patch.

The quit smoking patch is applied once a day and forgotten, at least until you change the patch next day.

This form of quitting smoking doesn't instil any new behaviors. If you don't have a new behavior you can't form a new habit. The daily habit of changing the smoking patch is attempting to replicate the hourly, or half hourly habit of smoking. It just doesn't work as well.

Even though you are getting a hit of nicotine, half of the habit of smoking is in the ritual... Taking out the cigarette, putting it into your mouth, lighting it, and smoking it until it's finished.

Is the Replacement Habit Healthy?

But, there's another problem. Even if you successfully quit smoking, the cigarette smoking habit is supplanted by the habit of chewing gum or smoking an e-cigarette.

If you know any smokers who have quit using these techniques, you'll know that they can easily fall into the trap of replacing smoking cigarettes with smoking e-cigarettes.

That's why in the long run, quitting cold turkey and replacing the habit with something healthier, is much more effective.

The disadvantage of this is that the person will feel some initial discomfort associated with breaking the old habit and establishing the new behavior. But once the new behavior has stabilized, it becomes habitual and it's very difficult to go back.

Dormant Old Habits

In fact, the old habit never really disappears. The new habit just takes over the neural pathways that the old habit once used.

How long does that take?

It depends on many different factors. It depends on the person, the habit, the individual circumstances, and so on.

In a 2009 study, conducted by researchers from University College London, 96 people's habits were tested over a period of 12 weeks. Over those three months, it was found that, depending on the habit, it took anywhere from 18 to 254 days for a new habit to stick. This was an average of 66 days.

Quickly Showing Habits the Door

Of course, there's always the possibility that you can break the desire of an old habit very quickly. I did.

My motivation for quitting drinking was very strong. As I have said, I was completely focused on the bad influence that I was having over my son. Something very simple happened which caused me to question my whole drinking life and how that drinking life was affecting him.

The conclusions I came to completely altered the way I thought about my habit and that made it possible for me to stop very quickly.

What's Your Incentive?

As we saw earlier, if you're locked up in a prison cell without access to alcohol, your habit will break very quickly. If you are given a big enough incentive to stop drinking, such as being offered a huge amount of money, you will have a lot less difficulty kicking the habit.

During the Vietnam War, many US soldiers who were stationed abroad were thought to be completely addicted to heroin. It was a drug that was readily available and many Marines willingly used it in an attempt to escape the worst of the atrocities they were going through.

The US government thought that there was going to be a massive problem once the war ended, with thousands of soldiers returning as heroin addicts.

It turns out that this was far from the truth.

Once the soldiers returned to the United States, and were away from the barbarity, only a few of them remained addicted to heroin. Most of them cut the habit quickly and easily.

This proves that addiction is not just physiological. It is largely psychologically driven, habit driven, and driven by circumstances. Once the psychological circumstances change, the habit is no longer required.

Dynamic Habits

So in answer to the question we started out with, if you don't have an alcoholic drink within the 30 days, by the end of that 30 days, you will notice significant changes. However, your overall drinking habit will still be lurking in the background.

Exercise

As a quick exercise, look at all the habits that you do on a regular basis, habits that you might not even think about. All day long, your life is filled with habitual behaviors, large and small. I bet you don't have to think about brushing your teeth in the morning, making that first cup of coffee, or even driving to work.

This essential part of our human make up allows us to be the fantastically diverse creatures that we are.

Now look at your alcohol use as a habit.

Think about how it started, how it has progressed through the years, and how much of your alcohol drinking behavior happens below the surface, without you even thinking about it.

Will Quitting Drinking for 30 Days Reset Your Tolerance?

How does quitting alcohol for 30 days affect your levels of tolerance?

Quitting drinking for 30 days will reduce your alcohol tolerance, but won't reset it. Resetting your alcohol tolerance would require your body to go back to the tolerance levels before you started drinking. This would be zero, or virtually zero, since the human body produces very small amounts of alcohol through digestion.

Unless you're only very mild drinker, this is just not possible within such a short period of time.

Habit Endurance

As we touched on in the last section, your alcohol drinking habit will not fully disappear.

This is not because it's an alcohol habit. And it certainly doesn't make you an alcoholic. The same principles apply to all habits. There's just a difference in degree.

Your brain continues to maintain a skeleton structure of the habit, if you like. It's a kind of watered-down backup. The triggers may change, the behavior definitely changes, and the rewards may change, but the underlying connections in your neural pathways remain, but they lose most of their strength over time

After a few months of not drinking, the power of your old habit will hardly be noticed.

The old habitual neural pathways can only re-establish themselves if the focus of the behavior returns to alcohol. In other words, if you don't start drinking again, there's no way that those neural pathways can reignite.

Tapering Tolerance

Going through the 30 Day Alcohol Reboot will lower your tolerance level. After the challenge, if you decide to start drinking again, it will take a lot less alcohol to give you the same buzz you were at before.

But there's a caveat.

Once you do start drinking again, your body will quickly reset itself back to the same previous tolerance levels. It will be as if you never stopped drinking.

Exercise

How has your tolerance increased over time?

Think about when you first started drinking. How much could you drink back then?

How much can you drink now?

This is tolerance in action.

Will Quitting Drinking for 30 Days Reset Your Habit?

Quick answer, no!

As we have seen before, it will take an average of 66 days to eliminate any habit. We've also seen that this figure depends on the person, the habit, and so on.

It's also fair to say that a drinking habit, or any habit involving a drug, will take longer to eliminate. 30 days is certainly not enough to reset your alcohol habit, but it is enough to get a handle on it. In other words, 30 days is enough time for you to gather some experience of what it's like not to drink alcohol.

New Experiences

In those 30 days, you will experience four full weeks including four full weekends. This is more than enough time for you to experiment with new different ways to relax, have fun, sleep, and so on.

After the 30 days has ended, the bones of your new habit should be emerging. And even though this new habit won't be rock solid just yet, you'll be well on your way.

Rituals, Routines, and Behaviors

Habits are made up of individual actions which form rituals, routines, and behaviors. After 30 days, all the actions, behaviors, and routines, which are attached to your new habits, will have gained some momentum.

You will have pushed past the initial period of habit gravity, which requires a lot of willpower, and you should be finding it a lot the easier to deal with not drinking.

The point is that although the *30 Day Alcohol Reboot* won't completely reset your habit, 30 days is enough time to break up some of the most binding actions, behaviors, and routines that make up that habit. With these broken down, it gets a lot easier moving forwards.

Exercise

Start thinking about which habits you would like to replace. For instance, new ways of relaxing. How can you relax without alcohol?

What Are Some of the Obstacles That Might Hamper Your 30 Day Alcohol Reboot?

As with any challenge in life, the *30 Day Alcohol Reboot* will throw some obstacles in your path. Some of these obstacles will come from things that are outside of your control, but most of them are self-made.

I'm not very comfortable writing a list of obstacles to your challenge.

Why?

Because I don't want to plant the idea of an obstacle in your mind. Once an idea takes hold, it can become an expectation, and that expectation then has a greater chance of creating an obstacle where there wasn't one before.

As I said, most obstacles are self-made. Just keep this in mind as we go through this material.

These obstacles are in no particular order. Also, the obstacles that might affect me, might not necessarily affect you, at least not in the same way or with the same intensity.

1. Mentality

The biggest obstacle that is ever likely to stand in the path is yourself. End of story. Everything else is minor.

If you have full control over your mind and your thoughts, life becomes what you create.

As I pointed out earlier, quitting drinking alcohol is very simple, quitting drinking alcohol = don't drink the stuff. The mental obstacle comes about when there is a conflict in this basic equation.

You already understand that to be successful in quitting drinking, you don't drink the alcohol. It's obvious, right!

The problem is that there is a massive difference between not drinking and not wanting to drink.

Most people don't start this journey by eliminating the want. As long as you want to drink alcohol, there will be a conflict. The only way to eliminate this conflict is to put yourself in a position where you cannot drink alcohol.

As we've seen previously, locking yourself up in a prison cell for 30 days will do the trick. It's extremely difficult to continue drinking alcohol in this environment. However, this is not something that most people would be prepared to do.

You might not want to get yourself locked up for 30 days, but there are many other, less forbidding ways to get leverage on yourself, ways of making it very difficult for you to drink.

We'll talk about this later.

2. Sleeping

Alcohol is a self-medication which many people used to fall asleep at night.

I was one of them. I didn't think of it as self-medication, but I nearly always fell asleep under the influence. It became a part of my habitual behavior. And it was difficult to fall asleep without it.

This is one of the most common obstacles to quitting alcohol.

Sleep is a fundamental need. The scenario that a lot of people find themselves facing when they quit drinking is lying in bed in the middle of the night, wide-awake, knowing that there is a simple remedy available, just take a few drinks.

Multiply sleeplessness over a few days, and it's easy to see how the decision to return to drinking can get very tempting.

3. FOMO

FOMO means Fear Of Missing Out. It's another common obstacle to quitting drinking, a common fear.

During the first few days of my new journey, I spent a lot of time worrying about what might happen. One of the areas I thought a lot about was how other people would react to me now that I didn't drink, how I would react in social situations, and if I would still be able to have fun.

This is typical FOMO thinking and it's a natural symptom of quitting drinking.

We fear losing what we know and understand.

As drinkers, we know how to socialize with alcohol. It's in socialising without alcohol that we find difficulty.

We've all been in social situations without alcohol at one stage or another during our drinking lives. In some situations you feel comfortable, in others you don't. It's the human condition. We remember the pain more than the pleasure. FOMO is a trick of the mind.

4. Cravings

Again, cravings are mind over matter.

Don't get me wrong, cravings are very real and they do have a physical element. But most cravings are psychologically based. They are in the head. That's why you can feel cravings in some situations and not in others. With some people and not with others.

And you can certainly alter how you react to a craving. You feel a craving, you change your frame of reference, and the craving will disappear.

Cravings convince us to take the path of least resistance, the easy way out. When you submit to your cravings, you get an instant gratification hit which feels good.

And therein lies the key to overcoming all your cravings.

Once you can push yourself past that initial urge for instant gratification, the craving disappears.

How?

Mind over matter.

I'll be showing you plenty of simple tricks that you can use to push past this particular obstacle.

5. Forgetting You Don't Drink

This is a fairly minor obstacle but it's something that can hit you frequently and unexpectedly in the early days.

Think about this scenario.

You haven't used any alcohol in a few days. Then you're invited out for a meal and you meet up at a nice restaurant with your friends.

You greet your friends, smile, take off your coat, and you sit down at the table as you would have done a hundred times before.

The waiter comes to your table and asks you what you would like to drink.

Your subconscious habitual brain will try to jumpstart your old habit. You find yourself almost forgetting that you don't drink any more.

You are just about to order what you would have ordered only a week before, a glass of wine, small beer, etc. It's on the tip of your tongue.

It's an easy one to overcome. You are just not used to asking for a non-alcoholic drink. Even if you blurt out an order for a beer, simply realize your mistake, laugh it off, and reorder.

6. Other People's Reactions

When you first tell other people that you're going to quit drinking, it can seem to them that you are making a "bizarre" decision.

Four years after I quit drinking and I still get strange glances when I order a water while everyone else is ordering wine. I'm quite happy being the odd one out when it comes to my health.

Getting this type of weird reaction from people is quite common and understandable. If these are your regular friends or family, they have their own expectations about how a normal evening with you is going to pan out.

This might include everyone drinking, everyone eating, everyone having fun, and ultimately everyone having a good time.

If you alter one of these things, changing the alcohol, the food, or the having fun part, it messes around with the other person's expectations, and they have an upsetting moment.

So what?

Who cares what they think about what you're doing.

You're doing this for yourself, not for other people.

Don't be swayed by social pressure.

7. Relaxation

Another roadblock associated with quitting drinking can be found when people associate alcohol with relaxation.

Again, it's all in the head.

You relax because of the relaxing surroundings, the comfy chair, the soft lighting, and so on. You relax because of the people you are with. Alcohol drinking is just one small element.

There are many more practical, healthy, and effective ways of relaxing than putting this awful poison in your body.

Another aspect of this is stepping outside of your comfort zone.

We automatically create habits in our lives for the things that we do over and over again. This means that we don't have to consciously think about them every time we do them, we just automatically go from one aspect of the habit sequence to another, from the trigger, to the behavior, to the final reward.

Breaking habits, no matter how small they are, pushes us out of our comfort zones. Being outside our comfort zones means we are not relaxed.

Because people equate drinking alcohol with relaxation, it's very easy to think that it's the lack of alcohol that is preventing the relaxation.

It's not.

It's the interruption of the habit.

Fortunately, you get used to it. The brain moves on. You need to move on. You have to accept the minimal discomfort and continue to forge ahead.

8. Social Anxiety

We've already looked at how other people's reactions can be a roadblock to your 30 Day Alcohol Reboot.

Another obstacle can be *your* reactions.

When we drink alcohol, our inhibitions lower, we become more talkative, a bit louder, and we are generally willing to say and do things that we wouldn't do while we were sober.

To a certain degree, alcohol gives us an ability to forget about what we're saying, how we look, or what we're doing.

In the beginning, being without alcohol in social situations can cause a bit of social anxiety.

Again, most anxiety is caused by a skills deficit.

You have been using alcohol as a tool to help reduce this social anxiety and you don't have that option any more.

You need to learn a new skill. You need to learn new ways to relax and to relieve that social anxiety.

The best way of learning how to do this is to just do it. Push yourself through the bit of discomfort that you will feel in the beginning and you'll find that, just as in your relaxation, it's the company and the surroundings that reduce your social anxiety, not the alcohol.

Don't worry if you think you're talking too much or not enough. Don't worry if this was or was not the right thing to say, if you're laughing too loud, or if your shoes match your pants.

None of this really matters.

Again, later we'll go through a few techniques to help you through this type of situation.

9. The Environment

One of the largest areas for sparking off alcohol triggers and putting obstacles in your way is your environment.

There are two types of environment, your personal environment and the wider environment.

Your personal environment is very controllable. This is your home, your office, or any other area in your life where you can control what goes.

For instance in your home, you control what alcohol or alcohol reminders or paraphernalia are present.

Your wider environment is a bit less controllable.

For instance, you can't prevent all the advertising billboards on your way to work. You can't shut down all the pubs or clear out all the alcohol aisles in your local supermarket.

But you still have a lot of personal control in how much influence these things have over your mind. And ultimately you can avoid many of them altogether.

10. People

In habit change, you have three areas of personal control. From greatest to least control, you have your mind, then the environment, and finally other human beings.

It's in this final area where you have the least amount of control. But it's also the area where you stand to gain the most amount of support.

Let's face it, people can be a massive spanner in the works, to put it nicely. Everyone else has their own agendas, their own way of doing things, and their own way of seeing their world.

As we've seen earlier, when you try to change, you at least put a ripple in the ideas of normality for those nearest and dearest to you. They have their expectations about how things are supposed to go.

When you change part of your lifestyle, it means that they also have to change a part of their lifestyle to accommodate you and your new way of doing things.

However, it's essential that you get people on your side, especially those who are close to you. Unfortunately, not everyone is going to want to be on your side.

But that's just life!

For those who are willing to be on your side, these people can really make the difference between success and failure.

Only *Potential* Obstacles

These are just some of the general obstacles that can potentially stand in your way.

As we've seen, the biggest obstacle is your own mind. Most of the obstacles we create because of the way we think.

Any other obstacle, anything happening outside of you, can still be controlled through your thinking.

Exercise

Take a look at your own life and see where some of these obstacles might show up. Can you think of any obstacles that are not presented here, obstacles that might be personal to you?

Take a sheet of paper and write out 10 different obstacles.

Now, see if you can come up with 10 different solutions.

As I have said, the first place you should look for any solution to your obstacles is in the way you are thinking, how you are framing things in your mind. If you can change the frame through which you see something, you change the perception of that problem, and therefore the problem itself.

How Can Your Fears Feed from Your Expectations?

We saw earlier that habits were essentially thoughts, actions, or behaviors which are repeated over and over again.

The Automated Driver

Think about driving a car. The first time you get into a car and drive it, you don't really know what you're doing or what to expect. The more you drive, the more experience you gain, the more confidence you get.

Eventually after driving the car over hundreds or thousands of hours, you can literally drive while doing something else: having a conversation, listening to the radio, and your awareness is only partially on the car or the road.

Automated Emotions

Exactly the same thing occurs with our emotions. Just as a particular action or behavior will become habitual, if it is repeated over and over again, the same will happen with your emotions.

An emotional habit will develop over time, and run unconsciously, unless you do something about it, and permanently in the background.

Think about the operating system of your computer. You don't see it, but you know it's there, running in the background, dictating how other programs on the computer are going to work.

Captured at Birth

The foundations of our alcohol drinking behavior have been laid down from the moment that we are born. We are sponges for the behaviors that we see around us.

If the people we grow up with are drinkers, this can easily become a normal part of our own behavioral culture and thinking.

The same thing happens with our fears.

When we are toddlers, we don't think in rational thoughts. We have a very narrow worldview, only partially perceiving what's going on. That narrow worldview becomes the basis for our beliefs.

Beliefs and Facts

A belief is not the same as a fact. A fact is a universal statement which is known to be true. A belief, on the other hand is a personal statement or idea which has been evaluated as true by that individual person.

If you put your hand into a fire and hold it there, you *will* burn your skin. That is a fact.

A belief can be anything and is only really sustained by that person. If the person doesn't exist, neither does the belief.

Early Fears

Many of our fears emanate from those early years, from those early beliefs.

If we are scared by those early beliefs, it can create a wound and a long-term fear.

There's nothing wrong with fear. Fear is the minds way of protecting us from harm. It's part of our security system. Fear is there to ensure that we don't continuously get hurt by the same things.

The problem with these early beliefs or fears is that eventually, over time, they become our reality. They become *our* truth.

Different Fears for Different Folks

As we saw earlier, we have emotional habits that have been developing since the day we were born. They run subconsciously and permanently in the background and influence everything we do.

What fears do you have about quitting drinking alcohol? The answer to this will be very different for everyone.

Some people fear how they will react in social situations without alcohol. Others will fear not getting enough sleep, feeling terrible cravings, or just missing out on the "good times".

Wreaking Havoc on Ourselves

Fear is self-inflicted. It doesn't exist in the real world.

Mark Twain said, "Do the thing you fear most and the death of fear is certain". Why is this true? Because fear is just an illusion of the mind.

Once you face your fears, and you realize that those fears are completely unfounded, you can never be afraid of that thing again.

The Expectation of Fear

Most fears about quitting drinking alcohol emanate from our expectations. We don't fear what will happen, only what might happen, or more pertinently, what we expect will happen.

Fear is another behavior which can easily form into a habit. And it's another habit which grinds away beneath the surface. The more you think about the fear, the more you feed the fear.

When something new happens in our lives, the automatic programming kicks in, and we find ourselves thinking about all the things that can go wrong.

One of the simplest ways of dealing with fear of change is to say to yourself, "I can do this and I will do this".

Then move forwards and take action. Action is the only antidote to fear. You have to take direct action towards the thing that you fear.

Exercise

Where are your personal fears?

What do you fear about quitting drinking alcohol?

Take a sheet of paper and make a list of five fears you have about quitting drinking. Then, try to find five alternative ways of framing those fears in your head.

How Long Will It Take for the Alcohol to Leave Your System?

Standard Drinks and Units of Alcohol

There is a lot of confusion about what comprises a standard drink. In the US, for instance, a standard drink contains 14 g of alcohol. In the UK, a standard drink contains 8 g of alcohol. The UK standard drink is also known as a unit.

When we talk about alcohol in units, one unit equals 10ml or 8g of pure alcohol.

Alcohol Metabolic Rate

On average, it takes the human body one hour to metabolize one unit (8g) of alcohol.

This metabolic rate depends on many factors including whether the drinker is male or female, the drinker's age, body weight, how much food they've consumed, and any medication that they might have taken.

Alcohol metabolic rate also depends on how long the person has been drinking. As we've seen, the human body develops a tolerance to alcohol over time.

Because alcohol is a toxin, it's likely to cause physical damage after long-term use. The physical damage to your metabolic organs, primarily your liver, can reduce the capacity of your body to deal with alcohol or any other toxin. This reduces the quantity of alcohol that your liver can metabolize over a set period of time.

This is another reason why your body's tolerance for alcohol will reduce with age.

Human Metabolic Evolution

Humans have evolved the capacity to metabolize small quantities of alcohol.

Your body naturally produces small amounts alcohol through its digestive processes. If your digestive system had no way of metabolizing these alcohols, they would build up in your system and become toxic, ending your life.

As you can imagine, the large amounts of alcohol that we put into our body quickly overwhelm our body's capacity to metabolize that alcohol. This contributes to the dangerous levels of toxicity. And that overload will result in all kinds of internal problems.

Let's be clear about the quantities of natural alcohol that your body produces. In any 24-hour period, your digestive processes will produce roughly 3g of alcohol. We might also consume another gram or two if we eat *a lot* of overripe fruit. But this is well within your body's alcohol metabolic capacity, which again is about 8g of alcohol per hour.

Also, this alcohol is introduced to your body over a long period of time. Your body doesn't need to shut down other essential processes in order to deal with this slow level of alcohol.

My Alcohol Consumption and Short Metabolic Capacity

When I was drinking, I could easily consume three pints of Guinness in an hour.

A standard pint of Guinness contains 2.3 units of alcohol.

2.3 (units per pint) x 8 (grams per unit) = 18.4 (grams per pint)

18.4 (grams per pint) x 3 (pints per hour) = 55.2 (total grams of alcohol per hour)

That's almost 7 times the amount of alcohol that my body could safely metabolize in any single hour.

Often, I could drink 15 or 20 pints of Guinness in one sitting. That amount of alcohol would take about 46 hours just to metabolize. And that's banking on the fact that my body had enough stores of the crucial enzymes it needed to continue the metabolic process.

All the while, there's a lot of unmetabolized alcohol floating around my system, doing a lot of damage.

We'll take a closer look at alcohol metabolism a bit later.

Exercise

Find out what your local standard alcoholic drink is.

How many grams per alcohol are contained in that standard drink?

How much alcohol would you normally drink in an hour?

Make a simple calculation of how much alcohol you are drinking in grams. How does this stack up to your liver's ability to metabolize this alcohol?

Will You Experience DTs?

Most people who quit drinking alcohol will never experience delirium tremens or DTs.

DTs normally occur a couple of days after you have quit and might include some shaking, irregular heartbeat, sweating, and shivering. You may also see things or hear things that aren't really there.

DTs normally happen when there has been a very high level of alcohol consumption in the month prior to stopping.

Prevention of DTs requires medication.

Again, only a very small minority of people who quit drinking ever go through DTs.

How Can You Know for Sure You Won't Go through DTs?

You should be the best judge of your own alcohol consumption, if you're honest with yourself.

If you have been drinking heavily every day for a number of weeks prior to quitting, you probably need to at least seek medical advice, if not medical attention.

You are unlikely to go through alcohol withdrawal if you have taken periods of rest between your drinking. For instance, if you have had no alcohol for two or more days in the previous week, you're highly unlikely to go through DTs or withdrawal.

Again, get some medical advice if you are worried.

Exercise

How many days alcohol free have you had in the last week?

How many in the last month?

If you feel worried about this, have a chat with your doctor.

Can You Follow the 30 Day Alcohol Reboot for More Than 30 Days?

Absolutely!

The more days you keep alcohol out of your system, the better you will feel.

Remember that 30 days is just an arbitrary figure. It's long enough to give you a taste of what it's like to be without alcohol, to experience some of the benefits. It's short enough to be doable to most people.

It's not really enough time to kick the habit completely or to experience many of the longer term life changing benefits.

Longer Plans

You can easily follow this plan for 30 days, 50 days, or 100 days. Perhaps you'll decide you feel so great after 30 days that you never want to drink alcohol again.

This is how I felt.

The more distance I put between myself and alcohol, the less desire I had to return to my old lifestyle.

At the end of the day, it's up to you.

You don't have to think about this yet. Just concentrate on getting through this first 30 days. Once you get through this part of the challenge, you can decide if you want to continue.

The benefits of being without alcohol will become more and more apparent the deeper into this challenge you get.

For now, take one day at a time, and above all - enjoy.

I'll be giving you a lot more advice about this towards the end of this course.

Can You Do This on Your Own?

What most people mean when they ask if they can do this on their own, is: Are they in any danger?

For most people, the answer is simply no: there is no danger. Yes: you can do this on your own.

How Do You Know You Can Quit Drinking Alcohol on Your Own?

It's really a very simple process. If you can go without alcohol for two or three days, if you get no symptoms of withdrawal, you can be fairly sure that you don't need medical attention.

If, on the other hand, you think you have a serious drinking problem, if you drink a lot of alcohol every day and you haven't taken a break in a while, you really need to get medical advice before quitting cold turkey.

Your own common sense will tell you. As I have said, if you are in any doubt at all, play it safe, go and visit your doctor. There's no point in taking risks with your health. Don't be afraid of reaching out for advice.

Big Alcohol

The alcohol industry wants to sell us this drug in as large a quantity as it can. They would have you believe that alcohol is not a drug, it's not a toxin, and it won't do you any harm if you drink it in moderate amounts. We've heard the same bullshit from Big Tobacco.

The fact is that alcohol *is* a drug and it *is* a toxin.

We've already seen that it's very unlikely that anyone who likes to drink alcohol will stick to the rate that your body can safely metabolize.

Also, once you start a drinking session, once the drug starts to take effect in your body, it lowers your inhibitions, makes you urinate more, which is a combination that is highly likely to give you the desire to drink more.

Big Quit Alcohol

On the other hand, we have a mirror industry which wants to help us to quit this drug, the quit alcohol industry.

The big players in this industry also have a business model which is designed to put profit first. The quit alcohol industry relies on persuading enough people to come through their doors, and pay hefty fees for the privilege.

Big Quit-Alcohol marketing is largely aimed at convincing you that quitting drinking on your own is not possible, from a personal or safety perspective.

Millions of people have successfully quit alcohol in their own.

What's the Real Risk?

For some people, there is a risk. There's no doubt about that.

For instance, if you drink 750 ml of vodka a day for a year, the advice presented here is not for you. You need to get medical attention first. Make sure you are safe, then come back here for more information. I can only help you deal with the psychological parts of this process, not the medical.

Drinking large amounts of alcohol over a long period of time virtually guarantees some physical damage. It's this physical damage that may require medical treatment. It's this physical damage that can cause seizures and even death.

However, most of us are not in this position. For the majority of people who drink a few beers a night, maybe a few glasses of wine, there is no real danger.

Having said that, your expectations can motivate mental distress which can cause physical symptoms.

I have to repeat again, if you are in doubt about your medical risk from quitting drinking alcohol, you should go to your doctor. If you have been drinking a lot of alcohol every day, you should go to your doctor.

Exercise

As a simple exercise, just think about your own immediate drinking past.

How many days a week do you drink?

How much do you drink on those days?

How many days a week do not drink?

I can't stress this highly enough, if you are in any doubt about your risk, don't take a chance with your health, go to your doctor.

Will I Get Alcohol Withdrawal?

What Is Alcohol Withdrawal?

According to WebMD.com, the symptoms of "Alcohol Withdrawal Syndrome" usually appear between 6 and 12 hours after the person has stopped drinking alcohol.

The symptoms include:

- Shaky hands

- Sweating

- Mild anxiety

- Nausea

- Vomiting

- Headache

- Insomnia

If you think about it, these are all symptoms that come with the natural cycle of alcohol drinking.

How do you feel after a heavy bout of drinking?

We don't usually call these symptoms "withdrawal symptoms", we usually call them "hangover" symptoms. These are recurring withdrawal symptoms that are the consequences of drinking the alcohol, not in quitting drinking it.

Hangover versus Alcohol Withdrawal

Heavy drinking is always followed by a period of alcohol withdrawal. Time period that is generally known as the hangover.

The point is that, you've already gone through alcohol withdrawal multiple times. Every time you get a hangover after a heavy drinking session, that's a mixture of the physical consequences of your drinking, the dehydration, the toxic poisoning, and is also a form of alcohol withdrawal.

The Gift of Pain

Don't forget, you feel all these symptoms for a reason. Pain and suffering are a gift. They are telling you that what you are doing is screwed up. They are there to force you to stop doing what you are doing.

Google Expectations

The first place most people go when they're looking for information about quitting drinking or alcohol withdrawal is Google or one of the other search engines.

The Internet can provide you with a lot of resources. But therein lies the problem.

The information that is provided in the first few entries of any search result are from websites who have paid to be there, in one form or another. The information that is presented on these webpages is heavily targeted towards the severe end of the scale, that small minority of people who require medical attention to quit drinking alcohol.

You come to this page looking for some guidance on the best way of going about stopping alcohol, and you are met with a lot of horror stories.

Too much negative information can alter your expectations. It can heighten your fears. It can lead you to believe that your problem is worse than it actually is.

And remember, ultimately your expectations can transform your experience.

Have Patience

So, as I have said, unless you are a long-term heavy drinker, meaning you have been drinking large quantities of alcohol every day for weeks or months, you should expect a very positive outcome.

Your "withdrawal symptoms" are usually nothing more than the normal hangover discomfort that you have gone through many times in the past.

Unpleasant as these symptoms can be, they are only temporary.

Have patience. Treat the first day or two of your quit as you would any other hangover.

Soak up the discomfort and think of the benefits that the *30 Day Alcohol Reboot* will bring you.

Exercise

Think about your previous hangovers.

How many of them have produced the symptoms of shaky hands, sweating, nausea or vomiting, headache, or mild anxiety?

PREPARATION

What Is Preparation?

Preparation for the 30 Day Alcohol Reboot means going through the process of getting yourself ready to quit alcohol for 30 days. The better your preparation, the more successful your experience will be.

The First 30 Days Are the Toughest

You might think that you don't need to prepare. You might be asking, isn't it simple to quit drinking? I have already said: you simply don't put any alcohol into your mouth and that's it, job done. Right? You're only quitting alcohol for 30 days, after all.

But, in the world of any habit change, particularly when quitting drinking alcohol, those 30 days are the toughest. It's in those first 30 days that you will experience most of the withdrawal symptoms, the sleepless nights, the cravings, and so on. Once you pass that 30 day mark, life gets a lot easier.

Behavior Change

I've also said that most of this challenge is not about the alcohol, it's about changing your rituals and behavior. In effect, you need to know what you are going to replace your alcohol habit with, even if it is for only 30 days.

Long story short, some form of preparation is essential. With good preparation, you give yourself the best opportunity for the best outcome.

What We Will Cover in this Preparation Section

Over the next few sections we are going to look at how you should prepare your mind and your body, your environment, and the people in your life.

We'll look at when you should begin your 30 Day Alcohol Reboot and how to set a date to begin.

We'll ask if you should visit your doctor, if you should reduce your alcohol consumption before you quit, and what you should do the night before the challenge starts.

We'll then go through a few tips on setting yourself up for the best chance of a successful outcome.

Do You Need a Plan?

"Fail to plan, plan to fail" Benjamin Franklin

Quitting drinking alcohol for 30 days requires a plan. It doesn't need much of a plan, but you do need some preparation, a little bit of forethought, and some basic planning.

Vacation Planning

Quitting drinking alcohol for 30 days is not a lifelong decision. After you finish the 30 days, you might feel so good that you want to continue on for a while longer, we'll look at that later. Initially though, we are only aiming for a single month.

In the grand scheme of things, a month is not a long time. So you don't need to draw up extensive battle plans, but you're still better off with something. As I've pointed out before, the first 30 days in any habit change are crucial.

Think about going on vacation.

If you're like most people, you wouldn't just head out the door without at least some rudimentary idea of where you were going and what you were going to do when you got there.

Taking the 30 Day Alcohol Reboot is no different, it's like taking a vacation from your regular life.

Get Your People on Your Side

One reason for some rudimentary planning is that you get everyone that matters on the same page.

In terms of your personal influence, people are notoriously difficult to control. They have their own ideas about how things should be done, their own spin on life, and how you fit into that picture.

Your job is to get your closest family and friends on your side. If you don't, they can quickly become obstacles. You don't want that!

Personal Accountability

Planning also forces you to be accountable to yourself.

We all make mistakes. It's part of life. But you'll make fewer mistakes if you have a general plan about what going to happen and when.

What are you going to say when somebody offers you a drink? What will you do when you feel a craving? What's your plan if you can't fall asleep?

Personal Direction

A plan also gives you direction.

Planning helps you to know where you're starting from. You start out as a drinker who from day one is going to become a non-drinker.

You also understand fairly well where you going to end up. After 30 days, you take the benefits of not drinking for a month, and that the end of it.

The question is what is going to happen in the middle, during those 30 days.

There's also the question of what you want to get out of it.

We touched on this in the section on motivation. Why you are doing this is important in terms of maintaining your motivation. It's also important for giving you direction. What do you hope to achieve at the end of it all?

Even though this is only a month, it's still enough time to get good results.

Simple Does It

Planning for your 30 Day Alcohol Reboot doesn't have to be elaborate. All you need is to spend a bit of time thinking about where you're starting from, why you are starting, what you want to get out of it at the end of the month, and to have an idea about some of the things that might happen during those 30 days.

Through some careful thinking, you will get your closest family and friends on your side, create more accountability for yourself, and give yourself a much better sense of direction.

Exercise

As a quick exercise, think again about your reasons for starting this 30 day challenge.

What motivates you?

What do you want to achieve at the end of the month?

Do you have any preliminary thoughts about how you going to tell your family and friends?

Do you have any previous experience of stopping drinking alcohol that you can use now?

What are your expectations?

How Should You Prepare Your Body and Mind for Your 30 Day Alcohol Reboot?

In this section were going to look at preparing your mind and body for the next 30 days without alcohol.

Your Range of Control

In your personal preparation, you have three areas of control. These are your mind and body, your environment, and the people in your life. We'll deal with each of these areas from greater to lesser influence, starting with preparing your mind and body.

Mind and Body Preparation

Your mind where you have most control.

In fact, all your personal control comes via your mind. Regardless of the "symptoms", "side effects", or "cravings", what type of environment you live in, or the humors of the people in your life, none of these can influence you if you set your mind up properly.

What I mean by setting your mind up is having a positive growth mindset from the beginning.

These Are Your Choices

Quitting drinking alcohol for a month is a choice that you've made. Between now and the end of the challenge, there will be many more choices.

For instance, do you go to bars with your friends? What do you do if you feel cravings? What if you can't sleep? How will you relax without alcohol? And so on.

In each of these areas, you have a choice.

Your mind works best when it has very simple, very clear instructions. Complexity breeds confusion. Too much confusion can be a recipe for disaster.

You can make things much simpler through effective preparation. Preparation trains your mind. It allows your mind to rehearse possibilities, to see what might happen and how to act when it does happen.

Techniques for Mind Preparation

Let's take a look at three simple techniques for preparing your mind. These techniques are approaching things from the right mindset, using affirmations, and making a reminder video.

Approaching Things from the Right Mindset

First let's look at how to approach things from the right mindset. A mindset is a way of looking at things, the lens through which you perceive the world around you.

For our purposes, we are going to look at four different mindsets.

Positive versus Negative, Fixed versus Growth

We'll start with the positive mindset versus the negative mindset.

We all know that there is a positive and negative way of looking at everything. A common way of expressing this is the glass half full or the glass half empty mindset. Most people have a tendency to perceive things as either generally positive or generally negative.

The fixed versus growth mindset is very similar.

In the fixed mindset, the person believes that the natural talents and abilities that they are born with are fixed and cannot be changed.

The growth mindset believer, on the other hand, looks at these natural talents and abilities as just the starting point, like the first step on life's journey.

People with a growth mindset believe that anything they want to learn can be learned. They believe that people can improve themselves exponentially from where they started out.

A positive and growth mindset will help to speed you through any obstacles that you'll meet along the way.

Cultivating These Mindsets

How do you use the positive and growth mindset?

Any time you run into a problem or an obstacle, try to look at things from a positive viewpoint.

Instead of focusing on the problem, focus on the solution. Look at the obstacle and see how you can overcome or circumvent it. Also, make sure you look at any obstacle or challenge in life, good or bad, as a learning experience.

Problems versus Solutions

What's the difference between problems and solutions?

Problems are usually backward facing. You have to look back in your timeline to what the problem is, when it started, what caused the problem, and so on.

Sometimes it's difficult to know what the exact problem is. It's even more difficult to understand the cause. The nature of the problem or the exact cause might be something in the distant past, long forgotten about.

It's much better to think about any challenges or obstacles in terms of looking for a solution. This is forward thinking.

It focuses your attention on the future not the past. When you come up with your solution, you apply that solution, and you learn something of value that you can take forward for the next time you come across a similar obstacle.

Overcoming Obstacles

Another mindset shift is to look at obstacles as something you can circumvent.

Many people approach obstacles as things that have to be dealt with there and then, figured out, a problem that needs to be solved. Instead, as you come up against an obstacle, ask yourself if there is a simple way to go over or around the obstacle, to move the obstacle out of your way, and so on.

An example of problem sidestepping is where somebody offers you a drink, you say no, but this idiot won't take no for an answer. The person becomes an obstacle.

What is the easiest way of circumventing this obstacle? Walk away. Conveniently spot somebody else on the other side of the room that you haven't talked to in ages, say "I'll speak to you later" to the idiot, and walk away.

Positive Personal Affirmations

Another smart technique for preparing your mind is to use affirmations.

Affirmations are simply positive personal sentences that you repeat to yourself over and over again. Think about affirmations as your personal catchphrases.

When you first create your affirmations, they should be positive, in the present tense, and concise.

Examples of positive affirmations are:

"I feel relaxed without alcohol"

"I feel fantastic just being with my friends"

"My body feels great and it feels better and better every day"

"I am in complete control of my habits"

"I am changing my life for the better"

"I only engage in habits that support my well-being"

You can repeat your affirmations whenever and wherever you want. Say them to yourself when you feel a craving. Repeat them when you're a bit down and you need a pick me up. Rerun them in your head when you are under pressure from your friends to take a drink, or take yourself off to a quiet place and read your list.

Affirmations refocus your mind back onto what's important. It's impossible for you to think more than one thing at a time. Affirmations take advantage of this. While you are repeating your positive sentences, it's very difficult to indulge in defeating negative self-talk.

My Morning Affirmations

While I was going through the first few days of my quit, I would spend 10 minutes every morning writing my affirmations. I still do it now. The only difference now is that my affirmations focus on a different area of my life.

I usually have 12 to 15 affirmations in total. I write them down on a blank sheet of paper while repeating them out loud. Once I finish writing them down, I repeat them out loud once more.

I rerun the same process in the evening. This routine helps to reprogram my mind for the things that I want to happen. It's a form of self-propaganda.

When I feel my affirmations are completely embedded into my mind, I scratch them out and add new ones.

Your Personal Catchphrases

No matter where we go in this life, we are surrounded by other peoples brainwashing. That's what advertising is, basic propaganda. Think about all the advertising that you remember from your childhood, all those little jingles and catchy sentences. It's brainwashing at its best.

It works because that's how the human brain works. Why not use this to your advantage? Brainwash yourself into the believing the things you want to believe?

Your Personal Pep Video

The final technique I want to talk about here is creating a reminder video.

We all have our reasons for quitting alcohol, and again I encourage you to write them down on paper. You can take out that sheet of paper any time you need motivating during your 30 Day Alcohol Reboot, reminding yourself why you started this journey in the first place.

A more modern and significant method of achieving the same end is to record a reminder video. You can also use this reminder video to create a personal speech, addressed to yourself.

In this video, you start out by addressing yourself by name: "Hi John". You then go on to explain to yourself why you are doing this, how you feel about yourself in that moment, why you are making the video, and how much you desire change.

You tell yourself that this person that you are now in the moment is not the person you want to be. You address your future self as if they have arrived at the place that you want to be. At the end, give them a cautionary note. Tell them that you know how good it feels to be in that place where they are now and how much you do not want them to go back.

The reason this work so well is because you can see, in front of your eyes, the person that used to be. When you look back at this video in four weeks, or four years, you will see the old "you" that you have succeeded in getting away from

This is a very simple technique for future motivation and it doesn't take very long to set up.

How to Set up Your Personal Pep Video

We all have access to some sort of video camera these days. At the very least we have a camera on our phone.

The only rule is to keep it simple.

You don't need a script. It will be more authentic and have much more impact if what you say is unscripted. If you want write down some basic notes, fine, but make sure that your delivery comes from the heart.

Setup your video recorder in a quiet spot, press the record button, and create your masterpiece.

Exercise

First, try to maintain a positive and growth mindset at all times. Prepare, plan, and speak to yourself positively.

Believe in your inherent desire for learning. Think about solutions instead of problems. What's the easiest way to circumvent or overcome an obstacle?

Second, plan your affirmations. Keep them positive, in the present tense, and concise. Write and repeat these affirmations once in the morning and once in the evening. Carry a copy with you that you can take out when you need motivation.

And finally, create your personal pep video. When you record your video, speak from the heart. Explain to your future self why you are doing this and what you hope to achieve.

How Should You Prepare Your Environment for the 30 Day Alcohol Reboot?

Your next level of personal control and influence is in your environment.

Your environment is responsible for most triggers in your life, not just your alcohol drinking triggers.

Locking yourself away for the entire 30 days might make this challenge a whole lot easier because you won't have to face large chunks of your environment, but that's not really a viable solution. You have to go to work, get the kids to school, and do your shopping, etc.

Your environment can be split into two parts, your personal environment and your wider environment.

Your personal environment is where you have the most control. This is your home, your office, your car, and so on. Your wider environment is everywhere else.

Your Personal Environment

You control your personal environment. In terms of quitting alcohol, one of the ways that you can control your personal environment is by eliminating all the booze and other alcohol paraphernalia. Clear your fridge of alcohol, box up the wineglasses and the corkscrews, remove any other alcohol reminders.

You can also engineer your home environment so that it promotes better relaxation, allows you to sleep well, and takes your mind off any cravings.

For instance, instead of settling down to your normal glass of wine in the evening, turn the lights down low, put on some soft music, light a couple of scented candles, and chill out with some herbal tea.

Look, I'm not a very creative person in that way. I leave that up to my partner, who does a great job. Different strokes for different folks. If you don't know how to create a calm environment, ask someone who does. As a last resort, you've always got Google.

Your Wider Environment

Your wider environment doesn't offer the same level of control as your personal environment. However, you still have some control.

As we have already seen, it doesn't matter where you are or who you're with, the real control over what you put into your body comes from your mind. Your mind can only be influenced if you allow that influence to happen.

You will see alcohol reminders all the time, that's just a fact. It's up to you to choose a positive framework through which to look at these alcohol triggers.

Your Personal Environment

Also, you cannot avoid alcohol advertisements. You'll see them on the TV, in magazines and newspapers, on trains and buses, in sports stadiums, on billboards. Everywhere you go, Big Alcohol is waiting for you.

Alcohol advertising is designed to stir your emotions. Each advert is contrived to get you thinking about drinking. And they are good at it. So, expect alcohol adverts to trigger some unwanted thoughts.

Only you can choose how you deal with those thoughts once they happen, how you deal with the trigger once it happens.

You can allow this advertising to trigger you into cravings, or you can reframe those thoughts and see alcohol as something you don't need any more, something you don't buy any more, something you don't want any more. You can also use these alcohol advertisements as reminders of how much money you are saving. It's all about reframing.

You can shift your perspective from that of a drinker to that of a non-drinker, from the perspective of somebody who used to succumb to these types of advertisements, to a person who is no longer led by the bullshit.

Avoidance

Another tactic for environmental triggers is complete avoidance.

You can simply ignore these alcohol reminders, turning the other way, or using your affirmations to distract your mind.

You can completely avoid environments that you know are going to trigger alcohol cravings. You don't go to the pub, for instance.

Exercise

Think about where you can make changes in your personal environment. Can you throw out all the alcohol and other drinking paraphernalia?

Do you have a partner who still drinks, making your challenge a bit more difficult?

How can you create a personal relaxation zone in your home?

What can you do in your wider environment to reduce the amount of alcohol drinking triggers?

Can you plan a different route to work, avoiding those triggers?

How can you reduce the impact of environmental triggers, such as alcohol advertising billboards?

How can you change your personal perspective?

How Should You Prepare the People in Your Life for Your 30 Day Alcohol Reboot?

Let's move onto your final area of personal control.

People Control

The people in your life represent the area where you have the least amount of control. Having said that, this is certainly an area which can have the most influence.

John Donne said, "No man is an island". He was right. We all need other people. Everyone relies on other people.

Although it's not impossible to achieve things on your own, it's much easier when you have the help of those around you, especially those who are closest to you.

You might not think that you need any help, and maybe you don't. I like to think along those lines. I like to think I can do anything on my own. I don't need anyone else's permission, I don't need their input, and I certainly don't need their interference.

Having said that, not taking other people into account can create unnecessary and sometimes substantial barriers to your progress.

As with your environment, it's possible to lock yourself away for 30 days and not see anyone. You can refuse to take phone calls, check emails, or access Facebook, Instagram, or Twitter. But again, this not a very viable or desirable option.

Most of us need regular social interaction in our daily lives. We have to work. We have to socialize. We need to be with our families, our friends.

Getting People on Your Side

It's very important to get at least some of these family and friends on your side.

When I quit drinking alcohol, I told my partner first, then I told my son, then my best friend, and finally I told my father and my brothers and sisters.

I ignored everyone else. Everyone that didn't need to know, didn't need to know.

The Challenge of Focus

It can be quite challenging to tell people that you are going to quit drinking, even if it's only for 30 days.

Think about it.

What's the first thing that they're going to think when you tell them that you're quitting drinking? You just know some people will automatically think that you must have a problem. It's what we have been trained to do. If somebody says they are cutting down or quitting alcohol, they are obviously drinking too much.

Of course this leads to labelling or generalization at its finest. You're a problem drinker. You're dependent on alcohol. Maybe you are an alcoholic!

The big reason for most people quitting drinking is that they are absolutely sick of putting this toxin into your body. They've had enough. They want to get away from this drug!

You drink your fair share, but you certainly don't drink any more than any of your friends. The problem is your starting to feel adverse effects from that drinking. You feel what the alcohol is doing to your body. You don't like how this alcohol is affecting your life.

Does that make you a problem drinker?

Does that make you dependent on alcohol?

Does it make you an alcoholic?

In my mind it makes you an intelligent person. You see a problem and you find a solution. It's what a smart person does.

"I have a terrible cough in the morning, I'll quit smoking."

"I have gained a few pounds. I'll go on a diet."

"I'm bored of my job. I'll look for a new one."

"My car is giving me problems. I'll buy a new one."

"My hand hurts when I stick it into the fire. I'll stop putting my hand into the fire."

How Do You Tell People You're Quitting Drinking

I think the best way to tell anyone that you're quitting drinking is just not to tell them you're quitting drinking.

Again, it's about reframing your situation and then refocusing their attention where you want their attention to be focused.

Of course you have to tell them something, it's difficult to just stop drinking alcohol and say nothing. People are curious. People want to know why you're not drinking any more.

The thing to understand about making your explanations about not doing something is that people will focus their attention where you focus their attention. You don't have to focus that attention on the alcohol.

You focus their attention on one of your reasons to quit drinking. For instance, you want to lose weight, run a marathon, or you have a big workload this month, and so on.

That becomes your main goal, not quitting drinking. As part of this main goal, let's say losing weight, you cannot drink alcohol.

You've refocused their attention away from the alcohol and onto your weight loss.

Is this lying? No. It's telling people your version of the truth

Putting People into the Picture

The reason it's so important to tell the closest people to you is because their life is affected, to one degree or another, by your choices.

Each person in your life has their own way of seeing things. They picture their lives within a certain framework. They also have their own perceptions about you within that personal framework.

When you take on a big challenge, such as quitting drinking for 30 days, the changes that you're making set off little alarm bells ringing in the minds of your nearest and dearest.

The first thing my partner said to me after I told her that I was quitting drinking, was that she wouldn't be joining me. She would continue to drink.

Even though she was 100% behind my decision to quit, and she told me that she would support me in any way she could, she still wanted to enjoy her glass of wine in the evenings.

However much I tried not to allow my decision to affect her, it did. We share our lives together. What we do affects each other. For the first couple of weeks, she was felt very uncomfortable drinking in front of me. Now, she's totally fine with it. It's a part of my life and her perception that I don't drink. It's a part of my friend's life and perception that I don't drink.

We Don't like Change

Human beings don't like change, and that includes your nearest and dearest. They especially don't like it when that change is being forced on them by somebody else, even if that somebody else is a close friend or relation. So what do you do?

It's all about communication.

Tell them about your plans, tell them as soon as possible, and reassure them that you will do your best to minimize the effect that your decision has on them.

As we've already seen, you don't have to tell them that you are quitting alcohol. All you have to say is that you're making a couple of changes over the next month and one of them includes stopping drinking alcohol.

Explain to them why you're doing this and that you're not going to force your decision onto them.

Who Do You Tell?

Again, who you tell is completely up to you. Tell who you need to tell and don't tell the rest.

Because you're only doing this for 30 days, there is not such a great problem if you only want to tell the closest people to you, one or two people, the ones who you think will help you out the most. If you decide to continue not drinking alcohol after the 30 days, you can reassess your situation then.

Exercise

Who you are going to tell?

How are you going to tell them?

What are you going to say?

Will you tell them you're quitting alcohol or will you explain it in terms of some other change?

Where do you foresee problems?

Are some people going to be tougher than others to tell?

Who are these problem people?

When Should You Begin Your 30 Day Alcohol Reboot?

Now you have made your decision to go through the 30 Day Alcohol Reboot, it's time to begin.

When Is the Right Time to Start?

Should you start right now? You can begin your 30 Day Alcohol Reboot any time you want. Don't wait for the right time, there's never a perfect time to begin any challenge like this.

The best way of starting this challenge is to first give it a little thought, prepare yourself, your environment, and the people around you for your quit. Then just go for it.

What's the Best Time to Start?

So, there is no perfect time, but you still have a choice to make. You have to find a suitable time.

The time from when you make your decision to take on the challenge to the time you begin shouldn't be more than a couple of weeks. If you wait longer than this, there's a chance that procrastination will set in, or you could just change your mind.

Let's look at some of the more popular times to begin.

New Year's Resolutions

January is one popular choice. Dry January is very popular these days.

It's the start of a brand-new year and a traditional time for the New Year's resolution. It's a time for making a fresh start, and giving your body a break after the Christmas madness.

In reality, January is as good as any other month.

If January is your month, go for it. If it's June, or October, that's fine as well.

The First of the Month

Another popular choice is the first of the month. You choose a month to do your challenge, begin on the 1st of the month and end on the 30th or the 31st.

It's fairly traditional to start a 30 day challenge on the first of the month. The advantage of beginning your challenge on the first of the month is that it makes it easier to count the days. It also looks better on a calendar.

However, there is really no solid justification for not beginning on the first as opposed to any of the day of the month. There are enough 30 day tracking apps out there to justify starting on any day. Don't feel that you have to wait until the first. If you're comfortable starting on the 16th, do so.

Stressful Days

Although there will never be the perfect time for quitting drinking, you should always choose a time when you have little expected stress.

You cannot avoid all stress. Your 30 day challenge will create a bit of stress of its own. But there's no need to put yourself under more pressure than is necessary.

Choose a date which is not coinciding with a major family event like a wedding or a big birthday.

Giving Yourself the Edge

Choosing the right date is all about starting out with as many advantages as possible.

Try not to choose a day with inbuilt stress. And don't choose a day when you would otherwise be celebrating. If January 1 is close, by all means choose that date. Otherwise, don't get too caught up on specific days on the calendar.

Exercise

Take out a calendar and choose a day in the not too distant future.

Try to give yourself enough time to prepare, but not enough time so you change your mind.

Choose a date at most a couple of weeks away.

Try not to choose a day with inbuilt stress.

Try not to choose a day when you would otherwise be celebrating.

If January 1 is close, by all means choose that date.

How to Find an Alcohol Reboot Buddy?

A very simple but effective way of preparing for your 30 day challenge, and giving you a better chance of success, is to find a reboot buddy.

Who Is Your Reboot Buddy?

A reboot buddy is somebody who will take this journey with you. They are your accountability partner.

We're naturally social beings. As part of our unwritten social contract, if we make promises to another person, we find it very hard to break those promises.

Not only will your accountability partner help you when the times are difficult, they will give you that extra push to set the date and make the start.

How to Choose Your Reboot Buddy?

First, find somebody whom you trust, someone you know is going to remain steadfast and loyal. There's no point in an accountability partner who doesn't follow through, someone who's going to leave you high and dry when the going gets tough.

First, try to choose someone close to you, someone among your family and friends.

Ideally, the person you choose should be someone who has a slightly different personality than you. That difference in personality means that they will probably have alternative ways of looking at things. You can bounce ideas off each other, share each other's experiences, and also learn from each other.

How do you ask them? Let them know what you're doing and see if they will join you.

Talk to them about what you want to achieve from the 30 Day Alcohol Reboot.

Get specific about the details. You can write up a challenge contract between yourselves. Is not for everyone, but it can help some people to stay on track. Talk about your goals, the rewards that you will each receive both during and after the challenge, and the consequences if either one of you breaks the contract.

How Can You Help Each Other?

Catch up regularly, either in person or by phone. Have a physical meet up maybe once or twice a week, then have regular phone calls, or even text messages during the rest of the challenge.

When you have those face-to-face meetings, try to revisit your goals and see how you are progressing. Look at any problem areas and see if you can help each other with finding the right solutions.

Another benefit of a reboot buddy is you have somebody to socialize with. It can be tough, at first, socializing without a drink. If you've got an accountability partner who doubles as a social partner, it can make life a whole lot easier.

Exercise

Can you think of somebody who may want to take up the challenge along with you? A personal friend or relative, maybe.

Don't be afraid of asking. You'd be surprised how many people would like to take an alcohol break, but might need a little push to get them going.

How Can You Measure Your 30 Day Alcohol Reboot Progress?

Measuring outcomes when you are eliminating a habit or trying to give something up is notoriously difficult.

How do you measure *not* doing something?

Big Red X

One of the best methods is to measure the days.

Use a calendar, marking the start date with a big red X, another X for each day of progress, and the big red X for your final day.

There are many free online resources for downloadable monthly calendars or you can use the progress chart found at http://alcoholmastery.com.

Track an Alternative

Remember that even though the focus of this challenge is alcohol, the reasons why we are doing this are normally not alcohol. We want to feel healthier, we want to improve our relationships, finances, or spirituality. We want to be better role models to our children. Or, we just think enough is enough.

So, it's often more relevant to track an alternative goal that you're trying to achieve.

For instance, if you're doing the 30 Day Alcohol Reboot to lose a few pounds, you can easily track your weight loss on a daily or weekly basis.

Weight Loss and Body Composition

A very popular and modern way of tracking weight loss is to take a body composition test. You have one test performed before you start, and a second once the challenge is over.

The body composition test evaluates your percentage of body fat versus muscle. There are a variety of different methods for doing this. Some are far more accurate than others but tend to be more expensive and difficult to find unless you live in a large modern city.

Sleep

Another alternative for measuring your progress is tracking your sleep.

With modern technology, this is fairly easy to do. You can use gadgets like the FitBit or there are a variety of apps that run directly from your smart phone.

Tracking your sleeping allows you to ascertain what type of sleep you are getting, if it's beneficial sleep, and how to best adjust your sleeping habits to find what is optimal for you.

Feeling Good

Finally, you can test your well-being.

One huge reason for taking the *30 Day Alcohol Reboot* is to improve your overall happiness.

There are several good online tests for tracking well-being. One in particular that I like is the eighteen question test provided by the British National Health Service (NHS).

This is basically a questionnaire which is designed to help you better understand how you feel. Based on your answers, you will be recommended some helpful resources.

You can find this by going to www.NHS.uk/tools/pages/mood – self – assessment.aspx.

Exercise

What are you going to track?

How will you track your progress?

Will you track how much weight you lose over the 30 days?

Will you track some other health related progress, like running, walking, or lifting weights?

Will you opt for a healthier diet, tracking your meals, mealtimes, and so on?

Should You Visit Your Doctor before You Quit?

One of the problems that people will face when they are quitting drinking for the first time is confusion about what to do and what not to do. The first port of call for many people when they are looking for help is the Internet. The Internet is a great resource but it has its own issues.

Online Problems

The Internet is massive. There are well over 1 billion websites. From one perspective this is great. We can virtually find any information we want online. From another perspective, the more websites and webpages there are, the more cluttered things become. Even though Google is very good at serving you the basic information that you want, when it comes to looking for in-depth material, you will have to search through pages and pages of material before you find what you want

There are over 6.5 million webpages for the search term "quit drinking alcohol". That is a complete data overload.

One of the problems is that most of the advice is conflicting. What one website advises you to do is completely different to what another website will advise.

Another problem with the presented material is that it's generally aimed towards those heavy drinkers who make up about 5% of the total alcohol drinking population, those who are at high risk of disease or death.

This can be scary and oppressive for some people. Most people are not at high risk from quitting drinking alcohol. However, the more you read about the negative aspects of quitting drinking, especially the lethal ones, the more anxious you are likely to be.

Some of quit alcohol webpages, and the advice that they dish out, is just plain scaremongering by the quit alcohol industry, looking to make a fast buck.

Health Advice or Not

For many heavy drinkers, seeking medical attention is advisable because of the large amounts of alcohol that they have been consuming. Their consumption has transformed a habit into a medical issue.

For 95% of drinkers, however, quitting drinking alcohol is more of a psychological problem.

That doesn't mean to say that most people are going to escape some form of physical discomfort. But, for the majority, this discomfort will be minor and won't last very long.

I'm not a doctor. I'm not a medical practitioner. I can't give you medical advice. And you shouldn't take this as medical advice. It's not.

If you feel worried about quitting alcohol, even if you're in no danger, I'd suggest that you take the time for a quick visit to your doctor. If this is what it takes to set your mind at ease, it's well worth it.

If you do spend the time and money on a doctor, you should explain carefully how much you drink and how often.

Please do not hold any of this information back because it could result in a wrong diagnoses.

Exercise

Should you visit your doctor before you quit? This is a question only you can answer.

If you have been drinking a lot of alcohol, go to your doctor before you quit. If you're worried about what might happen, go to your doctor before you quit. Always err on the safe side.

Should You Reduce Your Alcohol Consumption before You Quit?

There is a tendency for many people to approach an alcohol quit by bingeing before the start. These people feel that because they are going to be denied alcohol for a month, they might as well "stock up" now while they can.

Start As You Mean to Go on

I wouldn't advise that you do this. Think about why you took on this challenge in the first place.

Your reasons might be to lose weight, sleep better, reduce your dependence on alcohol, or just to experience what it's like not to have alcohol in your life for a while.

If you hit the alcohol like a lunatic before the challenge even starts, you're going to be in a hangover state for those first few crucial days. You're putting yourself at a disadvantage before you even begin.

You should start this as you mean to go on. You will put yourself on a more stable psychological footing. You start strong and finish strong.

Prior Reduction

Another way of getting a solid start is to reduce the amount of alcohol you are consuming during the week leading up to the *30 Day Alcohol Reboot*.

Reducing your alcohol consumption for a few days before you begin the challenge will help your body become accustomed to using less alcohol.

There are a couple of advantages to this.

First, your body won't be as shocked by the sudden absence of alcohol.

Second, your brain has a much better chance of recuperating over the next 30 days.

Finally, by not having a hangover to start out with, you'll be better able to cope with any negative events or obstacles that happen along the way.

Dummy Run

Another option is to have a dress rehearsal, maybe a couple of weeks before your 30 Day Alcohol Reboot proper begins. A trial run of two or three days without alcohol gives you a good idea of what is going to happen in the first few days.

Very few people will experience any ill effects from not drinking alcohol. This dummy run should quash your lingering fears. If everything goes smoothly during the dummy run, you are assured that your body can handle it.

Dress Rehearsal Tips

If you are going to reduce your alcohol intake in the weeks leading up to your 30 Day Alcohol Reboot, here's some tips.

Stay away from buying rounds of drinks when you're out in the pub. Buying rounds keeps you in a drinking cycle that is hard to break away from. When you stay out of buying rounds, you choose your own pace, which helps you reduce your consumption.

You can download a drinking app to track your alcohol consumption. This keeps you accountable to yourself. Take note of everything that you drink, and try to calculate your overall pure alcohol consumption.

When you order your drinks at the bar, choose smaller measures than you would otherwise. If you would normally order a pint, only order a half a pint or a small bottle. If you drink wine, choose a small glass of wine instead of a large.

Finally, alternate between alcoholic drinks and soft drinks.

Exercise

How will you manage your drinking in the lead up to the 30 Day Alcohol Reboot?

Will you cut down?

Will you have a dry run?

What Should You Do the Night before the Challenge?

In the last section we looked at how you are going to prepare yourself in the lead up to this challenge.

In this part, we'll look at the night before.

What Should You Do the Night Before?

The success of your 30 Day Alcohol Reboot will be laid down in the first few days.

Your motivation will always be strongest in those first few days. You've made the decision, you're raring to go, and you're hungry for success.

This is also the time when the discomfort of being without alcohol will be at its strongest. Maybe your sleeping patterns are upset, you may feel cravings, or you might have difficulty relaxing.

We will deal with some of these issues shortly.

For now, let's take a look at getting off to a good start.

Starting Right

There's an Italian proverb which says, "A good beginning makes a good ending". That's why I'm saying it's important to start as you mean to go on. Don't come into this challenge with a hangover. Try not to come into the challenge with any alcohol in your system from the night before.

One of the appeals of taking any 30 day challenge is it offers a quick burst of self-improvement. 30 days is enough time to eliminate large chunks of a bad habit and to start laying the foundations for your new habits. 30 day challenges also offers a very palatable yet challenging timeframe.

One of the keys to successfully completing any 30 day challenge is to start strong. Start strong, you've a lot better chance of staying strong throughout the journey, and then to end strong.

Drinking the Night Before?

The first question you should ask yourself is should you drink the night before?

You don't have to. There is nothing to say that you have to take alcohol the night before.

I know it's logical to think, "I'm doing a 30 day challenge and if I don't drink the night before that makes it a 31 day challenge!"

So what? That's just one way of looking at things.

If you are going to drink the night before, keep it to a minimum. The last thing you want is a hangover to start your 30 day challenge.

Setting up Your Environment

If you haven't set up your environment yet, now's the time.

Get rid of all the alcohol and alcohol paraphernalia from your home. Set up your house in a way which will not allow you to drink. If there is no drink in your house, you've put an obstacle in your way because you have to physically leave home to buy some.

This puts a snap in your thinking. It allows you some room to think things through.

We'll talk about this again later.

Speak up Now

You should already have spoken to the people in your life. If you haven't, do it now.

What are you waiting for?

Feed Your Mind and Body

Give your body a head start by eating some nutritious food the day before.

Eat a good breakfast, a good lunch, and have a great dinner.

Keep the carbohydrates up and the fats low.

Also, drink plenty of water. Keep yourself hydrated. As we'll see later, this is one of the keys of reducing your cravings.

Practice Your Catchphrases

The day before is a good time to start practicing your affirmations.

Start by writing your first set of affirmations before you go to bed the night before the challenge. This will allow your affirmations to settle into your unconscious mind and prepare your conscious mind for what's to come the next day.

Nobody knows this for sure, but there's a lot of evidence to suggest that your mind goes on churning over information in the subconscious as you sleep. There is even evidence that your mind can solve problems while you sleep.

Have you ever hit a snag with something, lost patience with trying to figure it out, gone to bed, only to find the solution has magically popped up in your mind the next morning.

We put this down to not being able to find the solution because we were tired the night before. There is enough evidence to suggest that your subconscious mind will have been beavering away at the problem while you slept.

Exercise

What are you going to do the day before?

Will you go for that one last blowout before you set off in this new 30 day challenge?

Or are you going to be smart and lead into this month of non-drinking, with an eve of non-drinking?

Treat the challenge eve as if you were getting ready for something really important.

This is important!

Don't drink, stay hydrated, eat well, and sleep well. Tomorrow is a brand-new day.

How Will You Deal with Cravings?

I'll be talking a lot more about dealing with cravings later. For now, let's just have a quick look into some of the most important aspects of dealing with cravings.

Each One to Their Own

The level of cravings you will experience will depend on you as an individual.

For some people, cravings are very mild, short lived, and can be dealt with pretty quickly.

For others cravings can cause a lot of stress and anxiety, can last a long time, and can be bloody awful.

What's the difference?

Well, there are obvious physical differences. Age, sex, how much you have been drinking, how long you've been drinking, and so on.

All these can play a part in how good or crappy you feel once the alcohol is no longer in your body.

Mind Feed or Feud

You've heard me say this multiple times, and I'll say it again here, your biggest friend or enemy throughout this whole process will certainly be your mind. So, your mind is bound to have the biggest impact on your level of discomfort from cravings.

If you think you are strong enough to overcome any cravings, you will be.

Oppositely, if you feel that the cravings will be overwhelming, then they probably will be.

Mind over matter is what matters.

So what can you do to deal with the cravings?

How to Deal with Cravings

The number one tool for dealing with cravings is just to have a plan. Forewarned is forearmed.

A month is only a short period of time. We all know roughly what we're going to be doing within the next month, so you should have a good idea about the likely situations that will pop up over your chosen month, the situations where alcohol will be involved.

Effective planning ensures that you know what to do while you're in those tricky situations or how to avoid those situations.

Don't plan the end result, always plan the action. Plan what you are going to do, not what the result is going to be, the end result will look after itself.

If/Then Scenarios

If you know the specific situation, you can use what are known as if/then scenarios.

These are very simple scenarios where "if" stands for a situation or event and "then" stands for what you will when that situation or event happens. Here's some examples.

If you walk into a party and somebody offers you a drink, *then* you will say, "No thanks, I'm driving".

If you feel like a drink on your way home from work, *then* you will go to the gym and run on the treadmill for 20 minutes.

If you see a billboard advertising your favorite drink, *then* you will think about what you are going to buy with the money you're saving by not drinking.

Stay in the Here and Now

Another way you can deal with cravings is to just stay in the moment.

Cravings are slight discomfort. They can be physical, mental, or both.

The thing is that cravings never last long. They come and go very quickly.

Stay in the moment, focus your attention on something other than the cravings, and the cravings will disappear within short space of time.

Exercise

Think about what you are going to do when a craving strikes.

Write up some simple if/then scenarios.

Practice saying no. Stand in front of a mirror and just repeat it to yourself. Your mind doesn't care whether you're doing this for real or you're only rehearsing. It has the same effect. With practice, your mind gets used to saying it.

Cravings don't last long. Their power will diminish over time. Eventually, your cravings will disappear altogether. When you get urge to drink, think about the short lifespan of your cravings. Close your eyes, breathe deeply, and let the craving pass.

How Can You Improve Your Chances of a Successful 30 Day Alcohol Reboot?

Investing in Yourself

There's an old maxim in the world of finance that says if you invest 3% of your income in yourself, you'll guarantee your future.

It's the same with most things in life. The more you invest in yourself, the better success you will find at the end of the day.

So, to significantly improve your chances of a successful *30 Day Alcohol Reboot*, invest a little bit in yourself. In this case, I'm talking about a regular investment of positive self-talk, nutrition, and exercise.

We'll talk more about these three personal investments as we go through the "four weeks" part of this material.

Positive Self-Talk

Positive self-talk is all about being your own personal motivator, talking to yourself like you matter, like you care about yourself.

There are plenty of people who will talk to you like you're a piece of dirt on the floor, please don't be one of them. Self-talk can have an overwhelming influence on your levels of confidence, and it works both ways, positive or negative.

One of the best ways I know of developing positive self-talk is to listen and become aware of what you are saying to yourself.

We can be our own worst enemies, telling ourselves all sorts of rubbish and nonsense, putting ourselves down when we should be our biggest cheerleaders.

You need to give yourself big huggable self-talks. You need to be constantly telling yourself that this *30 Day Alcohol Reboot* is going to be a breeze, and that you're going to have no problems.

This is one of the reasons why I suggest you create at least a dozen positive affirmations. Positive affirmations can be used to drown out the horrible, negative, and useless downer-talk.

Nutrition

The second investment I'd advise you to make in yourself, before and during your challenge, is to provide the essential building blocks that your body needs. This means providing yourself with good, wholesome nutritious food.

There's a second side to this. Wholesome nutritious food accounts for less than 10% of what is sold on your local supermarket shelves, if that. The rest is processed junk.

Stay away from that stuff!

It's detrimental to your body, your long-term health, and your new journey.

Give your body the fuel it needs to perform and your body will perform. Give your body the fuel that it needs to perform superbly and it will perform superbly.

Remember, you are what you eat!

Daily Exercise

The final investment I would advise that you make in yourself is consistent daily exercise.

Exercise builds up physical and mental strength. It also helps to take your mind off alcohol.

Exercise is a natural antidepressant, so you can expect to feel a natural high. You don't need alcohol or any other drugs.

The more you keep faith with an exercise routine, the more energetic you will feel.

Exercise will relieve your stress, help you sleep better, and even allow you to tap into your inner creative flow.

I walk between 10 and 15 km every day and I love every second of it. When I don't exercise, when I don't get out on my walks, I feel like crap.

Walking also helps me to think. It does something to my brain cells, keeps them spinning and churning. I take my phone with me to record any ideas that pop up in my mind with without breaking stride. Who says men can't multitask! :-)

Time is our greatest asset. Combining exercise and creativity is a great time saver.

Exercise

During your *30 Day Alcohol Reboot,* where can you make good investments in yourself?

Are you providing your mind with positive self-talk? What can you do to increase that investment?

Are you investing in good nutrition? How can you improve that investment?

Do you take the time for regular exercise? How can you improve those investments in terms of fun and regularity?

What Should You Replace the Alcohol with?

One of the typical questions I am asked from people who are about quit drinking is what should they replace the alcohol with?

It's a good question.

It's a question that as drinkers, we probably haven't thought about in a long time.

Water

I used to drink the same thing, day in and day out. When it was time to stop drinking alcohol, I didn't know where to turn. The only thing I could think of was water. How boring is that? It was boring to me. I drank water when I was thirsty. But that's the mentality of the drinker. We don't drink alcohol to cure thirst.

In fact, water is the best thing for you in terms of your body's physical needs and if you're looking for something to quench your thirst, you can beat it.

But there are far more tasty beverages out there.

Replacing the Intoxication

If you're not struggling with alcohol dependence, this might be a moot point. There are simply more than enough non-alcoholic beverages to suit any taste.

For other people, it's not so much the drink that they will miss, rather the feeling of being intoxicated.

I can't help you with that, there is no healthy replacement for the intoxication. Switching one intoxicant for another defeats the whole purpose of the *30 Day Alcohol Reboot.*

Hydration and Diuresis

One significant problem for heavy drinkers is the diuretic powers of alcohol. The more you drink, the more you need to pee. The more you pee, the less liquid there is in your body. The less liquid, the thirstier you are.

When I drank alcohol, I could easily down 10 pints of Guinness (a very heavy Irish stout), in three or four hours.

I couldn't drink that same quantity of water.

I live in Spain, and even during the hottest summers, I can manage about five or six pints of water.

It's a simple as this, water hydrates, alcohol doesn't. Orange juice hydrates, alcohol doesn't. Motivate. Hydrate. Feel great.

Oral Fixation

Another quirky fact that drinkers never think about is that heavy drinkers tend to consume more liquid. This means that not only is the person taking more liquid into their mouths over a longer period of time, they also tend to hold the alcohol container in their hands more than a non-drinker would. This means that drinkers can easily develop an oral fixation which can lead to an urge to habitually consume more liquid.

Of course, if you go to a party, it's good to hold something in your hand. This prevents unwanted attention from well-wishing drinkers who don't want to take no for an answer.

So, what are you going to hold in your hand? What are you going to sip on?

Watch Your Calories

What you drink depends on the outcome you want.

If you're doing this challenge because you want to lose weight, be careful of the calorie content in the substitute you choose.

Most manufactured soft drinks are loaded with sugar. These drinks will pack on the pounds if you are not very careful.

Also, be cautious about the zero and low calorie versions of popular soft drinks. They usually contain enough additives to warrant a chemical license of their own.

Exercise

What are you going to replace your alcohol with?

What you going to drink at home instead of your normal tipple?

What will you choose to drink when you go out on the town?

Search Google some of your favorite tipples and see if there are non-alcoholic alternatives.

SECTION 2: THE 30 DAY ALCOHOL REBOOT

WEEK ONE

The 30 Day Alcohol Reboot - Week One

The Journey Begins

"A journey of 1000 miles begins with a single step".

This quote from Lao Tzu is a great reminder that every significant journey you take in your life can only be done moment by moment, step-by-step.

It's also a reminder that each journey has a beginning, a middle, and an end.

The quotation is not just aimed at those who are about to travel, it can be paralleled in many areas of life. Whatever journey you are taking, inwards or outwards, you have to start somewhere. That first step almost always a very simple and straightforward step.

Of all the steps that you take in a thousand mile journey, the first step is the most important. It's the one which gets you started. You cannot start without it.

The first step is often the most difficult one to take. It takes determination, willpower, and courage to cross that line.

But once you take that first step, it's easier to take the second, and then the third. You build forward momentum, focused direction, away from where you were and towards where you want or need to be.

Review Your Reasons to Quit

As you begin this first week of the 30 Day Alcohol Reboot, take a little step back and review again your reasons for wanting to take this challenge.

What is the outcome you hope for?

What are the benefits that you expect to happen in your life once you have completed this 30 day challenge?

Let's Get Started!

In this section, we are going to examine some simple tips and techniques that can help you through this first week. Let's move on!

Welcome to week one and congratulations for starting this new journey.

What Can You Expect from Your First Week on the 30 Day Alcohol Reboot?

What's Coming Up?

For the most part, you should be excited. It's great to get started and you should be looking forward to completing the first week and feeling the benefits of not having alcohol in your system.

On the other hand, you might also be slightly nervous about what's going to happen. Don't worry, that's a normal part of the process.

A Simple Reminder

I'll remind you again that not putting the alcohol into your mouth is quite simple. That's the easy part.

The more difficult parts are integrating your new non-drinking thinking into your normal day-to-day life.

A Momentous Week

Week one is the most important week. Most people fail at quitting drinking within the first few days.

It takes time to build momentum. Until that momentum has acquired some energy it can be a lot easier to backtrack and make excuses for quitting.

To overcome this, week one will be about giving you the tools to stay the course, overcoming some of the more obvious obstacles that might stand in your way, and ultimately motivating and moving you towards your final destination in 30 days.

In this section we will take another look at how your self-belief can make all the difference. We will look at keeping things as simple as possible, maintaining positive self-talk, and finding some leverage on yourself... I'll explain this in a bit.

We will also revisit affirmations, look at how to deal with social situations, and how to deal with any criticism or ostracism from other people.

Finally, we'll look at cravings, rewarding yourself and celebrating your successes, and how you can use nutrition to give you the best possible start to your new journey.

Exercise

Give yourself a pat on the back for starting this new journey. Are you ready to take that all important first step? Let's go!

Believe That You Can Do It and You Are Halfway There

Believe

"Believe that you can do it and you are halfway there."

This motivational quote from the 26th US President, Theodore Roosevelt, has truth no matter where you apply it in life.

However, the opposite is also true.

If you believe that you cannot do it, you will certainly drag your mind in the opposite direction.

This journey is all about self-confidence. If *you* won't believe that *you* are capable of doing this, who will? The answer is nobody. You have to believe in yourself first. You will only ever go as far as your mind allows you to go.

Perfectionism is the Mother of Procrastination

Many people are reluctant to make changes in their lives unless, or until, they think that everything is perfect. The perfect time. The perfect situation. The perfect mood. The perfect star alignment!

Perfectionism is the mother of procrastination.

Seek perfection and you will most likely find only demoralization.

Suck in Your Doubts

On the other hand, when you start out this challenge, or any challenge, from a position of doubt, you'll find it very difficult to stay on track.

Most people are much stronger than they actually believe.

Your capacity to quit drinking for 30 days is not in doubt for me.

Even though I don't know you personally, I know you can do it.

Does that seem a bit far-fetched? How can I know that you are capable of doing this if I don't even know who you are?

Because if you were locked in a room for 30 days, if you were given food and water and a place to rest your head, but you had no access to alcohol, you would have no choice but not to drink. That is the argument for mind over matter.

Although you might fret and moan, tell the walls how unfair life is, you would soon settle down and forget about drinking alcohol until the 30 days was up.

So, anyone can do this, all they have to do is recreate that "locked in a room" frame of mind.

Create the scenario that no matter what happens, there is no alcohol available for 30 days, end of story.

Only You

Obstacles, problems, bad situations, or overbearing people cannot stop you. The only person who can truly stop you is you.

Your most powerful tool is your mind. It is the place where you have all the control. But, there's a caveat. You have to believe!

And don't be fooled into thinking that just because you have never quit drinking for 30 days before that you can't do it now. If we only ever did the things that we have done before, our species would never have moved out the primordial swamp.

Recap

Change will happen if you believe the change will happen. You are much stronger than you believe you are. You can achieve anything in life if you put your mind to it. The conditions have to be right, not perfect, only right. And you can create those right conditions for yourself. If you were locked up in a prison cell for 30 days, or if somebody offered you $1 million to quit drinking for 30 days, you would have no problem in not drinking the stuff. It's mind over matter. It's belief over doubt.

Exercise

Think about how you can recreate the "locked in a room" mentality. You have to create the situation in your mind where there is no way that you are putting alcohol into your mouth for 30 days. Alcohol is off-limits. If you drink alcohol, there's going to be trouble.

We'll talk a bit more about this when we cover the topic of getting leverage on yourself.

Keep It Simple

The Rewards of Simplicity

Human beings are complex creatures. However, when it comes down to it, we thrive on simplicity.

We see unambiguous purity throughout the natural world. Even though we admire the seeming complexity that nature can throw up or the complex achievements that we humans can achieve, it is simplicity that is rewarded over and over again.

Tony Robbins said that, "Complexity is the enemy of execution". The more complicated you make this journey, the more difficulty you will find, and the greater your chance of you not reaching your final goal.

Simple Truths

The simple truth of quitting alcohol for 30 days, or of quitting alcohol for the rest of your life, is that the only way to fail is if alcohol passes your lips.

The simplicity of the *30 Day Alcohol Reboot* can be summed up in four words: *allow no alcohol in*!

Another simple truth of this challenge is that it's only for 30 days, just over four weeks, one solitary month.

Anybody can do this.

Four weeks will go by very quickly.

So, the essence of the *30 Day Alcohol Reboot* in one sentence: don't put alcohol into your mouth for 30 days. End of story!

The Simplest Solution

As you go through this journey, look for the simplest solution to any problem.

Often the simplest solution to a craving is to get up and go for a walk or take a drink of water.

The simplest solution to somebody who won't take no for an answer is to keep repeating the word "no" or just to walk away.

These might not be the most eloquent solutions, but it is a simplicity which even a complete moron can understand.

Exercise

How simple you can make this journey?

When you look for a way around or over any obstacle, think about the simplest solution possible. Don't bog yourself down with complex ideas. Complex ideas need to too many choices. Too many choices make it more difficult to make a final decision.

Simple solutions create swift answers.

Keep Talking Positive

Negative Hijacking

When you go through any sort of challenge, it can be very easy to allow negative thinking to hijack your mind. This negative thinking can quickly spiral out of control.

Imagine a snowball rolling downhill, accelerating, quickly gathering snow, and growing in size. It's difficult to stop that negative snowball effect once it has begun.

The negative hijacking can take many forms.

You might start telling yourself that you're missing out on all the fun, that alcohol is not really a problem in your life, and that you don't really need the hassle of this type of challenge in your life.

Combating Negative Hijacking

To combat this negativity, you have to listen to what's being said in your mind.

It's easy to get caught up in the negativity without actually listening to the words, the phrases, the pitch and tone of voice, or the emotions.

All of these elements can influence your behavior, your attitudes, your beliefs, and your habits.

In fact, negative hijacking can have such a great influence on your state of mind that negativity becomes your norm. Thinking negatively about life becomes habitual, especially when it comes to our personal lives.

It Started with a Thought

As we've seen, the most powerful level of control is in your mind. Every action you ever take, every choice and decision you make, these all have to start out as simple individual thoughts.

When you cast a critical ear over your negative thoughts, start asking yourself questions.

Why are you thinking in this negative way?

What do you get out of thinking negatively?

Are you just feeling sorry for yourself?

Do you really believe these negative ideas about yourself?

Dig down past the words and listen to how they are being said. Listen to the voice.

Is it self-pitying?

Is it whiny?

Distancing Yourself

You can also put some distance between yourself and the negative self-talk by using second or third person pronouns.

Instead of asking, "Can I do this?" or "What am I missing out on?" You can replace it with, "Can you do this?" Or "What are you missing out on?"

This creates a psychological distance which can help you to lessen any discomfort you feel in that moment, rather than adding to it.

Replace the Self-Pitying Voice

You can replace the whiny, self-pitying voice with something a lot stronger.

Who is your favorite action hero?

Try replacing the self-pitying voice with that of one of your movie heroes.

Imagine your internal voice is that of Samuel L Jackson's character Jules Winnfield, from the movie "Pulp Fiction". "Say 'I can't do it' again. Say 'I can't do it' again, I dare you, I double dare you mother**ker, say 'I can't do it' one more Goddamn time!"

Or instead of using a dour, self-pitying voice, try changing it to sound like Daffy Duck or Jessica Rabbit. It's very difficult to be serious about your negative self-talk when you hear the words through this frame.

Imagine Daffy telling you that you're no good. Imagine Jessica saying that you're useless in those languid tones of hers.

Keep Responsibility in Mind

Finally, this is your life and you have to take responsibility for it.

Negative self-talk is completely under your control. You can change from the negative to the positive very easily. You do this by not focusing on the problem. Instead you focus on the solution.

Recap

Positive or negative self-talk is in your control. If you allow negative self-talk to take over, it can easily get out of control and quickly become habitual.

Your first antidote to any negative self-talk is to listen carefully and cast a very critical ear over what's being said. Only once you know what's being said, how it's being said, and the emotions that these thoughts are invoking, can you do something about them.

Put some psychological distance between yourself and the negative self-talk by using the second or third person. You can also change the tone and context of what's being said by replacing the whiny voice with something more forceful or more cartoonish.

Exercise

First of all, when you hear this negative hijacking self-talk, listen very carefully to your thoughts.

Look for any patterns.

Listen for the pitch and tone of voice as well as the content of what you are saying to yourself.

What words and phrases are you using to put yourself down or to talk yourself out of doing what you know needs to be done? You should be able to notice patterns after a while.

Change the voice. Choose a movie hero or comedic character as your inner voice. Arnold Schwarzenegger or Samuel L Jackson… Daffy duck or Homer Simpson.

You'll notice that once you change the pitch and tone of what is being said, the effect these words have on you will also change.

Experiment until you find the right combination.

Get Some Leverage on Yourself

The Power of Will

We've all heard that to achieve anything in this life, you have to toughen up and use your willpower.

We all need the power of our wills for dealing with cravings. We want something that gives us short-term pleasure but we know that there are long-term consequences.

Willpower is a necessary resource. But it's also in short supply. And sometimes willpower just isn't enough.

You are having a really rough day, things are just not going your way, and you're on the verge of slipping back into your old habits and taking a drink.

When you're on the edge like this, it's not very easy to maintain your motivation, to keep that stiff upper lip, or to snap yourself out of it.

You could tell yourself that you just need to be stronger, but that doesn't really help in the moment.

What you need in these moments is leverage.

Personal Leverage

Archimedes famously said, "Give me a lever long enough and a fulcrum on which to place it, and I shall move the world".

Personal leverage is a tool that gives you very little choice but to keep moving forwards.

If you have the right lever, and a fulcrum on which to place it, your commitment will stay strong.

Leverage creates a barrier between what you want to do and what you have to do.

Leverage makes it embarrassing, shaming, or just plain impossible for you to back out.

Humans are motivated by two basic things, pain and pleasure. Having good leverage on yourself means that you associate backing out with pain.

A Written Commitment

One of the easiest ways of gaining personal leverage on yourself is to make a written commitment.

There's something about committing a specific objective to paper in your own handwriting. It's such a simple thing to do, but it's very effective.

Your commitment doesn't have to be anything too long or complicated, a couple of sentences will do. Write it up and sign your name to it.

Signing your name to any piece of paper gives that document an air of ceremony, it feels more official, and can therefore add another layer of psychological advantage.

Add more leverage by giving a copy to one or two members of your own family or to a couple of friend.

A Friendly Commitment

Committing to a friend or family member is also another great form of leverage.

To give your commitment any backbone, you have to commit to someone who won't easily back off and let you off the hook.

You should commit to somebody who can withstand all your pleading efforts, but, at the same time someone who will be supportive and won't try to sabotage your efforts.

The entire goal of getting leverage on yourself is to attain your long-term gain, not theirs. So avoid people who discourage your growth.

A Money Commitment

Another way of gaining leverage on yourself is to put your money where your mouth is.

Take a chunk of money, an amount you cannot really afford to lose, and give it to a trusted friend. Tell them that if you don't stick to your 30 Day Alcohol Reboot, they can either keep your money or give it to a charity of *their* choice.

Alternatively, have them give your money to a charity that you hate, a benefactor who completely goes against what you stand for, the opposition political party, for example. Write a check out to the KKK. See how that feels!

A Forfeit Commitment

If you don't want to risk your money, have a forfeit that will be completely uncomfortable for you to do.

Some examples are eating a spoonful of dog food, singing nursery rhymes in an embarrassingly public location while holding a cap in your hand, or doing your shopping in a bright pink fluffy onesie.

Create a written commitment, including any leverage clauses. Sign it, date it, and ask someone close to you to add their signature as a witness.

Exercise

How are you going to get leverage on yourself?

The idea is to make it very difficult to drink alcohol.

Get creative. Remember that your leverage should be something that makes backing out very difficult, if not impossible.

Write a personal leverage commitment. On that document, write what it is that you're going to forfeit if you don't complete your 30 day challenge.

Sign and date it, and get one of your friends to co-sign as a witness.

Choose a friend who will support you, but at the same time will hold you accountable, and will make sure that you do your forfeit.

Affirmations

Conflicts

The first week is all about winning small battles.

First, there is the battle between your positive and negative thinking.

Then there's the battle between feeling the cravings and ignoring them.

There's also the battle between enjoying yourself and sticking to your plan.

All of these conflicts are at their peak during the first few days.

A very simple but very effective method of reducing the effect of these conflicts is to use affirmations. I know I have talked about this before, but I think it's worth revisiting here.

Single-Mindedness

Our minds can only pay attention to one concept at a time.

We are very good at some forms of multi-tasking. We can walk and talk at the same time.

We can breathe and sleep at the same time. A musician plays the guitar with both his right and left hand simultaneously.

I'm talking about your focus, where you put your attention.

It's impossible to focus your mind on two things at once. Instead, we tend to switch our attention between tasks, often very rapidly.

Even though it might seem that we are capable of thinking two thoughts simultaneously, we are not. Again, we are very good at rapidly switching between the two thoughts.

Guided Positive Thoughts

Affirmations short-circuit this rapid thought-switching process.

You can use affirmations to alter your thinking patterns. If you're thinking guided positive thoughts, it's very difficult to think negative unguided thoughts at the same time.

You can think a positive thought, then think a negative thought, but you cannot think both thoughts simultaneously.

Affirmations allow you to take a guided personal positive statement and use it to override any negative thoughts, focusing your mind in a specific positive direction.

You can also persistently repeat your positive affirmations until you drown out the negativity. Simply repeating, "I can do this", over and over, will drown out any negative thoughts.

Positive Simple Affirmations

As I have already said, you should always try to keep things as simple as possible.

Positive affirmations should be very simple. As soon as you hear a negative thought, repeat a positive affirmation in your head, the negative thought is drowned out.

The How to of Affirmations

Begin and end your day by writing out your personal positive affirmations.

Say them aloud as you write and repeat them once again after you have written them down. This helps to commit them to memory. The more you repeat them the more you will believe them.

They should be concise, to the point, in the present tense, and very positive.

Take a copy of your affirmations with you wherever you go.

You can fold up sheet of paper and put it into your wallet or your handbag, pulling them out whenever you need some positive reinforcement.

Once you have committed them to memory, you won't need to take your sheet with you anymore.

Realistic, Reasonable, Reinforcing

Remember that affirmations need to be realistic to be believable. If you don't believe them, they are unlikely to work.

You have to have reasonable belief in what you're saying, a positive belief that you can achieve these things. You don't have to believe 100%, that's the point of affirmations. They are used to drum your version of the truth into your brain.

Affirmations are also great for helping to reinforce your core beliefs and values.

For instance, you can energize your core beliefs by telling yourself that you are a good person, a healthy person, a good parent, a good friend, and so on.

Recap

So, affirmations make a great weapon in overcoming minor battles between your positive-self and your negative-self. Begin and end your day by writing down your affirmations, have a copy on hand for whenever you need, and remember that your affirmations must be based on a reality you can believe.

Exercise

How can you use your affirmations to quickly change the direction of your thoughts, from negative to positive?

If you haven't written your affirmations, now is a good time to start.

How to Deal with Social Situations in Week One?

Recognize-Avoid-Cope

Unless you lock yourself away for the whole 30 days, your *30 Day Alcohol Reboot* is likely to throw up some pressure on the social front.

Family and friends are usually very well-meaning, but can sometimes, often inadvertently, stick a spanner in the works.

In this section, were going to look at some a simple cognitive-behavioral therapy approach to this, known as Recognize-Avoid-Cope (RAC).

Recognise

The first step is to recognize the social pressure.

There are two types of social pressure.

The first is *direct social pressure*. This is where somebody directly offers you a drink or offers you the opportunity to go drinking.

The second type of social pressure is *indirect social pressure*. Indirect social pressure happens when you are with other people who are drinking and you feel the urge to drink because of that.

Avoid

The second step of this approach is to avoid situations, environments, or people that cause alcohol drinking triggers.

At times, especially in the early days, this is your best strategy.

When one of my coaching clients wants to quit drinking permanently, I almost always advise them to avoid any areas where they might feel the pressure to drink, at least vo or three months.

There is absolutely no point in putting themselves into these situations until they have enough confidence and coping skills to deal with the situations effectively.

Sometimes, you may even have to avoid friends or family members who you feel might tempt you to drink. If you can't avoid them, try suggesting alternative activities where no alcohol is involved.

Cope

The third step of the RAC approach is to think about resistance strategies.

One simple resistance strategy, when somebody asks if you would like drink, is just to be very blunt and say "no".

Another is to always have a non-alcoholic drink in hand when you're in situations when you would otherwise have an alcoholic drink in hand.

You can enlist the support from your family and friends for coping with temptation. This is where your Reboot Buddy will prove their worth.

You can ask other people not to pressurize you into drinking. You can ask them not to drink in your presence if this helps.

Finally, if you have to attend a boozy event, say it's a wedding that you cannot get out of, you don't have to stay until the very end. Have your escape plan ready.

As soon as you feel you can't take it anymore, make your excuses and leave.

This takes a little bit of planning before you get there.

What's your excuse for leaving early? You shouldn't really need an excuse to leave, you should be able to leave whenever you want, but you know what some people are like.

Some justifications include:

"I have an early start in the morning"

"I'm feeling a bit tired"

"I have a family emergency"

If you're anything like me, it's won't be important to tell anyone that you're going. Say your goodbyes to the host, as a courtesy, but then just do as you please.

Recap

We've seen that to deal with social situations in your first week, make use of the Recognize-Avoid-Cope (RAC) approach.

First, recognize what type of social pressure you're under, direct or indirect.

Second, avoid certain situations, people, or environments.

And third, have some resistance strategies on hand.

Exercise

Take a moment to think about the different types of social pressure that might affect you over the course of this 30 days.

Where do you expect to find the direct social pressures?

Where do expect to find the indirect social pressures?

How can you use the Recognize-Avoid-Cope approach?

Avoiding certain situations is one of the simplest strategies to implement, especially in the earlier days. If you cannot avoid, have some coping strategies ready.

If you need to go somewhere you know there's going to be alcohol, what excuses can you use for leaving early?

How to Say "No"!

Simple, Clear, Friendly

As we said in the last section, if you find yourself in a situation where you are being offered a drink, you need to have some very simple resistance strategies on hand.

The best strategy in most cases is simply to say "No, thanks", and leave it at that.

Many people get flustered when they have to say no. They start offering all sorts of excuses and long explanations. This makes situation more complex than needed. It also allows you the time to think about your choices and maybe change your mind.

Keep it simple, keep it clear, and keep it friendly. "No thanks" is usually enough.

"No" Rehearsals

I know this might sound weird, but sometimes just saying "no" can be quite difficult.

Some people don't how to do it. I don't mean that they don't know how to use the word "no", they probably use it all the time. But they are not used to saying "no" in these situations. Let's face it, when it comes to alcohol, we are all used to saying "yes".

If you find "no" difficult to say, spend some time practicing.

Also, take the time to practice asking for alternative drinks.

Mental rehearsal is something that is used in many different areas of life from sports to exams, from interviews to going on a date for the first time.

Imagine yourself in the situation where somebody is offering you a drink. Then, rehearse out loud what you will say and how you will say it.

Repeat the process until you feel comfortable.

The benefit of mental rehearsal is that you should get a positive response every time. This helps build your self-confidence before you try it out in the real world.

"No" Role-Play

You can ask a friend or family member to role-play with you.

Again, your reboot body can come in useful here.

This form of role-play can bring the actual situation to life, giving you some almost-realistic pressure to drink.

Another reason for having other people participating in your role-play is that you are likely to get some valuable feedback on your responses.

You might feel like a plonker doing this, but it's very valuable practice that will really help you when you get into the real situations.

When the day comes, and you're facing the "nondrinking" reality for the first time, you might still feel a bit uncomfortable.

It's normal.

Stick to what you have practiced and your discomfort will quickly disappear.

The more you do this, the easier it gets. Practice makes perfect.

I've done this so many times now, I don't even think about it anymore. It's second nature.

"No" Responses

Take into account that the people who are offering you a drink may not know your situation.

It can be a good idea to plan a variety of different responses, depending on the situation.

As I said, a simple "No, thank you" will suffice in most situations and with most people.

If the person is insistent, you might have to repeat this same response a few times, like a broken record, so the message sinks in.

You can also say: "Look, I'm not drinking because I want to look after my health and I'd really appreciate if you would help me out".

If all else fails, simply walk away. If someone's not willing to respect your decision, they don't deserve to have your respect.

Recap

In most situations where you are offered a drink, simply saying "no, thank you" is enough.

To gain confidence with refusing a drink, or ordering an alternative, you can practice using mental rehearsals. You can rehearse on your own, imagining yourself in a specific situation, saying "no". Or you can enlist the help of a friend.

Exercise

Stand in front of the mirror and practice saying "No, thank you".

Practice standing straight and maintaining eye contact with yourself.

Remain calm, positive, and friendly.

Practice a few variations.

Practice being insistent.

How to Deal with the Criticism or Ostracism?

Social Punishment

Let's face it, not everyone will understand your decision to stop drinking. Not everyone will support you.

The cold truth is that some negative people will even criticize or ostracize you.

Social punishment for perceived or real social slights is a natural tendency which is encountered throughout the animal kingdom. It's often seen as the dark side of cooperation. It deters free riders and can intimidate others into doing almost anything.

On a personal human level, criticism can hurt because it goes against our basic needs for control, recognition, belonging, and self-esteem.

However, the likelihood is that the level of criticism or ostracism you feel from your friends or family is likely to be fairly low, but it can still sting.

How can you help yourself in these situations?

You're in Control

First you have to realize that you are in total control of how you respond.

Don't respond by being defensive. This won't help.

Remain calm. Never take it personally, even if it's meant personally. Don't react aggressively, you'll only escalate things.

The same goes with trying to prove the other person wrong if somebody criticizes you for trying to improve yourself, that criticism is likely to be completely wrong.

Most of this nit-picking criticism comes from insecurity on behalf of the critic. It's more a reflection of them than you.

Look your critic straight in the eye, and in a calm voice repeat the criticism back to them.

Something like: "So, what you're saying is...," followed by the criticism in your own words.

Be factual and don't exaggerate or you will appear defensive. Always be reasonable and try to appear like somebody who is really trying to get to the heart of the situation.

The idea is to put the focus on the issue, not on the clash. This is the psychological equivalent of turning the other cheek. You are turning the focus away from you and what you're doing, and back onto them and their criticism.

Offer the critic a bit of credit by saying that you understand where they are coming from. Then say something along the lines of: "Maybe I haven't explained myself as well as I could have". Then assertively, yet calmly, state your position again.

Would Your Real Friends Do This?

As I said, the likelihood of you being ostracized from your group because you are taking on a 30 Day Alcohol Reboot is pretty slim. If somebody does try to ostracize you, you should be asking yourself if these people are your real friends.

Would your real friends try to ostracize you like this?

A persons actions tell you everything you need to know. The only people who are worthy of being in your life are the ones that help you through the crap times and then laugh with you when the crap times are over.

They say that you never really know who your true friends are until there's a problem. And then, you're often surprised who turns up.

Well, this is one of those times. If your so-called friends are responding with ostracism, get shut of them as quickly as you can.

Recap

To recap, we all fear criticism and being ostracized from our social group. If somebody tries to ostracize you from the group, it gives you a rare opportunity to see them for who they really are.

As for criticism, first of all you don't have to listen to it. Second, if you keep calm, look the person straight in the eye and repeat their criticism back to them in your own words, then give them your calm response, they will usually fold, tell you they didn't really mean it, or walk away.

Either response is good for you.

Exercise

Think about how you are going to respond to criticism. Always remain calm. Don't be defensive or aggressive. And never take it personally.

You can use the mirror technique that we used in the session on saying "no". Look in the mirror and practice how you will react when you receive criticism. Practice what you will say and how you will say it.

What Are Cravings and How to Deal with Them?

Normal Discomfort

Most cravings are nothing more than discomfort.

They are subjective, can sometimes be a little intense, and can last for a few weeks after you've stopped.

Most people will only ever go through minor discomfort. It's always important not to blow your urges out of proportion. You can quite easily use auto suggestion to send yourself down the wrong track.

Experiencing cravings is normal and quite common for most drinkers. It doesn't mean that there's anything wrong with you, nor does it mean that you are an alcoholic, or that you want to go back to drinking.

Triggering Cravings

First, let's look at some of the triggers for your cravings.

Your environment, the time of day, and the people around you; these are some of the most common triggers.

Getting paid at the end of the week or just having money can be another.

More triggers include taking other drugs, social situations, and feelings such as joy, depression, or anxiety.

Let's face it, if you are asleep, none of these things are going to trigger you. So, the real trigger is the thought which fires off in your mind.

The thought can be provoked by another thought, or something that happens outside of you, such as one of the above triggers.

The thought trigger then leads you to act out the drinking behavior.

And finally you get your reward which could be the buzz, not thinking about a problem, sleeping, and so on.

Time Limit on Cravings

It's important to see that there is a time limit on your cravings. In other words, the craving will peak and then disappear within an hour, normally a lot less than an hour, if not followed by alcohol use.

Think about this from your perspective.

This is week one.

How do the cravings feel for you at this stage?

How do you feel physically?

What emotions are you feeling?

How bothered are you by the urges?

How long does the urge last?

What are you doing to cope with the craving?

What is sparking off your urges?

What are the triggers?

Take a sheet of paper and make as comprehensive a list of your triggers as you can. At the very least, try to identify the triggers which are most problematic for you.

Dealing with Triggers Using RAC

As we saw in the section on dealing with social situations, it can help to go through the RAC technique (Recognize-Avoid-Cope).

We've already looked at how you can recognize your triggers.

How can you avoid some of the environments, people, or feelings which trigger your alcohol drinking?

Methods of coping with your drinking urges include distraction, talking to somebody about your cravings, riding out the urge to drink, and thinking about the negative consequences of your alcohol drinking.

Another coping method is to think about why you are taking on the *30 Day Alcohol Reboot* challenge in the first place.

You can also use positive self-talk and affirmations.

Above all, know what you are going to do in certain situation by planning ahead and using if/then scenarios.

And I'll reiterate again the importance of keeping things as simple as possible.

Recap

At the end of the day, cravings are nothing more than temporary discomfort.

The alcohol habit sequence comes in three parts: the trigger, the behavior, and the reward. If you don't give into the craving, it will peak and then disappear within a very short space of time.

If you use some of the coping mechanisms outlined above, your cravings will disappear within minutes.

And remember, your cravings will disappear whether you give in to them or not.

Exercise

Question your cravings in week one.

Where do they come from and how do they make you feel?

What do you feel physically?

How do you feel emotionally?

How long does the craving last?

How have you been coping with it up until now?

What exactly is triggering your cravings?

Take a sheet of paper and make a list of all your main triggering thoughts. Do the same for everything in your environment that triggers your drinking cravings.

Celebrate Your Successes by Rewarding Yourself

We all like to reward ourselves from time to time. We can use rewards to celebrate our successes, to motivate us into continuing through difficulties, and as coping mechanisms.

Finishing the Journey

In terms of the *30 Day Alcohol Reboot*, there are two types of rewards.

The first type is where you reward yourself for finishing the journey.

Think back to the benefits of quitting alcohol for a month. One of the more obvious benefits was the amount of money that you will save by not buying all that alcohol.

Depending on the amount you save, your final reward could be spending that money on pampering yourself, buying something that you have wanted for a while, or just blowing it on something frivolous.

Interval Rewards

Another form of reward is where you give yourself with a treat at a set interval, perhaps every couple of days, or the end of the week.

Again, what you choose for a reward is up to you. It's much more gratifying if the reward has personal meaning for you.

Always have a couple of options to choose from.

Remember that sometimes the best rewards are things that money can't buy. Taking an hour to yourself in the middle of the day to just read a book, take a walk, or cuddle your pet dog.

The smaller rewards, taken more frequently, will probably be much more effective than the one single reward at the end of the challenge.

Reward Caveats

A couple of small caveats.

First, try not to use food or drink as a reward, especially if you're trying to lose weight.

Second, don't fudge the numbers just to get the reward. You have to be honest with yourself.

Recap

Whether your reward is to motivate yourself, to celebrate your successes, or as a coping mechanism, there are two types of rewards to choose from.

The first is the short-term reward, given after a set interval, a number of days achieved, the end of the week, et cetera. The second is the long-term reward, rewarding yourself at the end of the challenge.

Choose rewards that are meaningful to you, small rewards are probably better than the larger ones, and don't cheat.

Exercise

What are you going to reward yourself with? When are you going to reward yourself? Think of some deliciously rewarding and very personal rewards.

Choose a long-term reward for when you finish the 30 Day Alcohol Reboot.

Then choose some short-term, interval rewards to provide ongoing motivation and support.

Remember, these rewards don't have to cost money. They can be very simple. In fact, like everything else in this course, the simplest rewards are often the best.

Good Nutrition for Long-Term Success

As far as I'm concerned, taking care of your body should be the number one priority in your life as a general rule. Your body is the only body you've got, and once it is knackered, that's it. It's game over.

It doesn't have to be that way.

Buffett Your Car

Warren Buffett has a great analogy for the way we treat our bodies.

He asks you to imagine that we live in a world where once a person got to driving age, they were given a brand-new car.

On your 18th birthday, or whatever the driving age happens to be in your neck of the woods, you're presented with a brand-new car. It's explained to you that this car is the only car that you will ever own in your entire life. You are told that this car will have to last you until the day you die.

What do you do? You would really look after it, that's what you'd do!

Imagine the business opportunities. There would be a whole sector of companies whose sole mission it was to help you maintain your car for as long as possible.

You would never miss an oil change. You would wash it and wax it as regular as clockwork. You would never leave it out in the sun, making sure it was covered if you had to leave it out in the open, and you'd park it in a garage whenever you could. You would never drive it in such a way that put your lifetime car in any danger.

In short, you would do everything in your power lengthen the life of your lifetime car.

The moral of this story is that when we are born, we are given a single body which has to last until the day we die. It's the only body we ever get.

Why don't we treat our bodies with the same level of respect that we would if we owned a lifetime car?

Some people do.

Most people don't.

A Slice of Life

Now, in the context of this material, we're not talking about a lifetime, we're only talking 30 days. But, as I have said before, this 30 days challenge gives you the opportunity to see how alcohol is affecting your life from broader perspective.

Alcohol is very harmful neurotoxin. When we are drunk, we gravitate towards further physical danger through the actions that we take, the additional rubbish food that we consume, and so on.

There are so many benefits to putting a small bit of effort to exercise every day, and looking after your nutrition. It's shouldn't be difficult.

Healthy Lifestyle Rules

There are a few simple rules, to make sure that you maintain a healthy and active mind and body.

Keep carbed-up on healthy whole foods.

Good carbohydrates, from fruit and vegetables, give you the natural energy that you need for maintaining your motivation. This energy will also expand your willpower and provide you with the fuel you need to keep pushing.

On the other hand, avoid junk food like it's the poison that it is. Avoid junk food in all its forms, solid or liquid.

Junk food does the opposite to natural whole food. It gives you almost no nutritional value. It provides energy in very short spikes, followed by an equally sharp decline. And in the long-term, eating junk food will sap your mental strength and damage your health.

Finally, drink a lot of water.

Water is essential.

Drinking water will not only keep you hydrated, it will help keep your cravings at bay. This is because many of your alcohol cravings are fuelled by thirst.

Recap

It's important to look after your body as if it were your lifetime car. You can do this in part through good nutrition and exercise.

In the long-term, good nutrition and exercise help you to live a longer quality life.

In the short term, good nutrition and exercise give you the fuel by which to drive your motivation, your willpower, and your abilities to do anything.

Exercise

I'm sure you want to get the best from the body you've got. I'm sure you want to live a longer life, a better quality life. And I'm sure you would be willing to change many of the damaging elements in your life to ensure that this happens.

Make a list of all the areas where you can make improvements.

How can you improve your nutrition?

How can you improve your levels of exercise?

WEEK TWO

The 30 Day Alcohol Reboot - Week Two

Congratulations if you have reached week two.

Momentum Is with You

Sales author, Charles J Givens, said "Success requires first expending ten units of effort to produce one unit of results. Your momentum will then produce ten units of results with each unit of effort."

You should have momentum on your side now you've reached week two.

Once you've passed that seven-day milestone, you have time and energy invested. That time and energy represents something tangible. It represents the effort that you have expended to get you through seven full days. This gives you momentum.

Experience is Vital

It's easy to say that a week is not much time, but in the realm of habit change, getting past the first week is crucial. With seven days under your belt, you have experience of what it's like to be without the focus of the behavior, in this case the alcohol. Without the behavior, the habit cannot survive.

You've gone through seven mornings without a hangover, seven evenings without taking a drink, and perhaps a few restless nights.

You've also gone through a whole weekend. Have you socialized? It can be tough. But you've done it!

The Storm Is Passing

If you felt cravings in the last week, the worst of that should be over. I'm not saying that you won't continue to feel cravings. You will. But now, your experience should give you a bit more self-confidence in your own abilities to overcome any cravings.

Experience also tells you that the cravings probably weren't as bad as you thought they would be. Mind over matter.

Week Two

In week two we are going to look at going to parties, comparing your drinking with others, and how to deal with any lingering cravings.

We'll look at how to keep yourself on track, how to avoid the temptation of giving in to that one momentary urge, and where to focus your mind for the best possible results.

Then we will look at keeping the end goal in mind, staying active, rewarding behaviors not outcomes, and finally what to do if you slip in week two.

Let's begin!

Going to a Party?

We've already seen that you should choose a time for your *30 Day Alcohol Reboot* when you are unlikely to have any commitments.

If we are lucky, our day-to-day lives are fairly predictable. But there are times when life is unpredictable. Surprises can always be found around the corner.

The Surprise Party

The surprise might be a party. A couple you know decide to get engaged, your best friend has just had an unexpected windfall, or your brother just got a great promotion.

Whatever the reason, parties are going to happen. It doesn't have to mean the end of your *30 Day Alcohol Reboot*.

When you find out about the party, use some forward thinking and planning. What are you going to drink? Will you bring your own non-alcoholic drinks? How will you react when somebody offers you a drink?

Being a Party Pooper

You don't have to go to every party that you're invited to. If you can avoid them, just don't go.

Sometimes these parties are impossible to avoid. They are just too important in the grand scheme of things. We all have important celebrations, milestone birthday parties, engagements or weddings, christenings, and so on. So, it's fair to say that not going to some parties will cause you more problems than going to them.

Only you can be the best judge of that.

Party on Dude!

But there is no reason why you cannot have a great time at any party without drinking alcohol, even if all your friends are. It can feel a bit strange to be on the soft drinks, but that's all it is, something you're not used to.

Let's face it, as a drinker, if you gone to a party in the past without drinking alcohol, it's probably because there's been a really good reason for not partaking. Maybe you have had to drive, perhaps you were on medication, or you just had to get up early the next morning for something important and you couldn't risk the hangover.

Now that you are doing the *30 Day Alcohol Reboot*, it's exactly the same final result. You attend the party and don't drink.

One of the reasons why it can feel a bit strange is because you know that you could drink if you really wanted to.

Don't Make a Big Deal Out Of It

The first tip is don't make a big deal out of.

It's only a month.

It's only a party.

If you take the alcohol out of the party, the party still exists.

The fun doesn't disappear just because the alcohol is off the menu. The fun continues. The fun remains because of the people, the atmosphere, the venue, the conversation. The fun is there because of all the reasons why a party is fun in the first place. We've just been brainwashed into thinking that a party without alcohol is no fun. We've been brainwashed into thinking that we are no fun without alcohol.

Don't let that brainwashing continue. Stop being a sheep.

You will surprise yourself at how easy it is to still relax and have fun without alcohol. You may even exceed your expectations, having even more fun.

Own the Room

The second tip is to own the room.

That means don't be a victim. Don't have that victim mentality that says poor you, you are the only one that cannot drink.

If you're looking for a way *not* to have fun, that's probably it. Hold onto that victim mentality and you'll be the most miserable one there.

However, if you want to have fun, keep your chin up, keep the smile on your face, and the maintain those positive thoughts running through your mind.

Don't Take Any Crap

As we have talked about in the last section, quitting drinking alcohol is your decision and people should respect that. So don't allow people to push your buttons.

If someone offers you a drink, say "No, thank you", and repeat that same simple statement as often as is necessary, sounding like a broken record if you have to.

Say it and repeat it calmly and with respect.

Say it and repeat it while you look straight in their eyes, with your head up and your chest out.

Plan, Visualise, If/Then

Before you go to the party, be sure to plan what you are going to do and what you will drink.

Picture yourself already there. Visualize the people, the drinks, the food, and your friends.

Create some if/then scenarios. If this happens, then I will do that.

And finally, remember that you always have the option of leaving early.

If I go to a party, I will stay until other people's drunkenness gets to a certain irritating level, then I make my quiet exit into the night.

Recap

Parties are a fact of life. The same simple rules apply if you are going to any place where drink will be served, any place where you would normally have had a few drinks in the past or maybe have even got drunk. At first, it will seem a bit strange.

Don't make a big deal out of it. You'll surprise yourself at how easy it is to get into the mood and have fun despite your lack of inebriation.

Don't be a victim of yourself. Own the room and don't be afraid to say "no". Don't be afraid to say "no" as often as you need.

Prepare beforehand, rehearse how to say no, and create some if/then scenarios.

Above all, you can still let your hair down and enjoy yourself. And take charge of when you are going to leave. You feel the need to go, just go!

Exercise

Think about going to a party and not having any alcohol. How do you feel?

Concentrate your thoughts on the lack of alcohol. Concentrate on how much you miss the alcohol, how much everyone else is enjoying themselves apart from you, and how much you can't wait for this stupid challenge to be over.

Now switch perspectives.

Again, think about going to the party and not having any alcohol. Concentrate on the room, on the people, on the music, and the laughter. Think about how much fun you are having, despite the fact that you aren't intoxicated.

Can you see how much your frame of mind makes a massive difference in how you perceive any given situation?

Compare Your Alcohol Drinking with Others

Taking Perspective

Sometimes it's hard to see the forest for the trees.

On a day-to-day basis, we tend to focus our attentional lens on the specifics, on the details. We also tend to focus our attentional lens on *our* specifics. This is good. It allows us to get things done, to get *our* things done.

But when you're too close to a particular situation, it can be difficult to see the wider picture.

It can be very instructive to step back a little bit and get some perspective.

What Are Other People Drinking?

When you drink alcohol, one of the major things that is out of focus for us is what other people are drinking.

Of course, you might know what your close friends drink or your family members, but you're not really taking notice of who is drinking what and how much they are drinking. This is even more so in the wider environment.

Why is this important?

When you don't drink alcohol, at first you feel like you're the only one who is not drinking. It's an uncomfortable feeling. You feel you're on your own and being left out.

It almost feels like you're the naughty child who hasn't eaten his dinner and, because of that, you aren't getting any desert.

However, after a while, a strange thing starts to happen. You start to notice that you're not alone, you're not the only one who isn't using alcohol.

In fact, it's quite amazing how many people don't drink any alcohol, ever. In the West, it's about 35%. In the whole world, almost half the population have never, nor will ever, drink alcohol in their lifetimes.

Look Who Is Drinking

When you're in a room full of people, in a restaurant for instance, take a look around and see who is drinking and who is not drinking. See how many people are only drinking water or some other soft drink.

Don't just look at what they are drinking, observe how much they are drinking, and how they act when they are drinking.

Compare that to the alcohol drinkers.

How are they drinking?

How much they are drinking?

How do they act when they are drinking?

Your Alcohol Drinking Comparison

Now, take a retrospective look back at your own alcohol use and make some comparisons.

As you observe, keep in your mind that alcohol is a drug, a very potent and potentially dangerous drug. Look at people from this perspective. Can you see drug use? Can you see drug users?

Recap

Not everybody drinks or wants to drink alcohol.

When you step away from drinking alcohol for a while, you get to look at your alcohol use from a different perspective. It's only then that you can start to observe and understand just how many people are not actually consuming alcohol at all.

These people don't need to drink and are still having fun without it.

Exercise

The next time you are in restaurant or at party, check out how many people are drinking and who is not drinking.

Sometimes it's hard to tell the difference. Some non-drinkers hide their non-drinking behind mocktails and lookalikes: alcohol free beers; Coke, ice, and lemon; tonic water, ice, and lemon.

Notice the difference in how people are behaving, the difference between the drinkers and the non-drinkers.

Do one group look like they're having more fun than another?

Now look back on your own drinking, and make some comparisons.

Are You Still Getting Cravings?

New Cravings

In week two, you should find that your cravings have declined considerably compared with the first week.

Having said that, new situations can trigger new cravings.

Remember that cravings are a normal process of any habit deconstruction.

Cravings don't just happen in connection with drug withdrawal, we experience cravings in many areas of our lives.

We experience cravings for food and other types of drinks, think sugary drinks or caffeine. We have cravings and urges as a natural part of our physiology. We crave safety, belonging, or feeling that we make a difference. We also get emotional cravings.

Of course, if you add a drug to the mixture, you generate a different dimension. However, all cravings essentially tweak the same strings.

Cravings Responding to Triggers

Cravings usually happen in response to a trigger.

An alcohol drinking trigger is part of your alcohol behavior sequence. First you have the trigger, then the behavior, and finally you get the reward.

A trigger can be anything. It can be a feeling, thought, something somebody says to you, something that has happened recently, or it can be anything in your environment.

Environmental triggers are the most common. But as with everything, all triggers are catalysts which kick start a thought process. It is that thought process that results in a decision being made, which leads to the behavior of alcohol drinking, and finally the result of you getting drunk, sleeping, relaxing, or whatever the reward happens to be.

Personal Trigger Recap

So let's take a look at your personal triggers once again.

If you feel cravings, think about what has happened immediately before you felt that craving.

What did you see, hear, feel, taste, or smell?

What did you think about?

Now, go back to your if/then scenarios.

In the future, what will you do when you are triggered by that sight, sound, feeling, taste, or smell?

What can you do when triggered by that thought?

You can use if/then scenarios, as I talked about before. "If I see an advertisement for my favorite drink, then I will think about how healthy I am feeling without alcohol in my system and how I would be jeopardizing my health by giving into those cravings".

Craving Acceptance

Sometimes you just have to accept the craving as it is.

A craving is only a naturally occurring discomfort, it's a part of the habit. It's also a part of learning to be without the habit.

Cravings cannot harm you. They won't kill you. All you will feel is a feeling of discomfort. And anyone can handle that.

Remember also that cravings are very short lived. They will peak and dissipate within a short space of time, normally after only minutes.

Accept the craving, accept the discomfort, accept the naturalness of it all, and allow it to pass freely.

Recap

We are in week two, and you're still feeling cravings. So what? It's a natural process that happens to us all. It's an inconvenient discomfort that you can handle perfectly well.

Exercise

To reduce the risk of future cravings, think about what preceded the craving. It could have been a thought, a smell, a sound, and so on. Isolate the triggering incident, then develop a couple of if/then scenarios to deal with these triggering incidents if and when they arise in the future.

How to Keep Yourself on Track in Week Two?

How do you feel now that you are in week two? Are you still feeling motivated? Let's take a look at a few more motivational techniques to keep you on track in week two.

The Seat of Motivation

Where do you find motivation?

Motivation is fundamental to achieving anything of value in our lives. Motivation is can only found internally. You might be motivated by outside events, people, things you hear and see, and so on, but the impetus to take action comes from within.

To get that motivational drive working, you need to move your thoughts in the right direction.

I am motivated by many things in life, but mostly by my son. I am motivated to be the best person that I can be to encourage him to live the best life that he can live and be the best person that he can be.

Is it him who is motivating me or are my thoughts about him motivating me? It doesn't matter.

Sometimes, motivation is just not enough. Motivation certainly helps you to achieve. It drives you forward through the good times and it can be crucial during dark times, when you're having difficulties.

Think about motivation as the wheels specifically designed keep your personal train moving forward on its designated track.

Let's take a look at a few more techniques to help maintain your motivation.

Narrow Your Focus

Don't overanalyze. Learn to ignore the unimportant.

If you spread your focus too wide, you run the risk of not putting enough effort into those things that are more important.

To help stay focused and productive, as well as freeing up some of your valuable time, ignore everything that won't directly contribute towards your success.

Pat Yourself on the Back

Keep reminding yourself of your strong points.

They say self-praise is no praise, I beg to differ. If you have to advertise your own virtues, then yes, self-praise is no praise.

What I'm talking about is understanding your strengths and giving yourself a pat on the back for those strengths. This is a good thing.

Being well acquainted with your potential is one of the keys to habit change. To understand what skills you need to learn, you also have to understand your weaknesses and strengths. You need to know where you're starting from in order to move forwards.

Self-praise is also a very helpful component of self-motivation.

One way great way of reminding you of your good points is through your daily affirmations. Use your affirmations to pat yourself on the back for all the hard work you're putting in, the lessons you are learning, and your growth as a human being.

Focus Forward

Focus your energies on building a new habit instead of destroying the old habit.

Positive forward focusing is much more motivating than negative backward focusing.

It's virtually impossible for your instinctual brain to think about not doing something. Your logical brain gets the concept, but the older and more powerful part of your brain, the reptilian brain or basal ganglia, only sees the thing that you're trying to remove.

When you think "I don't want to drink alcohol", what does your brain see? It sees see alcohol. You see yourself drinking alcohol.

For your brain to figure out what it's not supposed to be thinking about, it has to think about it. It's a Catch-22 situation.

If you think about not drinking alcohol, guess what you focus will be on? The alcohol, of course! Do it now. Think about not drinking alcohol. What images do you come up with? What do you see in your mind?

The only way around this not thinking about alcohol or quitting drinking alcohol is to focus your mind forwards to what you want to achieve.

I'm not talking about the thoughts of alcohol that will pop into your head from time to time. You can't help that. It's part of the change process. I'm talking about your deliberate thinking patterns.

When you are thinking about ways of overcoming this problem, focus your attention on what you want to replace your alcohol habit with, on the solution. Never focus on the old habit, on the old problem.

Focus on where you want to be not where you were. In the words of Tony Robbins, "Your life is controlled by what you focus on".

Take Regular Exercise

A third way of keeping yourself on track in week two is to get plenty of exercise.

Exercise doesn't have to be pounding away for an hour on the treadmill, or busting a gut trying to lift your own body weight in the gym.

Exercise means moving. Movement alters emotions. Movement can take you from a negative feeling to a positive feeling very quickly.

Exercise triggers happiness endorphins in your brain. When you're feeling happy, you're much more likely to feel motivated.

So don't waste your time sitting on the couch feeling demotivated, get up off your arse, get moving, and change your emotions through motion.

Recap

Sometimes it's difficult to keep yourself motivated in week two. You've gone past the initial drive of the first week, and you're settling into a routine, a routine that can sometimes be boring.

The three tips for keeping yourself motivated are:

Learning to ignore the unimportant

Reminding yourself of your strong points and focusing on those strong points

Exercise regularly

You can quickly alter your emotions through your motions.

Exercise

Make a list of your strong points.

What are you good at?

What have you done well in the first week?

What are you focused on?

Are you focusing on the alcohol that you cannot have? Instead, focus on the future goal that you want to achieve through this *30 Day Alcohol Reboot*.

What Do You Do If You Drink Again?

The last thing anyone wants when they're going through a challenge is to slip up halfway through.

Does this mean that this is the end of your journey?

What does it say about you as a person?

Learning Life's Lessons

Life is full of mistakes.

As human beings, it's how we learn. Far from making us fragile, making mistakes actually creates a stronger person. Making mistakes also helps us to deal with future adversity. You know that making a mistake is not the end of the world. Mistakes are proof that you can deal with life and everything that it throws at you. Mistakes are proof that you are trying

To paraphrase the American artist Beatrice Wood, mistakes are like the pebbles that make a good road. To have a good life, your own journey has got to be paved with mistake after mistake.

Taking that drink isn't the end of the world, nor should it be the end of your 30 Day Alcohol Reboot.

Viewing Your Mistakes

You have a couple of ways of looking at this.

You can look at your mistake as the end of your challenge. That's it, you screwed up, you took a drink, and now it's game over! You can feel sorry for yourself, feel guilty, and vow to do better the next time.

You can also say that this mistake was just that, a mistake, a detour, a slip or stumble.

Let's say that you are taking a walk down a road. Say you're doing 20 km. What do you do after you stumble off the road? Do you have to return to the start? "Do not pass Go. Do not collect $200."

Come on!

This is the real world. In the real world when you slip off the road you get back onto the road exactly where you fell off. You don't have to walk back ten feet, or a hundred feet, nor do you have to go all the way back to the beginning.

Games and Rules

We play silly games with ourselves, enforcing rules on ourselves which only serve to put unnecessary obstacles in our way. That's just bullshit! With any challenge in life, there will be mistakes.

You might be saying that the whole point of this 30 Day Alcohol Reboot is not to drink alcohol for 30 days. But if you do have a slip, why should it be the end of your journey?

If you ended after a single mistake, you've just wasted all those days and all that energy that have taken you up to this point.

It also means that you are robbing yourself of the opportunity of continuing. Why would you do that?

In our sometimes warped culture, it's considered cheating if you slip up and want to continue from where you left off. How dare you! How dare you think that you can cheat your way out of this! Get your ass back to the beginning! I didn't slip and you've no right to slip either!

At the end of the day who cares about that. This is not competition. This is your life. You only have one life. What's the point in erecting unnecessary barriers to your own progress?

I'm not talking about deliberately taking a timeout of your challenge so that you can go out drinking with your mates, then in hindsight calling it a mistake.

Nor am I talking about repeatedly "making mistakes". If these types of mistakes are happening, you have to seriously question your resolve. You have to ask yourself if you genuinely want to complete this challenge.

Revisit Your Reasons

Look again at your reasons for doing this challenge.

Seriously, if you having problems with your resolve, go back and look at the reasons you started this journey.

These reasons are all profound personal motivations. They have a significant meaning to you. They're not part of some game. They are part of your real life. Looking at things from this perspective, don't ever treat it like a game.

If you're learning how to ride a horse and you fall off, you get back up on the horse and continue where you left off.

You haven't lost any of the knowledge that you've gained. You don't go back to being a complete beginner.

You simply begin again where you left off.

It's the same here. You are taking this 30 day reboot because you want to change something about yourself, you want to challenge yourself.

Don't create unnecessary rules. The basic premise is that you want to last for 30 days without taking a drink. If you happen to take a drink within that 30 days, don't throw in the towel. All is not lost. You simply start where you stopped.

You might take an extra day to complete the challenge to make up for the day you drank. But the end result will *almost* be the same: you not having alcohol in your body for 30 days.

We can get pedantic about this, but the end result is the same. And don't let anybody tell you anything different.

Recap

Life is full of mistakes. Even if you make a mistake in this journey, don't treat it like it's the end. You don't even have to go back to the beginning, to start again. As in life, if you fall off the road, you get right back on where you fell off, you don't go back to the start.

Exercise

Stop thinking about this like it's a game. It's not a game. Gamification is everywhere. We love turning things into games, competing with ourselves, trying to beat our last score, to run faster, eat better, play longer.

That's okay if it works, if it drives us on. But when it doesn't provide something positive, it can make us feel like failures.

The *30 Day Alcohol Reboot* is a challenge. The challenge is to keep going, to keep aiming towards your end goal, in spite of obstacles along the way. Making a mistake might be one of those obstacles.

Again, stop thinking about this like it's a game. It's your life. And that means it's important.

WEEK THREE

Half Way There

Congratulations on getting to week three of your *30 Day Alcohol Reboot*. You should be proud of yourself. It's a great achievement. Not many people who quit drinking reach week three.

Where Are You Now?

At this point, I think it's a good idea to take stock of your alcohol drinking and what led you to take the decision to quit.

First of all, let's take a look at where you are right now.

You haven't touched a drop of alcohol for over 14 days.

How are you feeling?

Have you had any thoughts about taking a drink?

Have you had any cravings or other discomforts?

Do you feel like you are missing out on anything?

Take out your list of reasons to stop drinking. Does anything really pop out at you? Do you notice any big changes over the last two weeks?

For instance, if one of your reasons for quitting was to improve your health, have you noticed that that your health has noticeably improved in the last two weeks?

If one of your reasons to quit was to lose some weight, how much weight have you lost?

Take a few minutes to look over your reasons and see if and where there have been improvements.

How Your Alcohol Drinking Habit Is Changing

Asking yourself questions like these highlights where your alcohol habit was before you started this challenge.

When you see improvements in your health or in the way that you're feeling now, it shows that drinking alcohol *was* having an effect on you. It shows *how* alcohol was affecting you.

When you have fewer thoughts about alcohol, cravings, discomforts, or feelings like you're missing, it shows how your alcohol habit is changing.

Like any other drug, the human body reacts in a specific way when alcohol is consumed over a long period of time.

One significant effect that this drug has on your body is dependence, another is tolerance, and a third is psychological and physical withdrawal when the drug is no longer available.

Let's look at each of these in turn.

Dependence

Dependence on this drug means that you have a need to use this drug under specific circumstances, in specific environments, or with specific people.

Most alcohol drinkers are dependent on alcohol to one degree or another.

If you drink alcohol every evening, you are dependent. If you drink alcohol every weekend, you are dependent. If you cannot go to a pub without drinking alcohol, you are dependent.

Most people try to defend their alcohol dependence by giving examples of times and places they haven't drank alcohol.

It doesn't prove anything.

Just as you are dependent on the drug in specific circumstances, there are also specific circumstances where you don't use the drug, when you are not dependent on it.

Dependence is a part of the habit. Habits are learned and so is dependence. You learn to be dependent on alcohol in some situations, and not in others.

Of course, there are times when you may go to a bar or a party and not drink. You might even say that this proves that you are not dependent, that you can go without.

In most cases, these periods of abstinence don't prove the lack of dependence. This is because they are normally forced periods of abstinence.

You have to drive, you are taking pills, or the some of the reason. You don't drink because you can't drink.

The Alcohol Drinking Scale

Some will argue that there is a difference between dependence and addiction. They would be right. But that's like pointing out the difference between two different shades of blue.

Dependence and addiction are just different points on the same scale.

At one extremity on this scale is the occasional drinker who drinks once in a blue moon and doesn't actually need alcohol for anything. They could happily go for the rest of their lives without drinking. Or they might have one or two alcoholic drinks a month, just to satisfy social convention.

At the other end of the scale is the person drinks alcohol as soon as they wake in the morning and continues drinking throughout the day.

Dependence takes up many spaces in between these two extremes.

Who's Definition?

If during the first two weeks of not drinking alcohol you have had thoughts about taking a drink, cravings, or some other discomfort because you haven't been able to take a drink you are most certainly dependent on alcohol to one degree or another.

These are not very precise definitions, I grant you that. But there are no precise definitions when it comes to drug use. Who is alcoholic? Who is dependent? Who is a problem drinker?

Yet these are the definitions that are used by professionals to evaluate a person's level of drug use.

One professional's definition of a problem drinker, a dependent drinker, or addicted drinker, won't necessarily fit with another.

The only definition that matters here is your definition.

How do you think about your own drinking?

Do you feel that you need to drink?

When do you need to drink?

Under what circumstances?

With who?

Alcohol the Outlaw

If you asked an average group of people to list drugs in order of harm, alcohol would probably not even appear on that list. Yet, it is one of the most harmful drugs out there, and it's freely available.

If alcohol were a new drug being introduced to the market and had to go through FDA scrutiny, it would never pass. It would be placed on the banned substances list.

Yet, because it's freely available, we freely consume it. Is it any wonder? We assume that we are protected by our governments. Surely, if there was anything wrong with alcohol, it wouldn't be freely available? That's just not the case.

Tolerance

Tolerance is another aspect of alcohol use I would like to cover here. The more a drug is used, the more it needs to be used to get the same hit. It's as simple as that.

Your body builds a tolerance for the dose. To get the same buzz, you have to increase the dose.

We see this with all sorts of drugs, from prescription pharmaceuticals to alcohol.

Think back to when you first started drinking alcohol. How much could you drink? I'll wager it was very little in those early days. Compare that with how much alcohol you are able to drink now.

This is drug tolerance in action.

The Dangers of Tolerance

Don't make the mistake of equating tolerance with control. Tolerance does not mean that your body can handle more alcohol. It can't.

The average human body can only metabolize on average one unit (8 g) of alcohol per hour. Just because your body can tolerate a lot of alcohol, this doesn't mean your body can metabolize more alcohol. Your liver still has to grind through the alcohol at the same rate of one unit per hour.

Stand in any bar and watch the way people drink. The glasses of alcohol are emptied, one after the other, without the slightest thought for the damage that is going on beneath the surface.

But the whole point of drinking alcohol is to push our bodies past those fixed metabolic limits. Essentially, we have to overdose on alcohol. If we didn't push our liver past its natural limits, we wouldn't get drunk.

Alcohol Damage versus Alcohol Tolerance

And there's another component to this: age. The fact is, the older you get, the less alcohol your liver can metabolize.

Because alcohol is a toxin, it causes damage each time it is ingested. The more alcohol you consume, the more damage is caused. Some people presume that more tolerance equals less damage.

Wrong!

The damage caused does not correspond to your level of alcohol tolerance. The damage caused only corresponds to your level of alcohol consumption. The more alcohol you drink, the more damage is caused, end of story.

Tolerance only affects the immediate physical effects of the alcohol, the drunkenness. You drink more, you need more.

Defending Tolerance

My theory is that tolerance has evolved as a security measure.

Our brains function as if we were still living in the cave, in the wild, with all that that entails.

We might live in the modern world, with all sorts of artificial safeguards, but our brains are essentially wired to survive in those primitive and very hostile conditions.

In these primitive conditions, if you are incapacitated by alcohol, your ability to defend yourself or to run away is severely handicapped. The more frequently you experience this inebriation, the higher is your chance of landing yourself in the shit with some hunter-killer animal with big teeth. So it's in your own best survival instincts if your body can evolve a rudimentary immunity to this type of intoxication.

And that's just what happens.

The human body has evolved the capacity to cultivate a gradual resistance to the effects of alcohol or most other drugs.

Tolerance Is No Fun

Of course, this tolerance gets in the way of our having fun. And we don't like it.

This bloody tolerance thing goes completely against our motivations for using alcohol.

So what do we do? We counterbalance the effects of tolerance by increasing the dose, by overdosing.

We increase the dose, our body increases the tolerance, we increase the dose again, and again our body increases the tolerance.

All the while the damage is accumulating.

Your body has no idea that you are diligently and enthusiastically consuming more and more alcohol. It has no idea that you are using the alcohol to get a buzz, to feel drunk.

Your body only sees alcohol in one way, as a foreign invader, as a toxin, as something it needs to eliminate as soon as possible.

Psychological and Physical Withdrawal

And finally, what about the psychological and physical withdrawal when the drug is no longer available.

Are you feeling cravings or discomfort?

Do you feel like you are missing out when you're in a situation where you would normally drink and yet you are prevented?

This is a form of either psychological or physical withdrawal.

Just like dependence or addiction, the withdrawal can also be measured on a scale from very mild symptoms of withdrawal to extreme withdrawal syndrome where the person is at risk of death.

Be Aware of What You Are Doing to Yourself

The idea of this section is to make you aware of the risks you're taking whenever you drink alcohol, whether it's wine, beer, whiskey, or alcopops.

You are consuming a drug. To get drunk, you have to overdose on this drug. Alcohol is one of the most harmful drugs, even though it's legal.

In terms of annual worldwide deaths, only nicotine beats alcohol.

The worldwide deaths from smoking are about 5 million a year. The worldwide deaths from alcohol are approximately 3.5 million per year. Compare that to the worldwide deaths from all the other illegal drugs combined, which is 250,000 a year.

You should also be aware of your level of dependence. Alcohol affects so many different parts of your physical and mental self. It damages almost every organ in your body, and is one of the few substances which can pass through the blood brain barrier, gaining direct access to your brain.

Recap

Most alcohol drinkers are dependent on alcohol to one degree or another. It's very difficult to put a concrete definition on drug dependence, just as it's difficult to define an alcoholic or a problem drinker. Only you can truly evaluate your own situation.

Even if you go to a counsellor, they will only evaluate you based on what you say. This doesn't guarantee anything.

Tolerance is your body's way of defending itself against a toxic onslaught.

In the "real" world, intoxication will get you killed very quickly. We have evolved alcohol tolerance as a security against this.

The more alcohol you drink, the more you need to drink. The more you drink, the more damage is caused. Tolerance does not counterbalance this damage.

Exercise

Think about your past drinking, and ask yourself how your drinking has changed since you first started?

How many alcohol drinks can you drink now in comparison to when you first started?

And finally, you have had two weeks free of alcohol, how has that affected you, physically and mentally?

Has it been a struggle?

Have you had cravings or discomfort?

Have you missed drinking alcohol?

How Do You Think about Yourself As a Drinker?

Good News about Our Bad Habits

Who are you as a drinker and what has alcohol done for you?

For the most part, we think about alcohol as a part of our culture, as something we do to relax, to have fun, to celebrate, and so on.

It's only when we realize that there are consequences associated with drinking alcohol, particularly personal consequences, that we begin to open our eyes to the fact that alcohol might not be as beneficial as we had once thought, or we would like to think.

We like hearing good news about our bad habits, after all.

A Drug by Any Other Name

In the last section, we looked at alcohol as a drug.

The alcohol industry fights tooth and nail to prevent any alcoholic drink from being labeled as such. They prefer the term "beverage". And you can probably understand why.

How many people would stop using alcohol if it were reclassified as a drug? If that were to happen, it would be classified as "Class A" or "Schedule 1". This means that it would be in the same category as heroin, mescaline, ecstasy, and LSD. How many people would still use alcohol then?

This definitely puts a different spin on things, doesn't it!

William Shakespeare said, "A rose by any other name would smell as sweet". Well, a drug by any other name would kill as dead.

Meet Kevin, the Drug User

It's only when I stopped drinking alcohol that I realized how much of a drug alcohol really was, and how much of a hold the drinking habit had over my life.

I had never thought of myself as a drug user before, not in relation to alcohol or nicotine. I had dabbled in cocaine, speed, ecstasy, and had been a long-time cannabis smoker. However, I never really got into any of these drugs as much as I did alcohol, in fact I stopped taking every other drug years ago.

I didn't view myself as a drug user, even though cigarettes and alcohol were causing me many difficulties.

Alcohol in particular was robbing me of large chunks of my life. It wasn't until I finally quit, when I was free of the effects of this drug, that I finally realized just how much of my life had gone to waste.

Meet You, the Drug User

I think this is an ideal time for you to begin looking back at your drinking life. Take a trip all the way back to the beginning, when you took your first swig of that foul-smelling liquid.

Was it beer, wine, whiskey?

How much did you drink?

Who were you with?

What made you take that first sip?

Now move forward through your alcohol drinking life to where you are now.

Can you see how you have progressed from drinking a little to drinking your current consumption levels?

How much can you drink now on an average night?

What's the maximum you can drink?

20 Questions

Now, take an honest look at these questions below and simply answer yes or no.

1   Have you lost time from your work because of your drinking?

2   Is drinking making your home life unhappy?

3   Do you drink because you are shy with other people?

4   Is drinking affecting your reputation?

5   Have you ever felt remorse after drinking?

6   Have you gotten into financial difficulties as a result of drinking?

7   Do you turn to lower companions or environment when drinking?

8   Does your drinking make you careless of your family's welfare?

9   Has your ambition decreased since drinking?

10   Do you want a drink the next morning?

11   Do you crave a drink at a definite time daily?

12   Does drinking cause you to have difficulty in sleeping?

13   Has your efficiency decreased since drinking?

14   Is drinking jeopardizing your job or business?

15   Do you drink to escape from worries or trouble?

16   Do you drink alone?

17   Have you ever had a complete loss of memory as a result of drinking?

18   Has your physician ever treated you for drinking?

19   Do you drink to build up your self-confidence?

20   Have you ever been to a hospital or institution on account of drinking?

Why am I bringing up these questions?

These questions are known as the Johns Hopkins 20 questions for alcoholics. The criteria for problem drinking is if you answer yes to more than three of these questions.

These questions can help to see how your drinking patterns have changed through the years.

When I was drinking, I could probably answer yes to over a dozen, if not more. How many people have drank alone? How many people have drank to escape from worries or trouble? How many people have drank to get to sleep at night? How many people have had a hangover going into their job, putting pressure on that job? How many people have consumed alcohol because they were a little shy, to give them some Dutch courage?

Problems and Solutions

Let's get back to the challenge. You've been off the alcohol for a few weeks and you should now be in a position to see some of the benefits of not drinking. You should also be able to see areas where you are dependent.

The point is, casting an honest eye over your drinking life, lets you see the problems. Hopefully, the *30 Day Alcohol Reboot* will show you some of the solutions.

Think about the amount of time you have spent drinking, thinking about drinking, and overcoming the consequences of that drinking. Think about the hangovers.

Be brutally honest with yourself here.

Count the hours, the days, the weeks, and even the years that have passed by while you've been following this "normal" pastime.

How many opportunities have you lost in this time?

How much has your brainpower been affected?

How has alcohol drinking altered your self-respect?

How has your alcohol drinking affected the respect and trust you get from others?

Opportunities Lost

Losing trust is difficult to see or comprehend until you have quit. When I stopped, I began noticing people asking me to do things that they wouldn't have asked me to do while I was a drinker. I hadn't realized I had lost so much trust.

Once I'd stopped drinking, I thought about the amount of money I had been spending. I worked out that I'd spent about $300,000 over the 30+ years. Not just on booze. On everything that accompanies the booze, like dining out when I can't be bothered to cook at home.

And that figure doesn't take into account the opportunity costs.

How much money would I have made if I hadn't been suffering all those hangovers? How much more successful would I have been if I hadn't spent half my life in a perpetual fog?

Where I live in Spain, that type of money could buy a detached house on its own land, with a landscaped garden and swimming pool. And yet, I'm still renting. Already since I've stopped drinking, I've saved about $60,000.

Your Personal Alcohol Cost

The whole point of this section is to get you to think about your past alcohol use and how it has been affecting your life.

Take another look at the questions above.

How many have you answered "yes"? How much has your alcohol use changed over the years?

Just as we develop a tolerance for the effects of alcohol in our bodies, we also develop a tolerance to many other aspects of drinking alcohol in the long-term. The more you drink, the more you are likely to drink alone, to drink to escape your worries and troubles, and to have some form of memory loss because of your drinking.

The more you drink, the more alcohol will affect you in your wider life, in your sleeping, in your job or business, with your reputation, your family, and other people in your life.

The more you use this drug, the more tolerance will affect the timing of your drinking and how you are affected by cravings. Tolerance will alter the time of day you start to drink and think about drinking.

Eventually, your alcohol drinking will result in a doctor's visit or hospitalization.

I hope that you can accept that alcohol is a drug and alcohol use will follow the same patterns as any other drug.

I also hope you can see that as an alcohol drinker, you are also a drug user, and you are not immune to the patterns of any drug user.

All you have to do is look back over your own drinking history to see how your drug use has evolved over time, and not for the better.

Recap

Alcohol dependence, or any other drug dependence, happens over a long period of time. People don't realize how quickly so-called "normal" alcohol use can get out of control and cause problems.

The 20 questions are designed as an evaluative tool which can help you to see the problems alcohol can cause in your life.

Overall, how much has your drinking changed over the years?

Exercise

Take a look at how much your alcohol use has changed over your drinking life.

How much more do you drink now than you used to?

How has the alcohol tolerance effect changed over the years?

Can you see how much more tolerant you are to the effects of alcohol?

Can you see the areas where you are dependent?

Maintaining Your Motivation in Week Three

Here we are in week three. You already have a couple of weeks behind you and you're starting to see the light at the end of the tunnel. Only a couple of weeks left.

How is your motivation?

Are you still feeling urges?

Do you feel like you're missing out?

Do you get to Friday night and feel like you deserve a drink for all the effort you have put in during the week?

Here's some more techniques for maintaining your motivation and beating those urges.

Meditation

One of the benefits of quitting drinking is that you will have more energy. In the first couple of weeks, your energy levels can fluctuate quite widely. My take on this is that your body has gone into healing mode.

The toxin flow has stopped and your body can concentrate a fair share of its resources on first eliminating any remaining toxins, and then repairing some of the underlying damage.

With all that fixing going on, tiredness can become an issue in the first week or two.

Whether you're feeling tired or you have a sudden overflow of energy, meditation or breathing can help.

Sitting

The word meditation puts many people off. What does meditation look like? What are we supposed to do? Do we sit on the ground with our legs crossed?

There are no set rules to meditation. From what I have read and my own practices, I find one of the best ways of meditating is just to sit still, either on the floor or in a chair, close your eyes and simply concentrate on slowly breathing in and out.

Breathe in using your belly muscles. As you inhale, your stomach should expand, not contract.

Hold the breath at the top for three or four seconds. Then breathe out again, contracting your belly muscles at the same time.

Hold at the bottom for a couple of seconds.

Then repeat the whole process. You don't have to do this for long, five minutes is perfectly good.

Walking

Another great way of meditation is just to take a walk in peaceful surroundings. Mindfulness doesn't come so easily if there are many distractions

Where I live, we have a large area of pine woodland and that's where I have my best meditations. I simply walk, turn down my mind as much as possible, and just soak up the surroundings.

When you're meditating while walking, concentrate on your footsteps, your breathing, or just relax and let the environment carry you along.

Pranayama

A breathing technique which is good for clearing your head is called Pranayama.

There are many different types of Pranayama. The one we will concentrate on here is very simple and basic.

The idea is to alternate your breathing through your right nostril and then through your left nostril. This helps you to keep calm and gives you energy.

We always start the Pranayama by breathing through the left nostril.

With your eyes shut, close your right nostril with the thumb of your right hand. Now, breathe slowly and very deeply through your left nostril. When you get to the top of the breath, hold for a couple of seconds.

Then close the left nostril and breathe out through the right nostril, again very slowly and deeply.

When you have completely exhaled, hold for a couple of seconds, then breathe in through the right nostril, slowly and deeply, until you have reached the top.

Again, hold for a couple of seconds before switching nostrils, closing the right nostril and breathing out through the left.

Do this for a couple of minutes, switching between nostrils, and you should start feeling the benefits.

Focus on the Fix

Another concept in maintaining your motivation is to focus on what you're trying to fix.

There are several ways of doing this.

First, return to your original reasons to quit. Ask yourself:

Why are you doing this?

Who are you doing this for?

What are you trying to change?

Examine the health benefits of quitting drinking, the mental benefits, the physical benefits, and the intellectual benefits.

Second, repeat your affirmations. Keep going over your affirmations until they become second nature.

As you go through the *30 Day Alcohol Reboot*, remember that the whole process is dynamic.

Where you start at the beginning is not where you will end. You will evolve as a person. Your techniques should reflect that.

So if your affirmations begin to become a bit stale or redundant, don't be afraid to change them. Rework your current affirmations or completely scrap them and start over. There's no point in continuing to use a concept which is not working any more.

Visualize Your Future Self

Finally, visualize your future self in the place that you want to be.

Positive visualization can help you to keep the end goal in mind.

When you visualize, sit calmly, close your eyes, and project yourself into your own future.

There are two ways of doing this.

You can look at the scene as if you were hovering above, picturing yourself in the visualization, looking down on yourself. Alternatively, you can view everything in the first person, looking out through your own eyes. This is the one I prefer.

Use all your senses and your emotions.

Don't just see things, hear them and feel them. Feel the weather on your skin. Use your senses of smell and touch to further bring the experience to life. Feel the happiness, joy, love, and satisfaction.

This is a very powerful technique for daily practice.

Recap

I hope you found something there that will help you.

All these techniques only take a few minutes to complete. They are very easy and can be done anywhere. Yet, they are very powerful in that they can be used to alter your mindset from negative to positive.

Five minute meditations or a two-minute Pranayama sessions can alter the way you feel. They can reduce cravings or anxiety, or bring you back to being centred.

You can also use visualizations, your affirmations, or revisit your original motivations.

Memory is a funny thing. The discomfort you feel in the beginning, or before you started, soon begins to fade as you make progress through your *30 Day Alcohol Reboot*. It's very easy to forget why you're doing this.

Revisiting your original motivations helps to keep these discomfort memories alive.

Using your affirmations and visualizations helps you to focus on where you want to go.

Exercise

Picture your end goal.

Visualize yourself with lots of vitality, your skin is clear, your eyes are bright, and you just feel fantastic. You don't have any more alcohol cravings, in fact you don't think about it much at all.

Now, think back to the person you were a few short weeks ago, before you began this new journey. Try to picture your old self beside your new self.

Can you see the difference?

WEEK FOUR

Almost There!

Here we are in week four. Congratulations!

You have the worst behind you and only a few more days to go.

Now that you are close to the end, it's time to start evaluating your journey so far and thinking about what comes next.

In this section we will look at some more motivation techniques for that final push.

We will look at how far you've come, what this means to you right now, and what changes, if any, have happened.

Finally, we'll take a look forward, examining what could happen next.

Motivation for the Final Push

At this stage, you shouldn't need too much motivation. You have three weeks done, and the end is in sight. Most people have no problem finishing out one final week.

Once you get to week four, the alcohol routines, behavior, and habit will be seriously in decline.

Your sleeping patterns should have stabilized.

Any cravings you still feel should be much more manageable. Not only do cravings weaken with time, your resolve strengthens with time. Add the two together and you have a powerful combination.

You also now have the experience of going without alcohol in many different situations, circumstances, and with different people. This experience is essential moving forwards.

Focus Forward

To help you through this final week, keep focusing forwards.

Laser focus your mind towards that end goal.

One of the great things about being a human being is that we have the ability to think about the future and our part in it. We can project ourselves forward to see improved versions of ourselves. Not only that, we can figure out what those improvements need to be, and work out, step-by-step, how that personal evolution will transpire.

Think about how powerful this is.

You can project yourself forwards into a person who knows something that you don't know yet, who has achieved something that you haven't achieved yet, who has something that you haven't got yet.

Maybe it's a car, a house, an education, a ripped body, a drug-free body.

Not only can you imagine this, you can mentally rehearse the steps you need to take to get you into that position, and then bring that visualization into reality.

How Far Have You Come?

The only reason you should be looking backwards at this stage is to see how far you've come and how much you have achieved.

Viewing how far you've come, not how far you have got to go, is very inspiring and motivating. It's powerful because it motivates you to take more steps, to take more actions, and then look back and see how much further you have come.

It becomes part of a virtuous cycle instead of a vicious cycle, one step inspiring the next.

Keep Active

Finally, stay active. Do something that you enjoy doing.

Exercise doesn't need to be boring or very difficult.

Remember motion effects emotion. Just getting out there and moving is enough to alter your mood and your outlook. Your body knows how to balance itself while it's moving. That's fascinating.

The human body is built to move. We are made to walk, run, skip, jump, grasp, hold, hug, throw, and so on.

Movement is also essential for a healthy lymph system. Your lymphatic system helps your body eliminate toxins, waste, and other unwanted materials. Think about how essential this is in alcohol detox.

The primary function of the lymph system is to move lymph fluid around your body. This lymph fluid contains white blood cells for fighting infection.

Your body has three times more lymph than blood. But unlike blood, which has the heart to pump it around the body, your lymph fluid has no such organ. Lymph fluid cannot move around the body without body movement and deep breathing.

Recap

Congratulations on reaching week four. Now we are ready for the final push. Some simple techniques for motivation in week four are, keep focusing forward, only look backwards to see how far you've come, and keep that lymph flying around your body by keeping active.

Exercise

In this final week, try to keep your mind focused forwards. If you have to look backwards at all, focus on how far you have come, not on how much you have left to go.

A healthy lymph system requires physical movement. What you going to do this week to make sure your lymph is flowing strongly?

Where Are You Right Now?

At this stage in the journey, you may be starting to think about the end, about drinking again. Before you finish with the *30 Day Alcohol Reboot*, take some time to think about where you are right now and how you feel.

How Do You Feel in Week Four?

How does it feel not to drink alcohol?

How does it feel to get up in the morning without that hangover?

How does it feel not to have to think about alcohol?

How do you feel about the money you're saving?

What does your family think about you not drinking?

Your Reasons to Quit

Take another look at your reasons to quit.

Most people quit because alcohol is having negative consequences on their lives. Now that you haven't been drinking for a few weeks, can you see that some of these negative consequences have disappeared, at least lessened?

Do you feel that you have missed drinking alcohol?

What is it you have missed?

Have you missed the actual alcohol, the taste, the feeling it gives you?

Or are you missing something else?

Do you miss the camaraderie of drinking, the socializing, or fitting in?

Not Getting Drunk

How does it feel not to get drunk?

There are several aspects to getting drunk. There is thinking about drinking and getting drunk, actually drinking and getting drunk, and then there is the hangover... the consequences of drinking and getting drunk.

How does it feel not to have any of these things in your life for the past few weeks?

Do you feel more productive?

Do you feel like you have more time, more energy, more thinking power?

Your General Well-Being

How do you feel in general?

Most people express that they feel very positive after a spell away from alcohol. They have more time and energy to do things they want to do, and they also feel like they have had a great weight lifted off their shoulders.

I felt the latter.

I spent years trying to curtail and moderate my drinking. I would moderate for a while, succeed and feel good about what I was doing. Unfortunately, I would quickly and inevitably fall back to my old drinking habits. My willpower was fine, it was my thinking that was broken.

Controlling Your Drinking

Trying to control alcohol is difficult, if not impossible in the long run.

Alcohol is a drug!

Allen Carr, author of "The Easy Way to Stop Drinking", had a great analogy for controlling your drinking. He described the habit of drinking alcohol as a pitcher plant which all drinkers fall into.

The pitcher plant is a carnivorous plant, also known as pitfall traps. The pitcher plant lures its prey by presenting brightly colored leaves, coated in sweet nectar, at the top of the trap.

As the prey drinks the nectar, it doesn't realize that it is gradually sliding further and further down into the plant, becoming more hopelessly entangled.

Once it does comprehend the danger, it's too late! It can no longer escape.

The fly can only helplessly continue its downward journey, falling to the bottom.

The gruesome reality, waiting at the bottom of the plant, are the plant's digestive juices.

Carr explains that once you start drinking alcohol, you put yourself into a metaphorical pitcher plant. A weather-beaten, full-blown alcoholic is just at a different level than the novice teenage drinker who is just starting out. Both are prey of the alcohol habit.

From Harmless to Habit

Alcohol is a depressive and addictive drug. It's also an extremely powerful neurotoxin. Unfortunately, our culture doesn't see it in this way. Our culture sees alcohol as cool, sexy, and harmless.

We talk about drinking in terms of happiness, giving us confidence, or making us more sociable. We feel we can party hard without alcohol affecting our wider world.

This is the intoxicating nectar that alcohol plays in our lives.

And it's only when we are dependent on alcohol for our confidence, our sociability, for sleep, relaxation, or feeling happy, that we begin to comprehend the threat.

And even then it takes a long time before we are aware enough to truly see the danger.

Most drinkers will never see this far. Most drinkers will just fall deeper and deeper into the pitcher plant, believing the bullshit and ignoring the warning signs, until it's too late.

Alcohol drinking becomes the norm, it becomes the ritual, and it becomes the habit.

The Emperor's Just Very Normal

There is a big problem in how our culture defines alcohol drinkers.

On the one hand our culture defines us as a "normal" drinker, drinking for purely social reasons, just having fun.

On the other hand, as soon as we show problems with this "normal" alcohol consumption, we become "alcoholics", suffering from a disease, probably with a faulty gene, and we are likely to be in recovery for the rest of our lives.

You never hear anybody talking about the disease of the smoker, or the nicotine gene.

We know that nicotine is an addictive drug. It has been manufactured to be as addictive as possible. And the same is true of alcohol.

However, as far as alcohol is concerned, we live in a fantasy world. It's a modern version of "The Emperor's New Clothes". We are sucked deeper and deeper into the con until somebody shouts out the naked truth about what we are doing to ourselves.

Why Can't We See the Truth?

What's the alternative? You have had a few weeks now to discover some alternatives for yourself. It's not easy to find alternatives, to try other things, and to go against the norm.

That's another part of the alcohol trap. We believe that because everybody else drinks alcohol, it must be right.

Today, smoking is a big no-no. It's banned in most public places. You cannot smoke at work, in bars, in supermarkets, in banks, or in any public buildings. You not allowed to smoke in the workplace, even if that workplace is your own home. It's against the law.

But that wasn't always the case.

I remember 10 years ago, when I first came to Spain, I went into a local bank to change some pounds to pesetas.

I couldn't believe my eyes when I saw people smoking in the queue. There was an ashtray on the counter. People were putting their cigarettes out on the floor. They were polluting the air and nobody batted an eyelid. They were creating toxic fog for everyone else in the bank.

Go back 50 years and everyone smoked. It was the norm.

How many people have had to go through painful diseases, cancer, emphysema, heart disease, stroke, blindness, to get where we are now, where smoking is no longer widely tolerated?

If you smoke, you know you are playing Russian roulette with your life. You don't need to be told. The evidence is in. The evidence is clear.

Alcohol causes 3.5 million deaths worldwide every year.

Alcohol is responsible for over 200 health conditions.

Alcohol is responsible for the deaths of one quarter of our young people between the ages of 20 to 39.

Are There Any Alternatives out There?

So what are the alternatives?

You might say the same thing about cigarette smoking, what are the alternatives?

We have the same arguments for smoking as we do for drinking. Smoking helps me to relax, it helps me to have fun, to socialize. It doesn't interfere with my work, my family, or my children.

We now know that that's a pile rubbish.

There are plenty of alternatives, we're just not looking for them. There are better ways of relaxing, socializing, and having fun. We just have to put the effort into finding them.

Recap

This section has been about re-examining your drinking life, asking yourself how you feel in week four. Have you fulfilled any of your reasons to quit? How do you feel about not getting drunk over the last four weeks? How do you feel in general?

You might be contemplating future alcohol moderation. We looked at Allen Carr's analogy of the pitcher plant. It represents the lure of alcohol and the inevitable fall into the alcohol trap. Explains why alcohol moderation doesn't work. Alcohol consumption starts out with very harmless motivations. After continued use, it quickly develops into a habit, then into an addiction.

Why can't we see the truth?

Exercise

Think about your alternatives to drinking alcohol. I don't mean the alternative drinks, I mean the alternative ways of relaxation, socializing, or having fun.

Can you see life without alcohol? Can you imagine it? Would you miss alcohol? Examine your reasons for drinking alcohol, for relaxation, socializing, to sleep, and so on. Now try to envision some possible alternatives.

Where Are You Going?

To move forwards in life, you need a fairly good idea of where you are right now. This requires complete honesty. If you're not honest with yourself about where you are right now, and how you got here, all your thoughts and plans about the future will be based on faulty data.

I hope that you've done a bit of work over the last couple of sections to really cement in your mind where you are right now.

Where to Now?

Next let's look at where you want to go from here.

First, let's revisit the concept of visualizing. I think visualization is a great tool for peering into your future.

As I have said, once you have a basic idea of where you are and what got you here, you should be able to extrapolate that out into the future.

The purpose of this section is to look at your future from two different perspectives: on the one hand the future where you quit alcohol and on the other the future if you don't quit alcohol.

Visions of Your Future

I think we are all familiar with Charles Dickens's A Christmas Carol. I think this was the perfect novel for the human capacity to transform. In this novel, Ebenezer Scrooge is visited by three spirits... The ghosts of Christmas past, Christmas present, and Christmas future. We've already visited your past and present alcohol life. Let's take a few minutes to travel into your future.

Close your eyes and relax.

Imagine the ghost of Alcohol future whisking you into your own future. First, you are taken one year down the road, then five years, and finally ten years.

At each stop, you get to see what how your life has evolved over the period of time.

Ask yourself these questions:

- Where do you see yourself in ten years if you haven't quit drinking alcohol?

- How is your health?

- How are your family?

- Where are your family?

- Are they still with you?

- Who are your friends now?

- How many of them drink?

- How many of them drink as much as you?

- How many of your old friends are still around?

- Are you still working?

- How has alcohol affected you physically?

- How much are you drinking?

- How often?

- What are you drinking?

- How has alcohol affected you emotionally?

- How has alcohol affected you intellectually?

40 Extra Units

When I ran through this visualization, I first looked at how my alcohol drinking had evolved over the past 10 years and how much my life had changed because of it.

Then I ran forward 10 years, making some assumptions based on that past.

If I had increased my drinking by 40 units per week over the last 10 years, I could safely say that I would also increase it by roughly the same figure over the next 10 years.

My visualization, playing out based on those figures, was very scary. I involved my son and the rest of my family in these nightmare visions. They were the witnesses to my downfall. It was horrible to visualize the mixture of disgust and pity on their faces.

I used as many senses as I could, as well as my emotions. I created all types of nasty smells, nasty visions, nasty sounds, and so on.

Facing Your Reality

Why does this type of visualization work?

Because, like Ebenezer Scrooge, visualizing your future forces you to confront your reality as it stands. You are forced to face a possible future reality, something that might happen if you don't change your ways.

That was the basic idea behind the Ghost of Christmas Future. The ghost was showing Scrooge not what would happen, but what might happen.

These visualizations push you to confront your future in a way that you might not have done otherwise.

The Imperfect Habit

It's very easy to get stuck in a rut of just doing the same day after day, week in and week out. Unfortunately, this is the imperfect side of our habits.

At times, we need a shock to the system to show us our reality for what it really is. Sometimes it's difficult to see the mess that you are in because you are already in the mess.

Einstein famously said, "We cannot solve our problems with the same thinking we used when we created them". He also said, "Insanity is doing the same thing over and over again and expecting different results".

As we have seen, habits tend to force us down the path of repeating the same things over and over again, yet at the same time expecting our lives to change for the better.

The Moment of Honesty

Visualizing your future is a simple technique which can really give you a glimpse of what might happen, how much worse things can get for you if you don't do something about it right now.

Now is the only time that you can do something. You cannot ever do something tomorrow, or the next day, or the next day. Tomorrow is tomorrow. It will always be tomorrow.

You have to make changes in the moment. If you are not willing to do it now, when are you willing to do it? When can you do it?

You have to be honest with yourself. If you keep putting things off, what's to stop you from putting things off indefinitely? That spells disaster.

Your Brighter Future

On the other hand, it's just as easy to think about your future in terms of what will happen if you do change.

This is one of the best parts of visualization for me. I love looking forward and trying to see how things can change if I make a change today.

If I do this differently today, how will that have a knock-on effect down through my life in a week, or a year, or ten years?

Change only happens because you notice something needs to be changed. And change only happens because you can first visualize yourself in a position where the changes has happened. If you can't see it in your mind, how can you manifest it in your reality?

Visualize Your Future

With this in mind, close your eyes again, relax, and take yourself down that same route, one year, five years, and ten years. The difference is that this time you have stopped drinking.

Ask yourself these questions:

- Where are you in 10 years now that you've stopped drinking right now?

- How is your health?

- How are your family?

- Where are your family?

- How do they view you now you don't drink anymore?

- Who are your friends?

- How many of them drink?

- How many of them drink as much as you used to drink?

- How is your career?

- Are you still working in the same job?

- How has your life changed financially?

- How has quitting alcohol affected you emotionally?

- How has quitting alcohol affected you intellectually?

Recap

Visualizing your future, from the perspective of not having quit drinking and having quit drinking, gives you the opportunity to see how your life could turn out. This is one of the most powerful tools that I have used in changing any bad habit.

Try to bring all your senses into your visualizations. Include familiar places and people. See their faces, see and hear their reactions to what you are doing. What does your visualization smell like, sound like, look like, or feel like? What are people saying?

Exercise

The only place we can truly live is in the present moment. This is where you will find fulfilment and happiness. The present is the only place where you can do anything or think anything.

If you haven't already done these visualizations, take the time to do them now.

Explore both outcomes. You have quit drinking or you haven't quit drinking.

Travel one year, five years, and ten years into your own timeline.

Look at how your decision to quit or not quit has affected your life, your relationships, your career, your spirituality, your finances, and your intellect.

Tolerance, Addiction, and Normalcy

Before we leave week 4, I want to talk more about tolerance, as well as addiction and normality.

Tolerance and addiction are two sides of the same coin. Physical alcohol tolerance and addiction boil down to: the more you drink the more you need to drink.

But tolerance and addiction go much deeper than this.

Cultural Tolerance

Our cultural tolerance for alcohol begins from the day we are born.

Our cultural alcohol message is simple, alcohol drinking is normal. It's normal to see alcohol being widely consumed. We see alcohol consumed at every level of life from our parents to our teachers.

It's normal to see alcohol advertised widely across TV, magazines, and the Internet.

Alcohol is sold in supermarkets, bars and restaurants, liquor stores, and sports venues, fun parks, and so on...it's all 'normal'.

The more we associate with people who drink, the more we are affected by cultural tolerance.

As we go through childhood, into our teenage years and adulthood, this cultural tolerance expands. The more we are exposed to alcohol, the more we tolerate it.

Hallmark Drug

Let's go over some of the points that have already been raised.

Alcohol is a chemical substance that alters your central nervous system, causing changes in your personal behavior. Use alcohol for long enough and it becomes addictive.

In other words, alcohol a drug.

Not only is it a drug, it has all the hallmarks of a dangerous and harmful drug. Realistically, alcohol is in the same category as any Class A drug in the UK or a Schedule 1 drug in the US. In our culture, however, alcohol is classified as a beverage, just like tea and coffee.

The alcohol companies refuse to call it a drug when, in my opinion, it's the number one gateway drug. Even though it's illegal to sell this drug to children, they don't seem to have much of a problem getting hold of it.

Alcohol companies have massive amounts of money and influence and they actively campaign against redefining their product as a drug, for obvious reasons.

The number one reason is the devastating impact on alcohol profits that would result if this substance were reclassified as a drug.

A second reason is there is a good chance that once alcohol were reclassified as a drug in the marketplace, it would be redefined in our culture.

This in turn would provoke an intolerance as people began to re-evaluate their drug use. Again this would hurt the bottom line for the alcohol companies.

Cultural Addiction

Let's take a look at addiction from a cultural point of view.

Addiction doesn't happen after you have drank a lot alcohol. The cultural addiction happens a long time before you have even started.

I'm not talking about physical addiction here, I'm talking about the logical and emotional addiction.

If you see alcohol all around you when you are growing up, how is that going to affect you?

You don't have to imagine this scenario too hard.

As a young child growing up in our alcohol culture, we see alcohol as something reserved for adults only. If you are legally underage, you are banned from purchasing or consuming alcohol.

This sets your brain up for drinking in the future.

Grooming Our Children for Drug Use

Although children cannot actually consume alcohol, they must wonder what it's like to drink.

What does alcohol taste like?

Why does it make you drunk?

What does it feel like to get drunk?

Children observe adults drinking and they anticipate themselves drinking one day.

Most children will get to taste alcohol early in their lives. Either they'll be supplied by a well-meaning adult or they'll sneak a sip while the well-meaning adult's back is turned.

By the time a child reaches adulthood, or at least the legal drinking age, they are already emotionally addicted to that drinking culture.

Most studies reveal that underage drinking is at epidemic proportions, with over 80% of high school students having consumed alcohol. So the likelihood is that children will succumb to this emotional addiction much sooner in their lives.

And underage alcohol consumption is far more dangerous to premature minds and bodies.

Physical Tolerance and Addiction

The physical addiction and tolerance to alcohol happens later in life.

Because alcohol is a drug, the more you drink, the more tolerance your body creates, and the more you need to drink in order to get the same buzz.

Think about physical tolerance in the same way as a hand callous which has developed from a lot of gardening work. The repeated pressure or friction on the area of skin causes the skin harden and form a protective surface.

Alcohol tolerance is also a protection.

Trigger, Behavior, Reward

We always have reasons to drink. In the behavioral sequence of alcohol drinking, first comes a trigger, which leads to the behavior, and finally to the reward.

The trigger can be anything. It can be a thought, and action, a person, something you see, hear, or taste.

When you are young, your trigger could be pressure from your friends to take a sip. As you get older, your trigger might be tiredness, happiness, a special occasion, or an inability to sleep.

In between the trigger and the reward is the behavior of actually consuming the alcohol. In this sense, alcohol is the tool which takes you from A to B, from the need to the reward.

But as we have seen, the more you drink, the more you need to drink. Physical tolerance means that the amount of alcohol that used to be enough to get you relaxed, or asleep, or happy, or finding your buzz, is no longer enough. You need a higher dose.

Alcohol works like any other drug.

If you start taking sleeping pills, for instance, after a while, you will have to increase the dose or the sleeping pill won't work. If you take antidepressants, tolerances built up, then you need to take an increased dose or the antidepressant won't be effective.

Intellectual Tolerance

We also build an intellectual tolerance. The more you drink, the more you believe that alcohol plays a legitimate role in your life.

The longer we use alcohol, the easier it is to convince ourselves that we enjoy drinking alcohol. Not only that, we also convince ourselves that without alcohol our lives would be less enjoyable.

You didn't start out that way. When you first drank alcohol, you didn't like the taste. When you first drink alcohol, your life and happiness didn't rest on you drinking the stuff.

Intellectual tolerance allows us to make excuses for our drinking, no matter how much we drink.

"I love drinking"

"It does me no harm"

"There are health benefits to drinking alcohol"

"I can always quit"

Intellectual alcohol tolerance creates and inflates a frame of mind that your drinking is acceptable. The more you drink, the more acceptable *your* level of alcohol drinking becomes.

Emotional Alcohol Tolerance and Addiction

Then we have emotional tolerance and addiction.

Emotional addiction happens when alcohol and your emotions become intertwined.

We often use alcohol as an emotional tool. The problem with using alcohol in this way is you come to rely on an outside source for internal emotional control.

There are two ways that emotional addiction can happen. The first is you need to drink alcohol to escape or alter an emotion. The second is you need alcohol to feel an emotion.

Drinking to Suppress Emotions

Most drinkers drink to escape or alter an emotion to one extent or another.

"I'm feeling tired and lonely, I need a drink to feel better"

"I feel really pissed off, I need a drink to feel calm"

"I feel sad, I need a drink to feel happy".

As soon as an unwanted emotions shows its face, you drink enough alcohol so that that emotion goes away. Unfortunately, these types of emotion don't go away, they are merely suppressed. This is very unhealthy, physically and psychologically.

Your emotions are there for a reason. Even though these emotions might be unwanted at the time, they highlight a personal problem, a problem that needs to be resolved.

Using alcohol to suppress unwanted emotions means the underlying problem remains unresolved. Unresolved emotional problems cause those problems to fester, become worse, which can lead to further problems down the line.

My Alcohol Toolbox

I have used alcohol to suppress all kinds of unwanted emotions. I have used alcohol to gloss over relationship problems, work problems, self-esteem and self-confidence problems. I've used alcohol to suppress grief and sadness.

Most frequently, I used alcohol to procrastinate, to put off making decisions or choices, to avoid thinking about problems.

This is the one part of my drinking life which has probably done the most damage. When I look back, it's difficult to know all the things that were never achieved because of my drinking. How do I determine the thoughts and ideas that have never been never realized?

Drinking to Feel Emotions

On the other hand, alcohol users get to the stage where they need to drink alcohol in order to feel a certain emotion.

"If I can't drink at this party, I cannot feel happy"

"How can I celebrate without drinking?"

"I won't be able to feel relaxed unless I have my regular glass of wine"

"How can I feel myself if I'm not drinking?"

Once you start down this route of hiding your emotions through alcohol or linking your emotions with alcohol, eventually you arrive at the stage where it's very difficult to have practical control over your emotions.

Ultimately, your emotions begin to revolve around using this drug.

This is emotional tolerance.

As we've seen with all the other levels of tolerance, this is a gradual process. It doesn't happen overnight. It's a dynamic process which, over time, constrains and enslaves your emotional control.

Psychological Alcohol Tolerance and Addiction

Let me give you an example of how psychological tolerance works.

Imagine that you have just found your first job, a really good job. The job is 5 km away from your home and there is no public transport available. You have no money to buy a car, you don't know anyone who can give you a lift, so you have no choice but to walk.

The walk takes you the bones of an hour in the morning and another hour on your return in the evening.

During your walks to and from work, there will be ups and downs in the weather, ups and downs in your mood, and so on. Some days will be really crappy, you have to walk in the rain, and you have a miserable time. On other days, the weather is sunny, you can relax and enjoy your walk, appreciating the scenery.

Walking to and from work eats up two hours of every working day. Even though you listen to music or use the time to think, you feel that you could be spending that time a lot more productively.

After a couple of months, you have saved enough money to buy a bicycle. You feel ecstatic on your first day cycling to work. You feel a real freedom. The bike has reduced your travel time from a full hour to twenty minutes cycling there and back. You feel great.

You've managed to save an hour and twenty minutes every day. But you are still at the mercy of the elements. Again, some days you have a good cycle to work and other days you're getting wet and miserable.

For the first couple of weeks, you are in your element. You have a great feeling of freedom and speed. But gradually, over the next few weeks, this feeling of freedom diminishes, you see your co-workers arriving at work by car. They are dry, out of the weather, and they always seem to have much more time on their hands.

When you first purchased your bike, you felt as if your life had fundamentally changed. Now that you've had the bike for a couple of months, taking twenty or twenty-five minutes to cycle to work morning and evening is the new normal. You don't look at it as anything special, you are used it.

You carry on saving your money and cycling to work for almost a year. You have completely forgotten about how you used to have to walk to work and how long that would take.

Eventually you have saved enough money to buy a small car.

With your new car your life again changes fundamentally. It now takes you only ten minutes to arrive at work, five km away. Not only that, you arrive dry and with plenty of energy.

You feel like you have achieved something fantastic. You feel pride in your new car, washing and waxing it over the weekend, keeping it clean, maintaining its engine, keeping it out of the sun, and talking about it with friends.

After a few weeks, again the novelty wears off. Of course you are still getting to work in only ten minutes, dry, and full of energy. But now that the excitement of owning a car has diminished.

You have started to admire the other cars in the car park and you think that you would like to own something a bit bigger, faster, and flashier.

Again, you start saving.

This is psychological tolerance in action. Once you get the bigger flashier car, you'll feel that sense of invigoration. You'll feel like your life has fundamentally changed.

Unfortunately, those feelings too will gradually diminish and eventually depart. You are dreaming about your next purchase.

To get the same hit, you need to save more and more money, buying faster and flashier cars.

Using Alcohol as a Tool

Psychological addiction begins when you start to use alcohol as a tool for overcoming problems.

Let's take the example of feeling shy about meeting people. Instead of facing your fears and learning some coping strategies for dealing with your shyness, you turn to the instant relief that you feel you can get from alcohol.

Alcohol only ever relieves your shyness momentarily. It does nothing to alleviate the pain from your shyness in the long run. Nor does it teach you any concrete coping skills for overcoming your shyness. In other words, shyness remains.

The next time you feel shy, it's easy to fall back on your previous experience of dealing with the feelings through drinking alcohol. Again, you temporarily overcome your shyness. And again, you fail to learn any coping skills. You only succeed in reinforcing the alcohol solution in your mind.

You've added another building block to your psychological addiction to using alcohol in social situations.

This type of habitual thinking can then easily become the norm in many different areas of your life, from relaxation to problem solving. Once you have a perceived success in one area, is not difficult to see how you could transfer that perceived success to another area of your life.

"I can suppress my shyness by taking a drink, maybe I can suppress my other worries as well."

Lessons Skipped

I was psychologically addicted to alcohol at a very early age.

As in the last example, I quickly realized that alcohol could help me overcome my shyness and lack of self-confidence, among other things.

Later in life, alcohol became a tool for relaxing, a sleep aid, and an emotional fix-it-all.

Of course, alcohol never solved any of these problems. It only disguised the symptoms. It didn't do a great job of controlling my emotions either.

It's easy to see how any young person can quickly become psychologically addicted to using alcohol or taking any other drug.

A teenage life is tumultuous at the best of times. A teenagers thoughts are full of doubt and uncertainty. These years are also when we see some of the realities of life for the first time. And there are many hard lessons to learn.

Alcohol can seem to reduce the intensity of these lessons. It is a readily available tool, offering respite from their burgeoning emotional upheaval. The problem is, once alcohol is used to calibrate an emotional reaction, the lessons that your emotions are trying to teach you are never learned.

From Hash to Ecstasy

I remember an occasion in my mid 20s when I experimented with ecstasy. Early in our marriage, my wife and I smoked marijuana quite regularly. In one of our visits to a local hash dealer, we were offered an ecstasy tablet, a *brown biscuit*, as it was known.

We split the tablet in two and swallowed half each.

It took a while for the effects to kick in, but once it did, we both felt a very powerful state of euphoria. It was a very impressive high. It's very difficult, especially years later, to describe those feelings. I can only describe it as a profound feeling of absolute love for each other.

It was a feeling which was very far outside our normal emotional range. I had certainly never experienced anything like that in my life before that point. I adored my wife. I loved her to bits. But this was something completely different.

To be perfectly honest, it scared the hell out of me. I knew that this was a feeling that I wanted to repeat. At the same time, I also knew that these feelings could very quickly become very addictive.

We talked about it and agreed never to take this particular drug again.

Habitual Tolerance

Before we leave the subject of tolerance, let me say that there is no real escape from tolerance. Many people think that they can control their drug use, but in reality alcohol is very difficult to control. With already seen this in the example of the pitcher plant.

People also mistake tolerance with being able to physically handle alcohol. It's true that you can drink more alcohol once your body builds a tolerance to the effects, but that doesn't reduce the consequences of drinking alcohol.

Over time, the more you drink, the more tolerance you build for the physical and psychological effects of the alcohol. However, the tolerance for the physical damage that alcohol causes never increases, it always decreases.

Your body can only physically deal with a fixed amount of alcohol at any one time. As you age, that fixed metabolic rate declines. Your body ages, your organs age, and your tolerance reduces.

The more you drink, the more you feel psychological tolerance and addiction. The more you drink, the more you will feel emotional addiction and tolerance.

Eventually we need to drink alcohol to find happiness, to be sad, because we're sad, because we are anxious or worried, because we're shy.

Alcohol becomes an integral part of our view of the world. It shapes our world. It shrinks our world. The more we tolerate and need alcohol in our lives, the less we tolerate other things. Our lives begin to revolve around the booze. Tolerance becomes part of our habitual state of drinking.

Normal for the Wolf is Insanity to the Sheep!

Finally, remember that normality is just the definition for what everyone else is doing. It doesn't mean it's right. It doesn't mean it's logical. It only refers to what is actually happening, or one version of it at least.

More than two thirds of the United States adult population are considered to be overweight or obese. This means that obesity could be classified as normal. It doesn't make it good or logical.

In 1965, 42.4% of high school students and adults in the United States of America smoked cigarettes. Again, this could be considered normal. And again, it doesn't make it acceptable.

Pushing Alcohol Normality

When it comes to alcohol, those who sell the stuff aim to completely normalize alcohol consumption within our culture.

Their reasoning?

Profits, pure and simple!

And they're doing a really good job of it.

Alcohol companies care about one thing, and one thing only, getting at the money in your pocket.

Unfortunately for you, money is not the only thing that they will take. Through their product, alcohol, these companies will take your money. In many cases they will also ransack your health, your self-respect, your dignity, your courage, your self-confidence, and in most cases your future.

They don't care if you get sick, so long as you continue to buy their drug. They don't care that you will probably become addicted, in fact they are delighted with this good news, they are literally banking on it. The more addicted you become to their product, the less they need to spend in brainwashing.

And if you think their brainwashing is restricted only to adults, think again. Most alcohol advertising is not aimed at those who are already addicted. The guy on the bar stool doesn't need too much convincing to drink.

Even though it's illegal to sell alcohol to children, alcohol marketing is blatantly aimed at attracting the young.

Alco-dollars are much better spent influencing the next generation.

Think of alcopops. Alcopops are nothing more than a dangerous and poisonous drug hidden in sweet, brightly colored soda pop. Grooming at its finest.

Recap

Tolerance and addiction come in many shapes and sizes. We have cultural, physical, intellectual, and emotional tolerance and addiction.

Normality of alcohol use is pushed on us from birth. By the time we reach drinking age, we are already psychologically and culturally addicted to the concept of drinking alcohol. It doesn't take long before this psychoactive drug plays its essential part in our lives, expanding the addicts of the world, and the coffers of the drug companies.

Exercise

Take a look at your alcohol use. Can you see where you might be addicted to drinking alcohol?

Look at how our society tolerates alcohol use. Compare that with how we view other drugs. Look at our blind acceptance of alcohol as part of the rites of passage, from child to adult.

Look at how alcohol is now a component part of all of our celebrations. If we're not popping a cork, we're not really celebrating.

Alcohol consumption is becoming an integral part of our identities.

Examine your own motivations for consuming alcohol.

Do you drink alcohol to compensate for a lack of skill?

Do you drink to hide an emotion?

Do you drink to foster an emotion?

Where has alcohol become an integral part of your life?

Congratulations on Reaching Day 30

Welcome to day 30 and congratulations for reaching this milestone!

I hope I didn't scare you off too much with the last couple of sections. The reason I talk so much about the dangers of alcohol is because I see how much our society has been brainwashed by clever marketing, peer pressure, and the delusion of "normality".

What to Do Now?

If you feel like you want to continue on with this journey, over the next few sections I talk about what you can gain.

So, what are you going to do now?

How do you feel?

How do you feel about your whole experience of not drinking for 30 days?

Are you glad you did it?

Would you do it again?

Do you feel that it was a worthwhile sacrifice?

How has it affected you in your wider life? Your social life? Your family life? Your work life?

What have you learned and what, if anything, will you do differently?

The Benefits of Being 30 Days Alcohol Free

Even though it's only 30 days, this time without alcohol has presented you with a test ground for understanding yourself in relation to your alcohol drinking habit.

To succeed in this challenge, you have had to change many different aspects of your life. You've made changes in your thinking, your social life, in your relationships, and even in your work life.

Most of these changes will have been positive.

Can you see the benefits of not drinking alcohol?

Go back to the beginning of this material and take a look at the benefits that you hoped to achieve by quitting.

After not drinking for 30 days, you should be looking at them from a completely different perspective.

How do you feel now?

How many of those benefits have you achieved?

Do you feel like you could achieve more?

Again, congratulations on finding yourself at day 30. Before you start drinking again, if that's your choice, please take a few minutes to go over the next section. It won't take long, and it could change your life forever.

SECTION 3: AFTER

Don't Go Yet

For those of you who have finished the challenge and can't wait to get back to their poison, stick with me a little bit longer as we explore life after the *30 Day Alcohol Reboot*.

What's Changed?

Again, congratulations on finishing your challenge. Before we move forwards, one question you should all be asking yourself is: Do you feel an improvement or improvements in your life because of being 30 days alcohol free?

If the answer is yes, the next question to ask is do you want to drink alcohol again?

If your answer to the second questions is also yes, then ask yourself why? Why would you want to resume a habit which has been causing you problems? Why would you want to keep consuming this harmful toxic?

Look again the changes that have happened in your life since you stopped consuming alcohol.

Where do you feel your life has benefited?

Where have you had negative experiences from the challenge?

Where has this challenge helped overcome some of the problems you had at the start, your reasons for quitting?

Where has it not helped?

What Can Change?

How much more rewarding could this journey be after sixty days, ninety days, six months, or a full year?

Remember, alcohol is a drug and the benefits that you see now from not consuming this drug for a month will gradually diminish and disappear if you take up the habit again.

You have managed to last the full 30 days without alcohol. That's the hardest part of any habit change, those first 30 days. If you compare quitting drinking alcohol with climbing a mountain, those first 30 days are the actual climb.

Now you're at the top, you get the reward for all your effort, catch a breath, take in the views, and see things from a completely different perspective.

Your First Drink

If you've come into this challenge with the mindset of just taking a break from alcohol, you might be looking forward to your first drink at this stage.

I remember I stopped drinking for 10 months. I had been planning on a full year, but my brother was getting married and he asked me to be his best man.

My first petrified thoughts were about the best man's speech. I remember thinking that there was no way I was going to do this without having a couple of drinks to pacify my nerves. Thinking back, it was downhill from there.

Once I'd made the decision to start drinking at the wedding, I couldn't wait for the party to get started. All I could think about was that first pint of Guinness.

After being alcohol free for ten months, it finally came to the morning when we were to travel across to the UK from Ireland. I drank my first drink, two pints of Guinness at 7.30 in the morning, at the departures lounge bar in Shannon airport.

I thought I had everything under control. I thought that being ten months alcohol free proved that. As I've said before, habits have a tendency to remain at some sublevel of the human mind. And it didn't take long before I was right back to my old drinking habits.

That's the way alcohol works. It's the way the habitual brain works. It's got nothing to do with the alcohol, yet everything to do with the habit.

I had been drinking for almost thirty years at that stage. That's a lot of time to build a pretty significant habit-base. And that habit doesn't go away overnight.

What I learned after those ten months of not drinking was that such long-term habitual behavior doesn't go away after ten months. As soon as you start drinking again, the habit retakes its residence in your brain, moving back in as if it's never been away.

If you're thinking about going back to the booze, stay tuned until the end of this section and I'll give you some helpful tips on how to reduce the damage that alcohol causes.

Exercise

What benefits have you realized through your 30 day challenge?

Where has this challenge helped you in overcoming some of the reasons you took on the challenge in the first place?

Can you see yourself achieving more if you expanded the thirty days to sixty days?

My Alcohol Story

What's My Story? Why I Stopped Drinking?

My life can definitely be broken into two separate parts, before I quit drinking and after I quit drinking.

I am still the same person in many ways. But, I've also changed my life in many more fundamental ways.

It's actually a running joke in my family that if there was somebody among us (there are five boys and four girls in my family) who would quit drinking alcohol, take on a whole foods plant-based diet, start walking for miles every day, take a degree course in psychology, write books, and teach people about habit change, it most certainly wouldn't be me.

Before T-Day

Before my Transformation Day (T-Day), I was the person who made the most of any party. I was the one who drank the most. I was the one who got the most drunk. And I was the one who said and did the most outrageous things while drunk.

If one word can be used to define who I was back then, or how I think about my old self back then, that one word would be embarrassment.

Most of the heavy mistakes that I've made in my life have happened either during or after drinking alcohol.

Most of my fallouts with other people have happened either during or after drinking alcohol.

Most of my cringe-worthy moments have happened while I was drunk.

Most of the insults I've given to other people have been thrown while I was drunk.

And the majority of personal injuries have happened while I was under the influence of alcohol.

Before T-Day, while I was sober, I still had a lot going for me. I was ambitious. I wanted to achieve great things during my life. I wanted to be a good role model to my son. I wanted to be a kind and caring member of my family. I wanted to be a good friend. And I always worked hard at trying to achieve these objectives.

But alcohol was always the spanner in the works. It always interfered with everything that I tried to do.

My alcohol drinking behavior, the rituals, and the overall habit, virtually guaranteed that my life would never be as successful as it could have been, nowhere near.

My drinking killed a lot of my success before it even had a chance to happen.

After T-Day

Comparing before and after T-Day, 2013, is like comparing chalk and cheese. There is no comparison.

Almost from the time that I made the decision to quit, my life began to change.

The day before T-Day, January 1st, 2013, my family and I were celebrating New Year's Day with dinner at my sister's house.

We all enjoyed a lovely home-cooked meal, and my sister served up some "excellent quality" local red wine. In the past, this would have been the only invite I needed to drink as much as possible.

Instead, I found I couldn't even finish one glass. The change was already starting to affect the way I thought. Even though I didn't know it at the time, my thinking was changing.

Needless to say, I started the day on January 2 without a hangover. The first of many. To date, I have over 1400 alcohol free and hangover free days.

Drinking Thinking

It's taken a long time for me to completely eradicate most of my drinking thinking. There are some elements of that drinking thinking still lodged in a dark recess of my brain. I know this because they surface every so often, unwanted habit memories. However, given time, these thoughts will also disappear.

I still love eating out and going to a good party. The only embarrassment I cause myself now are through my corny jokes. I am mostly positive, mostly forward-looking, mostly caring, giving, and open to new adventures.

I say mostly, because we all have our off days. I'm not a monk or a saint, and I sometimes lose my rag. There are days where the dark veil slips over my head, and I don't feel like speaking to anyone.

But these days are the exception rather than the rule. Before T-Day, these days were becoming the norm. The alcohol was the drug which hid my depression, but at the same time it was feeding my depression.

Whatever it was that opened my eyes to change, that gave me a different perspective and the inspiration to change, I am forever grateful.

Since T-Day, my life has changed beyond measure. I'm so happy in my own skin and I wouldn't go back to drinking if you paid me a million dollars

After the 30 Day Reboot?

So, what now?

Could you do more days? Could you go for longer? Why not continue? What's stopping you? If you feel good now, are you not just a little curious about how good you might feel after two months, three months, six months, or a year?

Part of the Herd?

Many people feel that quitting drinking alcohol is going against the grain. And, it is.

We have seen that normality doesn't necessarily represent a situation which is inherently good, it simply represents the volume of people for whom a particular behavior happens to be "normal".

It takes a lot of courage and mental fortitude to step out of that normality. Refusing to take part in anything which is otherwise socially acceptable can be very difficult.

It's a challenge to stop being a sheep, to stop following the herd. If all your friends are doing something, it almost behoves you to do the same.

This is especially true with deeply ingrained cultural habits such as consuming alcohol.

Even though you say to yourself, "I just feel so much better on every level without alcohol", it's not enough.

Peer pressure is a super strong mental barrier to change. It is probably what got you started in the first place.

Peer pressure can prevent you from making massive changes in your life, and it can exert a lot of pressure to force you back into following the herd, even though you know this is going to be against your best interests, and that there may be serious consequences as a result.

You feel like you can't help it. It feels like you are helplessly floating down a fast moving river, sitting in a boat with no oars. You've got no choice but to go with the flow. Even a dead fish can go with the flow.

The Courage to Stand Alone

British philosopher, Bertrand Russell said, "Collective fear stimulates herd instinct, and tends to produce ferocity towards those who are not regarded as members of the herd"

Let me tell you that you most certainly do l
You can most certainly change the way you
change the way you think. You can absolutel
you put into your mouth.

Remember that the good old days were never the good old days, it's simply a trick of the mind. Those reasons that you had at the beginning of this journey for quitting alcohol are still the same. That old part of you, the part that you're trying to get away from, will swiftly resurface again once you start reusing this drug.

Exercise

As a quick exercise, just think about the possibility of taking this journey for a few more weeks. You don't have to commit yourself to a lifetime of not drinking, just four more weeks.

How does that sound to you?

How Can You Protect Yourself

Okay, let's say that you have decided that 30 days is enough. Despite my pleas and protestations, you are going to go back to drinking alcohol and there's nothing I can say to change your mind.

How can you protect yourself?

An Ounce of Prevention

You are always going to be fighting an uphill battle when trying to protect yourself against any physical damage from the long-term use of any toxin, especially such a nasty toxin as alcohol.

Allow me to give you another small play. The best way to protect yourself, your first line of defense, is always going to be prevention.

Benjamin Franklin said, "An ounce of prevention is worth und of cure".

You are the only one that can prevent alcohol toxicity. You do that by not allowing the toxin to enter your body in the first place.

Failing that, you have to rely on the strength of your metabolic and immune system.

To minimize the damage of this toxin, it will help to understand how your body metabolizes alcohol. So let's take a look at a very simplistic breakdown of the process.

Alcohol Metabolism

Alcohol metabolism starts with the breaking down of the alcohol (ethanol) using an enzyme called alcohol dehydrogenase. The resulting product is a toxic compound called acetaldehyde.

Acetaldehyde is more toxic than the alcohol itself.

Acetaldehyde must be quickly broken down using the enzymes acetaldehyde dehydrogenase and glutathione.

The mixture of these two enzymes result in the non-toxic acetate. Acetate, which is similar to vinegar, is then harmlessly expelled from your body.

As we previously seen, your liver is only capable of metabolizing one unit of alcohol per hour. A unit of alcohol is a British measurement equaling 10ml or 8g. This is roughly the alcohol content of a small glass of wine or small beer.

Measuring Your Personal Alcohol Metabolic Rate

This metabolic rate is also only an average.

Among other things, the individual metabolic rate will depend on the health of the liver, the health and age of the person. The longer a person has been drinking, the more damage there is likely to be to their liver. The more liver damage, the less proficient the liver will be at metabolizing the alcohol.

As a person ages, the liver metabolic rate also declines.

Regeneration

The liver is a mighty organ with legendary regeneration capabilities.

Because there are so many people on the waiting list for liver transplant, many of them die before they are chosen for surgery.

A miraculous solution is to take a healthy liver and divide it into two. This is known as a split liver transplant. This one single donor liver can then be transplanted into two patients.

It's almost as successful as whole organ transplant. Amazing!

The Abused Liver

Unfortunately, the liver is also one of the most abused parts of the body, especially in the body of alcohol user. A healthy liver is not something which is often found in the body of heavy drinker.

Legendary as its regeneration capabilities are, the liver's capabilities are finite. Eventually your liver will become unable to cope with the stress of dealing with the constant incursion of any toxin.

Liver damage is also a silent assassin. You won't know you have liver damage until things are serious

Acetaldehyde Breakdown

Let's go back to our breakdown of the metabolizing process. As we saw, one of the substances required to break down the acetaldehyde, this very toxic by-product of alcohol, is the substance glutathione.

The body stores of this substance are finite. They quickly run out when large amounts of alcohol enter the system. This causes acetaldehyde to build up, leaving the body exposed for long periods of time.

As a side note, one of the leading drugs used for helping people quit drinking, Antabuse, is designed to block the breakdown of acetaldehyde. This can result in hangover symptoms, worse than any hangover the drinker has ever experienced before.

As another side note, women have far less acetaldehyde dehydrogenase and glutathione than men. This means that, along with smaller livers, the alcohol metabolic process in women takes longer. Women are prone to more prolonged periods of acetaldehyde exposure, leading to longer and deeper hangovers, and possibly more physical damage.

Long Live the Liver

Once the liver damage is done, your life is gone.

There's always a possibility of a liver transplant. However, if you are the cause of your own liver damage, there would be very strict preconditions before you were even considered for the liver transplant list. One of these would be to completely stop drinking alcohol.

Now, I can bullshit you and say there are foods that can counteract liver damage, but that's all it would be, bullshit.

The only thing that can prevent liver damage is to prevent the toxins from getting into your body in the first place. The only way you do that is by stopping drinking.

And that precludes the fact that you have to stop drinking before the liver damage has gone too far.

Fatty liver can be reversed. Cirrhosis cannot be reversed.

Again, the best advice I can give you is to stop drinking altogether. This is the only way of really guaranteeing no more damage.

If you are going to continue drinking, then the best advice I can give you is to drink as little as possible. The more you drink, the more damage you cause.

Consuming Less

One way of drinking less is to drink fewer units of alcohol. So, you cut down on the overall amount that you're drinking, or you choose drinks which are lower in alcohol volume. This is a bit like smoking cigarettes with lower tar and nicotine.

Another way of cutting down your overall alcohol consumption is to alternate your drinks.

For every one alcoholic drink you consume, drink one non-alcoholic drink, preferably water. Even better, have a ratio of one alcoholic drink to two non-alcoholic drinks.

Another way to mitigate the damage is to directly provide your body with the right tools it need for fighting off the toxins.

The two most potent tools are exercise and nutrition.

Vigorous Motion

Exercise, any vigorous motion, helps your body prevent disease and helps to rid your body of chemicals, toxins, pollutants, and additives.

Imagine that your circulatory system is like a network of highway tunnels which serve every part of your body. If you get a traffic jam in one area of that network, it can cause a lot of pollution, big delays, and the risk of accidents.

You have two types of circulation, your cardiovascular circulation and your lymphatic circulation.

We've all heard of the cardiovascular circulation and we've a pretty good idea of how it operates.

This circulatory system involves your heart, pumping your blood through blood vessels and supplying your body with all the nutrients and oxygen than it needs.

Even though we might have heard of the lymphatic system, not many of us know how important it is.

Your lymphatic circulation works in conjunction with your cardiovascular system. One of its main functions is to circulate immune cells throughout the body, essential for defending against infections.

The difference between the two systems is that your lymphatic system doesn't have a major organ to help pump the lymphatic fluid around your body. It relies on gravity, breathing, massage, hydrotherapy, and, most importantly, exercise.

Any activity that you can think of which will contribute to your overall fitness level, also strengthens your immune system.

Try to practice both aerobic and resistance training. Aerobic exercise is good for your circulatory system. Resistance training increases muscle mass, which in turn makes your cardiovascular and lymph circulation much stronger and more efficient.

Nutrition

The second tool is nutrition.

Nutrition gives your body the vitamins and minerals it needs for repair and recuperation.

Nutrition gives your body the building blocks for a longer and better quality life. These are also the building blocks which will help your body to mitigate some of the damage caused by alcohol.

Combining exercise and nutrition will give you an end result which is much more than the sum of its individual parts. We'll talk about this more later.

Water

Another way of reducing the damage caused by alcohol is to drink a lot of water.

Up to 60% of the human adult body is composed of water. The brain, liver, and heart are composed of about 75% water. We rely on water for all our physical and mental functioning. Water also helps to flush out the toxins.

Drink water regularly, even when you're not thirsty. Thirst is the first sign of dehydration.

Another way of checking dehydration is the color of your pee. If it's yellow, you need to drink more. The yellower it is, the more dehydrated you are, the more you need to drink.

Spreading Out Your Alcohol

Stretch your drinking over a few days.

Give yourself an alcohol limit. Restrict the amount of alcohol that you can consume in any one week and spread that consumption over a longer period. Don't consume your whole week's rations in a day or two.

Don't drink every day. Have at least a couple of clean days during the week.

To make this work in the long-term, you've got to track the amounts that you're consuming.

There are plenty of alcohol tracking apps available. Short of that, a small notepad and pen that you can put into your pocket or handbag, will suffice.

Who Are Your Friends?

Another way of reducing your risk is to diversify your friendships. When I was a drinker, almost all of my friends were also drinkers.

Having heavy drinker friends can lead to you consuming more alcohol. If all your friends want to go to the bar, how can you cut down?

Try to cultivate friendships with people who have other interests, interests that don't involve alcohol. When you're with these people, you don't drink alcohol.

It gives you a break without having to argue the toss every time you don't want to drink.

Recap

The human liver is one of the most abused parts of the drinker's body. It works overtime under normal circumstances. For the heavy drinker, the liver works double or triple time. There's no way it can maintain this level of function without serious side-effects and long-term consequences.

The best way of reducing the risk for your liver, and for your body in general, is to abstain from drinking alcohol altogether.

If you don't want to do that, at least make sure you are supplying your body with the tools it needs to protect itself: exercise, nutrition, and water.

Drink fewer units of alcohol, alternating alcoholic drinks with non-alcoholic drinks, and try to establish friendships outside your normal drinking circles.

Exercise

If you are going to continue drinking, where can you lessen some of the damage?

Can you reduce your overall drinking?

Can you spread your alcohol use over more days?

Track everything that you drink, every day, for a month. Download an alcohol tracking app for your phone or use a simple notebook and pen.

What do you see?

What can you improve on?

The Under Control Trap

Alcohol Moderation

Let's take a look at moderation. Moderate alcohol consumption means holding yourself back from drinking to excess.

What does excess mean?

In drinking alcohol, excess means exceeding the recommended dosage guidelines. These dosage guidelines differ, depending on where in the world you are, or who you listen to.

These guidelines average out at approximately 14 units of alcohol per week for men and women.

How much is this?

A typical strength bottle of wine, white, red, or rose, has 10 units of alcohol. So, if you drink more than one and half bottles of wine per week, you are drinking in excess.

The benefits of even these "moderate" amounts are contested by many leading scientists.

Alcohol Control

Controlling any drug is an illusion. More appropriately, it's a delusion.

Alcohol is very difficult to control because it is a drug, because of tolerance, because of rituals, behaviors, and ultimately habits.

It's easy to maintain control of alcohol in the first few days, or even weeks, after you've taken a 30 day challenge.

You say to yourself things like,

"I'm in full control of my drinking now, I have proved that by not drinking for 30 days". Or "I understand my alcohol drinking habit, therefore I can control it."

Moderation doesn't work if you enjoy the buzz of alcohol. If you drink to get merry, to get drunk, or to get slaughtered, moderation is essentially unattainable. At least it's unattainable without a lot of hard, hard work.

Moderation is perfectly achievable if you are a person who doesn't drink much in the first place.

If you only drink for social inclusion, or you have a drink every so often for special occasions, then by definition, you are a moderate drinker. However, a moderate drinker doesn't have to think about moderate drinking. It comes naturally.

For a heavy drinker to moderate, it becomes a constant battle.

Feeling the Buzz

When I drank alcohol, the whole point was to feel a buzz. I didn't see the point of drinking just for the sake of the taste, or if I'm being honest, for the socializing. The point for me was always to get drunk.

I didn't always have to drink to get obliterated, but I always felt that the point of drinking was to get high, to feel the buzz. I wanted to feel that heat, the light-headedness, the tipsiness if you like.

Whenever I tried to moderate my drinking, the buzz was either missing or so reduced as to not be worth the effort. In other words, moderation made me feel cheated.

And I think most drinkers feel the same way, if they're being honest.

What is Your Reason for Drinking?

It takes a lot of effort and time to get used to the taste of alcohol. Why would you continue to pour this foul tasting liquid into your mouth if there wasn't another motive?

Many people come to think about moderation when alcohol starts causing a problem.

They begin to feel some health consequences in one way or another, physical or mental. They're spending too much money on the stuff. Somebody has said something to them about the amount that they are consuming or how they are acting once they're under the influence. Perhaps these people have even given them an ultimatum.

Heavy alcohol drinkers like to drink, they like to have fun drinking, but they don't like the consequences.

Unfortunately, drinking the quantities of alcohol that allows people feel they're having "fun", getting high, or feeling that buzz, are always going to come with consequences, both long-term and short-term.

My Moderation Attempts

I was drinking alcohol for 30+ years. In the latter part of those years, I tried to moderate my use on many, many occasions.

I never wanted to quit alcohol completely because, in my mind I was having "fun". I saw myself as a drinker. I rejected any personal associations with alcoholism, being an alcoholic, or even having a drink problem.

I always believed that I was in full control of my drinking. If I drank twenty pints of Guinness, it was because I wanted to drink twenty pints of Guinness, not because I was habitually drinking, not because I was a heavy drinker, and certainly not because I was an alcoholic.

My moderation attempts also followed what I would call a fairly standard sequence.

Abstaining for a day or two days was the easiest form of moderation for me. I could hold my self-control together, not have any alcohol in the house, and concentrate my mind on other things.

Moderating while drinking, within a session, was always more difficult. Once I had consumed one or two drinks, it was more difficult to refuse the third or fourth.

I could make this type of moderation possible at home because I could arrange it so I only had a limited amount of alcohol on hand. If I wanted more, I'd have to walk to the nearest shop. That would usually be enough to hold me off.

Being in the pub was way more difficult, especially if I had extra money. In the long run, I would moderate for a week or two, maybe a bit longer, but eventually I would always return to the same amounts I was drinking before.

This is not "fun". It just served to make me feel pathetic.

Using for the Buzz

The majority of drinkers use alcohol for the buzz.

Moderation is not just about abstaining from the alcohol, it's about abstaining from the buzz. Once you have one drink, it gets more difficult to say no to the second.

There are a couple of reasons for this.

First, alcohol is a drug, it passes into your brain and impairs your judgment.

Second, one or two drinks is unlikely to give a seasoned drinker a booze buzz. He needs more. Alcohol tolerance takes care of this.

After the second drink, it's more difficult to say no to the third, and so on. Although you might start feeling the buzz after one or two, it's not likely to be enough. All the while, the alcohol is further reducing your inhibitions.

Each drink reduces the barrier to the next.

Long-Term Scrap

Alcohol moderation is a fight for anyone who likes the buzz. And this fight is not short-term.

It will last you for the rest of your life.

You will always have to battle between your needs to reduce the amount of alcohol you are drinking because of the consequences, and increase the amount that you are drinking because you want to have "fun".

Also, each time you quit moderating and return to your previous drinking habits, a part of you feels like you have failed. A part of you doubts your abilities. This in turn affects your future moderation attempts.

It's easy to see why some people start thinking about themselves as alcoholics, that they have an alcoholic gene, or some other bollocks.

That's why I maintain that quitting alcohol was the best thing that I ever did. It saved me from that lifelong fight.

With that one decision, I won the war. As far as alcohol was concerned, I didn't have to do another thing.

I didn't have to fight the moderation battles any more. It took me awhile to get the alcohol thinking out of my system, but once I got to that place, there was really no looking back.

Recap

Alcohol moderation is an illusion. Most people who drink heavily, drink for the buzz. They don't drink for the taste. They don't drink to socialize. They don't drink to relax. They drink for the effects of alcohol on their central nervous systems. Although these elements might come into it, they are not the main act. The headline show is always about the buzz.

For moderation to work with the heavy drinker, it has to be a lifelong commitment. This means battling to reduce the amount of alcohol when all your habit wants to do is consume more, and you have to keep this up forever.

Exercise

This 30 day challenge has given you a taste of what it's like to be without alcohol for a sustained period of time.

During this challenge, you have seen what it's like not to have to think about alcohol. Maybe you did think about alcohol, but you knew it wasn't an option, so you put it out of your mind.

You found that once you put alcohol out of your mind, you could easily get on with your life, taking advantage of your new found mental freedom, your healing body, and all the other benefits of not having this toxin in your life.

The longer you go without alcohol, the easier it gets.

Now, imagine that instead of quitting alcohol 30 days, you had to moderate your drinking.

You are never allowed to drink more than the maximum, "responsible" dosage... No more than fourteen units of alcohol per week, with at least two days alcohol free.

Binge drinking means having more than eight units of alcohol for men, six units for women, in any one sitting. So you can have fourteen units of alcohol per week, roughly a bottle and a half of wine, and no more than eight units of alcohol per sitting. How long do you think you would be able to continue with this?

Could you last 30 days?

Could you last a full year?

Could you do this for the rest of your life?

That's what moderate drinking entails. It's not for 30 days. It's a lifelong commitment.

The Benefits of *Drinking* Alcohol

Is there anything such a thing as a healthy drink of alcohol?

The alcohol industry would certainly like you to think so. Most people who drink find it very easy to convince themselves that *their* "moderate" drinking is healthy.

Healthy drinking is a concept which is actively promoted by the alcohol industry and is readily accepted by most drinkers. We all want to hear good news about our bad habits.

Deep down we all know that alcohol is bad for us.

How can we not understand that?

We feel physically ill every time overindulge. Even mild indulgences cause problems. We want to believe that we are different. We want to believe that our overindulgence have no consequences.

Brain Retardation

Remember that alcohol is a psychoactive drug. It is one of the few substances which can easily pass through the defenses of your Blood Brain Barrier. This is the natural fortification that surrounds your brain, keeping all manner of nasty things from causing you cerebral problems.

We all have small amounts of alcohol in our bodies which are present through digestion or overripe fruit that we eat. This is no problem. The human liver can easily and effectively deal with this amount of alcohol.

However, the amounts of alcohol that we deliberately expose our bodies to, far surpass this safe level. When the alcohol passes through the Blood Brain Barrier, it interferes with the natural brain functioning.

The brain is the driving force behind everything that you do. All movements, all actions, thoughts, emotions - these all rely on a consistent and fully functioning brain.

Alcohol, in combination with the behaviors, rituals, and habits of drinking eventually restructure your cerebral pathways. This restructuring alters how you think, feel, and act.

In the long-term, much of this brain alteration is reversible.

When you stop drinking, when you change your drinking behaviors, rituals, and habits, your brain restructures itself accordingly.

Long-term brain damage can be permanent, unalterable, and devastating.

Short-term damage can be just as devastating in the form of opportunity cost. How much more can you possibly do with your life if you are not deliberately handicapping your brainpower?

My Reactivated Brain

I'm a testament to this. Since I've stopped drinking, my brainpower, for what it is, has increased exponentially. I'm discovering more things about myself and my abilities all the time. I'm able to do things now that I never thought were possible.

I don't get side-tracked by binge drinking sessions.

I don't have to worry about getting up in the morning with a hangover and that hangover ruining my day.

I follow through consistently with my plans.

If I start my week off with a plan, I know most of it will be achieved. If I start my year off with a plan, I know most of it will be achieved.

In my 30 years of drinking, I made a variety of plans and resolutions that never came anywhere near fruition.

I used to be a smoker. I quit smoking over a hundred times. The one factor which hampered all my quit smoking attempts was alcohol.

Your Golden Opportunity

Why am I telling you this? Because now that your brain and body haven't been subjected to alcohol for 30 days, you are in the best position to think about how alcohol is affecting your brain and your life.

Your brain is everything. Without your brain, you are nothing, a chunk of meat.

You can do nothing.

You can be nothing.

When you poison your brain, you restrict who you are. You restrict what you think, what you can think, what you're capable of thinking. And by extension, you restrict what you're capable of doing.

You have an opportunity now to rethink yourself as a drinker. Ask yourself if alcohol has any part to play in your life from now on?

I hope you take some of these words to heart. I hope at least you can think about the implications of your alcohol use to your long-term physical and mental health.

I hope that these few thoughts help you to reduce your alcohol consumption, if not cease it altogether.

In any case, I wish you the best of luck in the future.

Recap

The benefits of alcohol are very suspect, to say the least. For every piece of murky evidence attempting to prove a benefit, there are a hundred pieces of clear evidence directly pointing to harm.

Alcohol causes short-term and long-term brain problems. Most of this mental retardation happens without you knowing about it. Some of this mental retardation is reversible, some is not.

Life is short. Everything you do to inhibit your brain function, by extension is inhibiting your life.

Exercise

If you are determined to start drinking again, I'd like to make this last attempt to get you to change your mind.

Think about what must be going on in your brain for this toxin to affect your speech, your movements, your vision, and all your other senses.

Think about the memory loss that you suffer, not only the next day, but for the rest of your life.

Now think about the possibility that this toxin, passing through the Blood Brain Barrier, and directly interacting with your brain cells, can have a long-term impact on every thought you make, even after the alcohol has been eliminated.

Again, if you decide to carry on drinking, I wish you the best of luck.

What Are the Benefits of Being Alcohol Free?

To end, here's a quick word for those who like what they've seen in themselves and want to remain alcohol free or who just want to extend this period of alcohol freedom.

Look at the difference that quitting drinking for 30 days has made in your life. Now multiply that by five or ten.

Living the Life You Want to Live

Now that you've decided to quit drinking for longer, you have the chance to begin to live the life that you want to live.

You will have the clean-running brain to power that life. You will have the clean-running body to go out and get whatever that new life has to offer. You will have all that time and money you were wasting on alcohol to fund that new life.

Removing alcohol from your life is not a magic bullet. There is still some work to do. But you're giving yourself a massive foundational kick start.

I think the main benefit of quitting drinking is that you have allowed your body the freedom to do what it's supposed to do, to feel how it's supposed to feel. You have given your brain freedom to think how it's supposed to think, without all that alcoholic toxin spoiling the show.

My "Benefits" of Drinking Alcohol

There is a lot of misinformation out there about the benefits of drinking alcohol. When I was drinking alcohol, there were many occasions when I seriously felt close to death.

I never felt as isolated, ill, poor, indulgent, unintelligent, and useless.

My alcohol behavior infected my mind and body.

My alcohol habit infected my spirituality and my relationships.

My drinking habit stole from my bank account and robbed me of many, many years of my life.

Each of these areas of my life have improved since I quit drinking. Some of them have improved beyond all my expectations.

What Is Worth Remembering in a Life?

Now that you've decided to quit drinking, you will start to remember the most important times in your life.

One of the saddest things is that all my alcohol consumption cheated me out of what should have been some of my most cherished memories. Memories that I will never get back.

Remember that alcohol is used at those moments in our lives which are the cause for celebration.

For the drinker who likes the buzz, any celebration equals alcohol use. Therefore these special moments also coincide with brain fog and memory loss.

These are the cherished times that create a life worth remembering. Unfortunately, these are the exact moments which are lost forever in the alcohol fog.

What you're left with is a lifetime of memories consisting of the dullest times.

You remember work, the household chores, the daily grind.

You forget family vacations, get-togethers, births, marriages, graduations, birthdays, Christmases, and all the other times of importance when we use this drug to celebrate.

You might have vague impressions that these events happened, but the details are gone. And it's the details that make the memories. Anyone can look at the calendar and say, "Yes, this event did happen", but that won't bring a smile to your face. It's the details that do that.

It's a sad thing to say, but the only memories that I have of some of the most special occasions in my life are the photographs that other people had taken.

When I look at these photographs, I see me smiling and happy, but I have no recollection about what was making me smile.

Thankfully, I am building a robust collection of the most vivid memories of the times in my life that are worth remembering.

What Can I Do Now? So Many Choices!

Now that you've decided to quit alcohol, you have just vastly increased your choices.

Another fundamental benefit from quitting alcohol is that you greatly amplify your choices in life.

Alcohol use, the drinking behavior, the rituals, and the habits, restrict you in so many ways. Your choices become reduced to what fits in with those behaviors and those habits.

I'm not just talking about not been able to drive because you've had a skinful of alcohol. I'm talking about not been able to live a full life because your everyday existence is peppered with the influence alcohol thinking.

As I said, alcohol is a mind altering, toxic drug.

Imagine replacing the alcohol with any other drug, heroin, cocaine, angel dust, PCP. Now imagine trying to live a full life while consistently using one of these drugs.

You might think that alcohol is a more benign drug. Most people do.

The fact is, alcohol is more harmful than any of these drugs. 3.5 million people die each year as a result of alcohol consumption.

Over 200 medical conditions are caused through drinking alcohol.

Why do people think that regularly and consistently using this dangerous drug won't have a detrimental effect on them?

Why do they think that consuming this toxin for short-term gratification is not going to produce long-term consequences?

Why do people think that decades of drug use will not reduce their lives to a shadow of what was once possible?

Thankfully, most people have the opportunity of grasping those possibilities once more.

The Possibilities Are Open

Now that you have made the decision to quit drinking alcohol, you have greatly expanded your opportunities. You have improved your chances of living a long and quality life. You have greatly improved your chances of passing on that positive life message to your children and your wider family.

The benefits of quitting drinking alcohol are that you just opened your life to all possibilities.

You get to make intelligent clearheaded choices about your future.

You get to make intelligent clearheaded choices about your present.

You once again put yourself in a position where today matters. What you do today matters, not only for today, but for tomorrow, and the rest of your life. And you get to do this in a positive way.

Of course, drinking alcohol makes today matter, it makes tomorrow matter, it makes your life matter, but it matters in a negative way.

As we've seen, moderation is a never-ending battle between what you know makes sense and your desire for the buzz. As we've seen with tolerance and addiction, this will never be an easy battle, and there is only ever likely to be one winner.

The benefit of stopping the flow of this poison is that you put yourself on an unerring path of forward momentum. You put yourself on a new path where you can progressively and consistently change your life for the better.

Who Can I Be Now?

Now that you've made the decision to quit drinking alcohol, you have greatly expanded your capacity to learn, to acquire new skills, to be the person that you want to be.

The benefits of quitting drinking alcohol mean that you have the time and the energy and the money to learn the new skills that you need to learn to create that fantastic new life for yourself.

You have the necessary resources to manufacture any future that you desire. Your self-control returns *to you*, where it belongs. You regain mastery of your mind. Once you are the master of your mind, everything else will follow.

Onwards and Upwards!

Now that you've made the decision to quit drinking alcohol, these are just some of the benefits that you stand to gain.

I congratulate you for your wise decision and I salute you on your onwards journey.

Onwards and Upwards!

Next?

Thank you for reading this book. I hope I have given you at least some food for thought. And I wish you very well on your onwards journey.

Quit Drinking Alcohol Resources

Before we end, let me give you a couple of fantastic resources that might help you building your new journey.

One is *AlcoholMastery.com* where you will find upwards of 500 videos to support you in your new life.

These videos range from understanding and overcoming your cravings, sleeping at night without alcohol, and ways of dealing with those annoying friends who just won't accept that you've quit alcohol for good.

You'll also find many videos on inspiration, building your determination and motivation, and how to maintain your.

We have the Alcohol Mastery newsletter. This is a daily email, each containing a video to help and inspire you on your new journey. You can sign up for free by going to *AlcoholMastery.com*, leaving your first name and email address. As a bonus for signing up, you'll also receive a free video course on relaxation and de-stressing after you've quit drinking.

If you're looking for a community of like-minded people, we have a private Facebook group, *Onwards and Upwards*.

This very successful group of people are doing an awesome job of helping each other thrive and survive in their new alcohol free life. Regardless of where you are in your journey, you'll find the right help here.

This group is by invite only. If you would like an invite, you need to sign up to our newsletter. Once you have signed up, I'll send you a note about what to do next.

All of the above resources are absolutely free.

For those who want a step-by-step approach to quitting drinking, Alcohol Mastery has a range of step-by-step courses covering quitting drinking alcohol, preparing to quit drinking alcohol, and finding relaxation and de-stressing after you quit. You'll find all the information about these courses in the Alcohol Mastery Store.

Again, thank you very much for giving me your attention, and I hope that you have found some help here.

Until next time, I'm Kevin O'Hara for alcoholmastery.com, onwards and upwards... Take care.

AlcoholMastery.com

Come to AlcoholMastery.com where you'll find a ton of helpful videos for quitting the booze.

Other Books by Kevin O'Hara

How to Stop Drinking Alcohol - A Simple Path from Alcohol Misery to Alcohol Mastery

Alcohol Freedom - 7 Powerful Mindsets to Kickstart Your Alcohol-Free Journey!

Made in the USA
Middletown, DE
12 December 2020

a novella

alone

the woman at the well

a novella

alope

the woman at the well

GOLDEN KEYES
PARSONS

WhiteFire
Publishing

This is a work of fiction. All characters and events portrayed in this novel are either fictitious or used fictitiously.

ALONE: THE WOMAN AT THE WELL

WhiteFire Publishing
13607 Bedford Rd NE
Cumberland, MD 21502

ISBN: 9781939023056 (digital)
9781939023049 (print)

*To women who might have felt trapped, or alone,
or who needed forgiveness or healing—
who felt as if no one cared, or even knew their names.
An encounter with Jesus turned women's lives around
then—
and meeting Him still does today.*

Dear Reader,

This series about nameless women in Scripture has been in my heart for 30 years. I wrote the first book about the adulterous woman approximately that long ago. I was an amateur writer then and made many mistakes on the technical side of the craft, but the story was there. And I kept pitching the idea to publishers and editors, but at that time the popularity of biblical fiction was waning. Or more well-known authors had a series out there that was too similar. But the series wouldn't let me go. It seemed interesting to me that some of the major encounters Jesus had in his ministry were with women, and that those women were not even named in the accounts. However, they were important enough to be included in the canon.

In the meantime, I got a contract for another series, based on my family genealogy in 17th century France, the Darkness to Light series, and subsequently published a Civil War novel set in Texas, *His Steadfast Love*. One day via a writers loop I learned that WhiteFire Publishing was interested in biblical fiction. They bought the series and they are now reality.

I hope you will find touchstones in these stories that will ring true to you as a woman. Jesus broke many cultural and social mores of the day to relate to women—women who felt trapped by laws and tradition; those who needed forgiveness; some who had been abused.

I love to hear from my readers. You may contact me through my web site at www.goldenkeyesparsons.com or by email at golden@goldenkeyesparsons.com.

May the One who has our names engraved on the palm of His hand minister to you through these novellas.

Blessings,
Golden Keyes Parsons

chapter 1

I see a stranger. He sits on the edge of Jacob's well in the blistering heat and watches as I walk toward him. Undecided, I turn and look back in the direction of the village. The man is a Jew. He wears the tallit *of a Jewish rabbi. What is a Jewish rabbi doing in Samaria? A younger man stands by his side. Perhaps I should return later. I don't care to encounter the upturned noses and sneering lips.*

Marah hesitated, the afternoon sun beating down upon her. They needed water, and Marah chose to come to this particular well at this particular time of day to avoid the gossipy women from Sychar, their frowns and whispers. She lowered the water pot to her hip and shielded her eyes from the the sun's glare. He stared back at her. She expected him to rise and turn his back. However, the smallest hint of a smile tugged at the corners of his mouth.

Dust swirled around her feet as she veered to the right to go around the strangers.

"Would you give me a drink?"

Startled, Marah nearly dropped her water pot. A Jewish man speaking to a Samaritan woman—and in public? She glanced about to see if anyone was watching. Beads of perspiration formed on her upper lip.

"You're safe. No one else is around. My friends have gone into town to purchase food for us to eat. They left us here…" He motioned to the young man with him. "John and myself." He stood. "You come to this well to avoid the accusations of the other women. It hurts you. I am sorry for that, Marah."

Her breath caught in her throat. Her heart thudded. How did he know her name? She was certain she had never met this man. She knew the lecherous glances, scorn, and mocking eyes that passed judgment on her as she walked through the streets of the village. Those lying, hypocritical lips that would form words of vulgar propositions. Pious, pompous, prideful men. She hated them. But this man was not one of the men from the village. This man seemed different. How did he know she had been the object of scorn her whole life, as far back as she could remember?

8-   Marah's mother's screams echoed in her head as her earliest memories. She was three years old. Her baby brother, Benjamin, stirred in his sleep, flailed his tiny fists in the air, and started to cry. At first she thought the cries were his, but then she realized the wails came from her mother across the room.

Marah covered her ears, but the shrieks wouldn't stop. Her mother rushed out the front door into the night—still screaming. Marah rubbed her eyes and peered through the darkness. What looked like a bundle of clothing lay in the middle of her parents' pallet. No, that wasn't clothing. It was her papa. Why was he bunched up like that? She crawled over the hard dirt floor and shook his shoulder. "Papa? Papa, wake up."

But Papa didn't wake up. He didn't move. He lay very, very still.

Beautiful, curly brown hair tousled over Phoebe's head, and dark inquisitive eyes peered at Marah. Her mother had married a distant cousin with two younger boys and a baby girl less than a year old. Obed was a widower whose wife had died birthing Phoebe. What Marah remembered about him was that he yelled at her. He yelled at her brother. He yelled at her mother. He yelled at everybody. Nobody could ever please him. They were always in his way. Dinner was not hot enough or spicy enough. The baby kept him awake. The boys were too noisy. And he would bellow, sending the children scurrying for cover.

Then her mother had died in childbirth, along with the baby, and Obed expected Marah to take care of all the younger ones. She was only ten years old when he went to a neighboring village one day and left her in charge of the children. The baby was fretful, so she carried her around on her hip most of the afternoon.

Phoebe seemed to sense all was not well, and her protestations emerged in continual whimpers. Marah broke the hard crusts of bread that Obed had left and gave pieces to the children for the noon meal. She poured goat's milk into a bowl to soften the bread, while passing Phoebe back and forth from one arm to another. Every time Marah put her down, she cried and held her arms up. "Ma-a, Ma-a." She couldn't say her name correctly, so it came out almost like "Ima." Mother.

Marah looked down to check on the boys who were playing happily in the dirt beside the stable under the living quarters. The three boys looked like stair steps when they stood shoulder to shoulder—Benjamin, Noah, and Asher, her brother the oldest at seven, the other two five and three. They played together as typical boys did, rough and tumble, even

9

the three-year-old, but at the moment they seemed fascinated by a hole they were digging in the dirt. Asher held a piece of a broken pottery bowl into which Benjamin and Noah spooned the dirt they collected. Then Asher would take it to the corner of the stable where he dumped it into a burgeoning mound. What fascinated them about transferring dirt from one place to another escaped her, but at least they were entertaining themselves.

Marah finally coaxed Phoebe to lie down for a nap by curling up beside her. The next thing she knew, Obed stood over her, blustering as he jerked her up by her arm. "You lazy, good-for-nothing urchin! Sleeping while you were supposed to be watching my children. Where are the boys? Where are they?"

His wine-infused breath assaulted her nostrils as he dragged her to the door. "Where are they?"

"I–I don't know. They were playing there in the dirt just a moment ago." Marah ran outside and pointed down to the hole beside the stable. The pile of dirt they were constructing at the corner had grown into a recognizable wall around miniature houses. In spite of the "Obed threat," she paused to think, How creative. The empty bowl lay on its side, but no boys were in sight.

Obed pulled her back inside, shouting, spraying spittle over her face. "Just a moment ago? How long have you been asleep? You don't really know, do you?" He raised his hand and brought it across Marah's face. Pain exploded in her cheek, and her head flew to the side, wrenching her neck. The attack knocked her into the table and chairs behind her. A chair fell onto the pallet where Phoebe sat, rubbing her eyes as she began to fuss.

Obed pulled Marah up by the shoulder of her robe and slapped her again and again until everything turned fuzzy—and then black. When she roused from the beating, Phoebe was climbing over her, howling. Obed staggered outside and down the stairway, roaring for his sons.

She breathed a sigh of relief when she heard the sound of their feet hitting the dry, packed earth as they came running from behind the house. She picked Phoebe up, stepped out the door, and looked down. The boys came to a halt at the corner of the house, dust flying. They carried branches of a nearby palm tree in their arms. Their eyes widened as they stopped and stared at Obed. Asher dropped his little stack of palm fronds, and his chin started to quiver. He ducked behind Benjamin.

"Where were you? Where have you been?" Obed lurched down the steps waving his arms.

Benjamin stuck out his chest and stepped forward. "We–we, uh—we were building a fortress and needed some…"

Obed interrupted the boy with a slap to his shoulder that knocked him to the ground. He swung at Noah, but the agile child bobbed aside and avoided the blow, which threw Obed off-balance. The veins in the man's neck bulged, and his face grew purple with rage.

Benjamin scrambled to his feet and stepped in between his stepfather and the two younger brothers. "Run! Run to Lois's."

Noah and Asher dropped their branches and ran out of harm's way toward the neighbor's house. Asher stopped and looked back as Obed began to beat Benjamin with one of the branches that had fallen to the ground. Marah ran into the house and huddled in the corner with Phoebe until Benjamin's cries ceased. All was quiet except for the boy's sniffling as he came inside. Marah reached out her arms, and he crumpled into them, all three of them trembling and sniveling.

"I'm sorry, Benjamin. This is my fault." Marah

wiped the dirt streaked with sweat from his face and his bloody nose with the corner of her robe. "I fell asleep with Phoebe. I'm so sorry."

"It's not your fault." This brave seven-year-old, far more mature than his years, tried to comfort her. A seven-year-old and a ten-year old attempting to protect each other. It wasn't right. Even in her childish reasoning, she knew it wasn't right.

chapter 2

"Give me a drink."

Marah scoffed and set her water pot down on the edge of the well. "How is it that you, being a Jew, ask me, a Samaritan—and a woman—for a drink? You Jews ordinarily want nothing to do with us Samaritans." Her tone sounded harsh and impolite even to her own ears. Softening the sharp edge in her voice, she asked, "And how do you know my name?"

"Marah!" Naomi called over her shoulder as she took bread out of the oven. "Check on the fire in the oven outside."

Obed had married again the year following her mother's death—a stern, no-nonsense widow with two older children of her own, a fifteen-year-old son, Jonathan, and a married daughter, Leah, who lived in the village with her husband and new baby. Naomi was not unkind to them, but she hardly ever smiled or offered a kind word. The first signs of daylight saw her up and about, starting the fires—both the inside and outside ovens—before the day got too hot, grinding wheat and baking bread. Naomi was a good cook, and was neat and organized. She kept the household in order, which pleased Obed—for a time.

"Marah! Did you hear me?"

"I'm coming."

alone

Marah had never liked her name. Why would someone name their child "Bitter"? She remembered asking her mother why they labeled her with such a name. Her mother would simply smile and pat Marah's cheek with her rough, reddened hand and say, "The Lord turns our bitterness into joy, our mourning into dancing. You'll understand someday." Then she would chuckle and return to her tasks, humming as she worked. Marah wondered why they didn't name her "Joy."

All of the children were assigned chores, even the little ones. Benjamin and Noah's responsibilities were to help with the livestock, feeding and watering. Asher tagged along with them, and assisted them in his own way. Actually, he proved to be good help. They learned quickly that things would go better for the family if they performed their duties willingly and without question. Marah's primary job was to take care of Phoebe, but she also was to help with the laundry and baking when Phoebe was down for a nap.

Marah started down the steps to the courtyard. Phoebe was still asleep. The sun shimmered pinks and oranges in the eastern sky as if it couldn't decide whether or not to continue its journey on this new day. She bent over to pick up the few pieces of wood that were left to put on the fire Naomi had already started.

"Where is your shadow?" Jonathan's changing voice burbled between deep resonance and the ever-present threat of a screech. This morning it was deep and soft. He cleared his throat as he dropped his armload of wood next to the oven. Tall and slender, he had dark, beady eyes that flitted over her with lecherous glances. Her skin crawled when he was around.

Marah stood up and backed away, tripping as her

foot hung in the hem of her robe. "She—she is still asleep. I was just going in to get her. I'm sure she's awake by now."

She regained her footing and moved toward the steps leading up to the living quarters, but Jonathan blocked her path. He grinned at her with a mouthful of crooked teeth. "I don't hear her. She's probably not awake yet."

She glanced over Jonathan's shoulder. "Where's your mother?"

He indicated with a toss of his head. "In the stable with Obed. That old ewe decided to have her lamb this morning."

"Oh."

He pinned Marah's shoulders against the wall. Leaning hard against her, he rubbed his hands up and down her body. She flinched and tried to twist away from him, but his grip was like iron. "Hmm. The young flower is beginning to blossom." His words came out between clenched teeth, his breath stale and rank. The thudding of her heart filled her ears. She pushed against him, but he was too strong. Her head came just to his chest. "You'd best not resist me or cry out. I'll simply tell Obed that you seduced me, you little wench."

She didn't understand why he would treat her like this. She didn't even know what "seduced" meant. Her knees trembled and turned to water. She could barely stand up.

Obed and Naomi's voices preceded them as they came around the corner from the stable. Jonathan released Marah and hurried to the pile of firewood, but not before hissing, "Remember what I said. I'll get back to you later."

She ran up the steps into the house and gathered a still-sleeping Phoebe in her arms. Marah huddled in the corner on the pallet, rocking the toddler in her arms until her trembling ceased. What had just happened? What did Jonathan want? She didn't know, but the sick feeling in her stomach told her it wasn't proper.

Naomi came into the room with the little lamb in her arms. "Look what I have here." She frowned as she sighted Marah in the corner. "What's wrong with you? Why haven't you lit the lantern?"

"N–nothing. I just stumbled on the stairs."

"Well, get up and get some light in here." She strode over to the pallet and knelt down beside Phoebe as Marah struggled to her feet. She lit the lantern with a stick from the fire.

Phoebe sat up, rubbing her eyes. "Ooo." She grabbed the neck of the wooly lamb and pulled it to her.

Naomi barked at the child. "Be careful. Don't wrench its neck off. You can play with it for a bit, but we'll need to return it to its mother pretty quickly. He needs his breakfast, just like we need ours." She stood and wiped her hands on her robe. "And I must be about that." She bustled to the oven. "Oy, the bread got a little brown, but it will have to do."

With Naomi's attention diverted to the duties of the day, Marah sat on the floor with Phoebe and the lamb and played with them, but her hands continued to shake.

"Take the lamb back to the stable, Marah. It's time to eat." Naomi kept her back to them.

"Yes, in a minute." She didn't want to encounter Jonathan, whom she pictured lurking in the shadows of the stable to corner her once again.

Naomi whirled around with a wooden spoon in her hand. "Excuse me? Now, young lady."

Marah scrambled up, took hold of Phoebe with one hand, and held the lamb in the other. She stood in the doorway and looked both ways. No Jonathan.

"What's the matter with you this morning, Marah? Take that lamb to the stable and get back up here and help me with breakfast. Go! Shoo!" She waved her apron at Marah and shook her head.

She half-ran, half-stumbled down to the stable, dragging Phoebe along with her. The little girl started to babble and whimper. "Ma-a. Ma-a." Marah stopped and picked her up with one arm and carried the lamb with the other, both of them protesting. Depositing the lamb with its mother, she ran back up the stairs with Phoebe into the house.

Jonathan came in with Obed for morning prayer and breakfast. Marah kept her eyes downcast. She didn't even want to look at him. The men eagerly tore the hot bread into pieces and stuffed their mouths, alternating with dates, mangoes, cucumbers, and cheese, washing it down with fresh milk. The boys bantered back and forth, swatting at one another until Noah knocked over his cup.

Naomi wiped it up with a towel, grumbling the whole time. "Clumsy boy. Haven't I told you boys over and over to quit your fighting while you're eating?" She pulled him up by his arm.

Noah squealed. "Ow! You're hurting me."

"I'll do more than hurt your arm if you don't quit knocking your milk over. You'll have no more this week. Maybe then you'll learn." She shooed him away. "Go on. Wait for your brothers outside."

Noah grabbed a piece of bread as he ran for the door. He stopped for a moment and looked back, grinning, then ran down the outside stairs to the yard.

Jonathan snorted at the young boy. "Thought you were through with naughty boys spilling milk, didn't you?" He rubbed his head. "I might even have some knots left from the thumpings you gave me."

Naomi swung her towel at him. "You're not too old for me to still thump."

He ducked as Obed swatted at his head. "Don't talk back to your mother. It's disrespectful."

Jonathan returned to his breakfast with a crooked smirk to match his crooked teeth.

Marah shuddered. She didn't want to be in the same house with the nasty boy, but she didn't know what to do. She couldn't tell Naomi. He was her son, and she would take his side. And she couldn't tell Obed anything personal. He was a man, and although he was her stepfather, she knew he really didn't care about her except that she took care of Phoebe for him. Benjamin was too young to share something like this with. Marah felt completely apart and alone.

She fed Phoebe her breakfast and then took her outside to feed the chickens. The child loved doing that. She would toddle up to them and try to pet them, but, of course, they simply scattered. Except the rooster, which chased her on occasion. But when there were chicks Marah usually caught one of the fuzzy yellow balls for Phoebe to play with. She was petting a particularly small one when Obed approached Marah later that morning. "How old are you now?"

"I–I'll be thirteen next month."

"That's what I thought." He held an axe in his hands. "It's about time we talked about your wedding."

Marah's cheeks warmed. She looked around to find Phoebe. The little girl sat under the shade of a scrawny tree playing with her chick. "But I'm not…I haven't…"

"You're plenty old enough. I shall speak to David's father this week." He swung the axe and plunged it into the splitting stump with a clunk. Picking up a log, he proceeded to split it, wood chips flying. He tossed it into the woodpile. "Plenty old enough that young men are starting to take notice of you." He spewed spittle onto the ground and glared at her.

Had he seen what happened earlier—or had Jonathan told him?

He waved her away, his dark brows furrowed over his bulbous nose. "Go on and gather the eggs."

She knew this day was coming. And she knew it was coming soon, but even so, she simply was not ready for it. Marah had been betrothed to David from infancy, as was the custom of their people. He was four years older than she, and she liked him very much. He was quiet and shy, with dark curly hair and gray eyes. Their families celebrated festivals like Passover together when they were children. They had been playmates. But as he got older, they weren't so much. He began to separate himself and go with the men.

It wasn't that she didn't want to marry David. Under the laws of betrothal, they were already bound together as husband and wife. She looked forward to going through the wedding ceremony and in reality becoming his wife—someday. Just not yet.

However, the incident with Naomi's obnoxious son earlier that morning made the prospect of leaving Obed's household more appealing. She would be safe with David—at least for awhile.

Chapter 3

The days before her week of rejoicing, Marah watched Naomi scurry about from sunup to sunset preparing the wedding garments, cooking, and cleaning. Obed had lost no time going to the priest to begin the process to move from the betrothal to the nissu'in, the wedding. The "opening Sabbath" of the rejoicing—the beginning of the wedding ceremony—commenced within a month.

Marah pressed herself against the cool earthen wall as Leah and a gaggle of female relatives pushed past her into the kitchen. They had all arrived yesterday to assist in the volume of work to be done. Even Obed seemed in a jocular mood. Jonathan avoided Marah entirely. He acted as if she didn't exist.

Normally she loved the week of celebration surrounding weddings—the singing, the dancing, the food, the beautiful bride and groom. The entire village joined in the festivities. But being the too-young bride, she walked about bewildered, not really knowing what was expected of her. Naomi actually seemed happy about the upcoming wedding. Marah supposed the woman was glad to be getting rid of her.

One evening as she was playing with Phoebe, Leah approached, holding her baby, and sat beside her. A younger version of Naomi, but without the hard etchings of time on her face, she smiled and touched Marah's hand. "What's wrong with the bride-to-be? You don't seem very happy." Her baby stuck his thumb in his mouth and peered out of the tightly wound blanket around him that left only his face visible.

Leah withdrew her hand as Marah folded hers in her lap. She stared at them as if they could speak for her. Shaking her head, she tried to respond with something that made sense. "I...I don't really know what's wrong. I've always known that David and I were betrothed and would be married one day. And I do love him. But I didn't expect it to happen so soon." She raised her head and looked at Leah. Her eyes reflected kindness, but embarrassment heated Marah's cheeks. "I haven't...I'm not really a woman yet."

Leah chuckled softly. "We all know you've not had your niddah yet. You've not begun joining the women during your time of uncleanness. The family is aware of that—as is David. He is kind and cares for you. He will be patient until your time of monthly flow comes." She patted Marah's hands and smiled again. "You'll know. All will be well. You shall see."

Marah supposed the ancient custom of niddah seemed mysterious to all the little girls, but they were particularly baffling to her with no mother to guide her through it. She didn't know how she would know when her monthly flow came, and she didn't know what to do when it did. She remembered her mother appearing one day a month carrying a chair, which was the only place she could sit for fear of contaminating other pieces of furniture. Then the family wouldn't see her for a week. Her father—or later, Obed—would have to provide meals, or an aunt or kindly neighbor woman would come and care for them. Mother would return at the end of seven days and resume her household routine as normal.

"Where have you been, Mother?"

"It was my niddah." Her mother would smile at her and pat her head.

"What is that?"

"The time of my uncleanness. You'll go through it when you get older."

"What do you do?"

"Oh, visit with the other women who are on their niddah. Rest."

Marah whined. "Why can't I go with you?"

She would tweak her cheek and laugh. "You will soon enough."

But then her mother died and left Marah to learn about the ways of women on her own.

She stared at Leah as the young mother put her baby to suckle. "Leah, may I ask...I don't know..." Her words stuck in her throat, refusing to emerge. She sighed as tears gathered. Squeezing her eyes shut didn't make them go away, it simply made them tumble down her cheeks.

Leah pulled the baby from her and lifted him to her shoulder to burp. She covered her engorged breast with her shawl. "What is it, Marah? Why the tears?"

Marah took a deep, ragged breath. "I–I don't know what to do. I mean I know a wife cooks and takes care of the house and the children, but I don't know how to...how to be a wife to a husband."

Leah put the baby to the other side. "Oh, that part comes naturally. Just let David guide you through your wedding night. It will be fine." She smiled and busied herself tweaking the infant's chin and goo-gooing at him. The sucking noises from the baby punched holes in the tense silence. She hesitated. "When you first become husband and wife...I mean when you consummate the marriage..."

Marah waited. Leah fingered the edge of her baby's blanket, and Marah realized she was embarrassed too. "Well, at first, the first time...it's painful, but as you learn to accommodate your husband, it becomes more pleasurable."

Marah didn't know exactly what "it" was, but she acted like she did. She nodded her head. She assumed "it" had to do with the noises she heard during the night from Obed and Naomi's bed. She wanted to ask more questions, but Leah got up and patted her arm. "I must get back to my house. Always chores to do. Everything will be fine. You'll see. Don't fret about it anymore."

Marah took a step toward Leah but hesitated. The young mother blinked at her, then ducked her head. Marah wanted to throw her arms around Leah and thank her, but she was too unsure of herself. She cleared her throat. "Thank you."

Leah smiled and walked away, and Marah didn't feel so alone anymore.

Shouts and laughter flew from house to house amidst much backslapping and joking. The appointed Sabbath had come, and the men were gathered at David's house. The priest read a portion of the law, followed by all of his relatives walking through the village inviting the villagers to participate in the week-long celebration.

Marah felt like she was in a boat on the Sea of Galilee being carried along by the sharkia winds that whipped the waves into whitecaps. She couldn't get out of the boat. She simply had to hang on. She could see the shore from afar, but she wasn't sure what awaited her once she got there.

That afternoon the men met again at David's house and celebrated with a great banquet. Then that evening the women gathered at Marah's house. She stared at the lavish gifts and abundant food—nothing like she'd ever seen in their home before. Obed had made sure the relatives and friends were impressed with his ability to provide properly for his daughter.

She giggled to herself thinking of the next men's gathering for the singing, verse by verse, of Rebekah's marriage to Isaac from the Holy Scripture. Of course, she wouldn't be present, but she knew the bridegroom sang last and couldn't imagine her shy David performing in front of all those men.

"What are you giggling about?" Leah put her hand on Marah's arm. "It's time to eat."

"Oh, nothing. I was just thinking about David singing tomorrow night." She drew her veil up around her face. "I'm certainly glad I don't have to do that here tonight."

The two girls laughed and found their places at the banquet table.

On the evening of the third day, Marah stood in the middle of a covey of women as they dressed her in the red garments for "the red night" celebration of the women. Naomi fussed with the sleeves. "If I'd had more time I could have made it more elaborate. I simply ran out of time."

Leah took the headdress that was a wedding gift from David. "Everything is beautiful, Mother. You did a wonderful job."

"Yes, I agree, Naomi. Thank you." Marah nodded.

Leah fitted the headdress over Marah's hair, which had been twisted into long, thin braids. The coins, strung together on a thick piece of tapestry of rich colors, rested on her forehead. She stepped back. "You know, Marah. You really are quite beautiful."

She was shocked. She'd never felt beautiful in her life. David had told her one time that she was pretty, but she didn't think much about it.

"Really? I look beautiful?"

Leah gave her a quick hug. "You are beautiful."

Marah peered down at her cumbersome costume. She felt like the red garments were wearing her rather than the other way around. Fumbling with the belt, she knotted it around her waist and adjusted the red robe, symbolizing her purity. What else would one expect from a thirteen-year-old?

If Marah thought the food was lavish on the first night of the celebration, it was doubly so on red night. The high point of the evening came when Johana, David's mother, performed the dance of the bridegroom's mother holding a parcel containing his wedding garments. The clang of the tinny music prevented Marah from thinking and seemed to become a visible force in the sweltering room. The faster and louder the music played, the faster Johana whirled and twirled, lifting the beautifully wrapped package above her head until she came to a stop in front of Marah. The music stopped, and the room fell silent. She gasped and looked at Leah, not knowing what she was expected to do. Leah lowered her head in a nod, so Marah did the same. As she did, a cheer went up among the women, and the dance ended.

Marah's heart pounded beneath her elaborate costume. She was ready for the ceremonies to be over with, but then that meant the wedding ceremony would have to take place, and she would have to be a wife. She looked at the multiple bracelets on her arms, and they felt like shackles. Her headdress of coins hung heavy on her forehead. She was a prisoner in her beautiful red wedding costume. If she hadn't known she could trust David, she would have run.

Marah sat in the middle of the room with her

hands folded in her lap, the bridal veil over her face, fearful that if she moved she would mess up her wedding garments. She watched through the folds of the veil for Naomi to give the signal to arise. After what seemed an eternity, she waved from the door and emitted what sounded almost like a squeal. "It's time! Come. It's time!"

The women grabbed their tambourines, ushered Marah out the door, and began singing the song of Miriam, dancing and rejoicing as the entourage made its way to David's house. Jostled about by the women, Marah prayed she wouldn't stumble on the dusty road with all the finery in which she was clothed. She felt as if she were walking in a dream and soon she would wake up and be lying next to Phoebe on their pallet at home. How did all of this happen so quickly? She felt numb—out of her own body. Looking to the left and then to the right, there was nowhere to run. And then she thought of David. She was being foolish. He was a dear boy, and she did love him. They would be happy. She breathed deeply and held up her chin. Everything would be as it should be.

Two women held on to her arms. One was Leah, but she couldn't see who the other was through the veil. She just kept her eyes cast down at her feet. The coins on the headdress jangled as she walked.

"We're almost there, Marah. Soon you will be wed!" Leah's voice resonated thick with excitement.

As they entered David's house, the priests broke out in song and marriage psalms. Then a quiet settled over the gathering. David rose and handed the marriage contract to the high priest, then kissed his hand. David glanced her way and sent her spirit soaring. Love brimmed in his eyes. Marah lost herself in the sea of emotion she saw in them.

The priest laboriously read through the marriage contract, then praised the families and handed it to

Obed for safekeeping. David kissed the priest's hands again and paid him his fee. Then the priest handed a wedding gift to David. Marah wondered what it might be. He handed the package to a bystander and walked toward her. Her heart thudded, and she found it difficult to catch her breath.

David stopped in front of Marah and awkwardly lifted the veil which insisted on falling over her face. She smiled at him, chuckled even, and he grinned. His eyelids fluttered closed as he bent to kiss her. She didn't know what to do with her hands, so she simply let them hang to her side. He took her gently by the shoulders as his lips brushed against hers. It was the lightest of embraces, but it sent her reeling. She'd never experienced a sensation like this before.

Being married might not be so bad after all.

Chapter 4

"If you only knew how generous God is and who this is who is saying to you, 'Give me a drink,' you would have asked of him, instead, and he would give you living water." The soft, deep tenor of the stranger's voice beckoned her.

"Do I know you?" Marah squinted to get a clearer view of the man. He didn't look familiar. *Living water? I know about the ritual cleansing in living water, but is that what he is talking about?*

She scanned the area around the well. He had no bucket with which to draw water. How was he going to give her water when he was empty-handed? "Sir, you don't even have a bucket to draw with, and this well is deep. So how are you going to get this 'living water'? Are you a better man than our ancestor Jacob, who dug this well?"

The stranger waved his hand toward the well. "Everyone who drinks this water will get thirsty again. Anyone who drinks from the water I give will never be thirsty again. The water I give is like an artesian well, springing up within, gushing fountains of endless life."

"Well, that would be wonderful. Then I would never have to come back and draw water again." The man glanced at her and raised an eyebrow. Her caustic remark died on her lips.

"Go call your husband, then come back."

Marah turned over and bumped into David's shoulder. Her heart banged against her chest, and she held her breath as she peered through the dark. She sat up and touched his back. The netherworld of sleep had spread a temporary veil of forgetfulness over her. Now she remembered—they were married. David rolled toward her and sighed. He folded his arms around her and pulled her to his chest. "It's not morning yet. Go back to sleep." His voice sounded thick and husky.

Marah hadn't known what to expect on their wedding night. David led her to the guest room in the back of his parents' house. He hadn't had time to finish their house, so they would stay there until the task was completed. David smiled at her in the glow of the lantern that he held as he closed the door. She ducked her head and stared stupidly at her feet. He put the lantern down on a wooden table which held a small earthen vase of flowers and a flask of wine. He cupped her face in his hands. His fingers were shaking. "You are so beautiful, Marah. I am proud to be your husband." The singing and music and the guffaws from the celebration in the main part of the house carried up to the guest room.

He began to loosen her wedding headdress. "Do you like it? I thought it was very beautiful—just like you."

"Yes, I love it, David." She reached up to help him remove it. Marah held the headdress in the flickering light as it glinted off the coppery coins. "I will treasure it always." She laid it on the table along with her veil.

David took her hands and turned them over, kissing her palms. "Come, let's have some wine." He poured two goblets full and motioned for her to sit beside him on a pallet lined with so many pillows she could not count them. She really did not want any more wine, but she took the goblet and sat with him.

He stared at her. "Marah, I—I want you to know that I…" He swirled the wine around in the goblet, then looked back at her. "I have loved you ever since we were children and have longed for the day when we would be wed. I've always known that God meant you for me." Caressing her arm, he continued. "You are so young and innocent. Uh, I know that you haven't…er, ahem…" He cleared his throat. "I'm aware that you've not had your niddah yet." He stood and began to pace and then, stopping in front of her, took another gulp of wine. He put the goblet back on the table and wiped the perspiration from his forehead. Taking Marah's hands, he knelt in front of her. "I will not require you to be a wife in the full sense until you do receive your niddah."

She nodded, having a vague sense of what he was talking about. He traced her cheeks with his fingertips, his gray eyes searching hers. He gently laid her down on the pallet, kissing her forehead, her cheeks, lightly—and then her mouth. His kisses became more insistent, and then the posture and change in David's body alarmed her. She drew back from him and sat up. "You're frightening me."

David leaned up on one elbow. "I apologize. This is not going to be easy for me, but I will honor my commitment to you. Come, lay with me. I want to hold you." Marah complied, and they fell asleep in each other's arms.

Marah stood in front of Johana clutching her stained clothing. "How do I tell David? What do I do first?"

She went to Johana after she woke up that morning with a smudge of blood hidden on her robe. She was embarrassed to show David. She had wished for her niddah to come and at the same time hoped it would not. But after only about three months, she had become a woman in the eyes of the community.

David had honored his commitment. He did not insist on consummating the marriage. Instead he educated Marah in the ways of a man and his wife. He guided her hands to explore his body, so she would understand what would take place when they would be able to truly become husband and wife. He laughed at her shock and gently teased her.

His mother, Johana, gave her wise counsel as well. Not only was Marah at last secure in the arms of her adoring husband, she reveled in the safety of a loving household as well.

"You won't have to say anything, child. Just go gather your bedding and eating utensils, along with a chair, and join the other women in their niddah." She hugged Marah tight. "You are now a woman." Then she stepped back and smiled. "David will be glad to welcome you back in seven days." Marah felt her face burning from embarrassment as she shuffled off to become a part of the community of women.

No husband could have been kinder, more patient or understanding than her David. Even as young as she was, she relished their evenings and nights together as they truly became husband and wife. David busied himself during the day finishing their little house, and she would help Johana with chores or go to play with Phoebe and the boys. They would have their evening meal with David's parents and then retire for the night to their little guest-room haven. Those were probably the happiest days of Marah's life—those early years with David.

alone

A few months after they married, Naomi showed up at the door of Marah's new house with Phoebe on her hip and the boys in tow. "Well, now that you have your own place, you can take care of these brats."

Asher tried to put on a brave face, but his dark eyes betrayed his anxiety. Phoebe reached for her. "Ma-a."

Marah took Phoebe from Naomi and kissed her cheek. "What happened?"

"Nothing happened. I've raised my children and don't want to do it a second time. I'm too old to be chasing a toddler around. Besides that, she cries for you all the time." Naomi fussed with Phoebe's tangled locks, brushing them out of the child's eyes.

"I do miss the children, but I don't know what David will say." Marah's heart melted as she took the little girl into her arms and gave her a kiss on a dirty cheek. If Marah were entirely honest, she had been concerned for the welfare of the children under the care of Naomi and Obed.

Naomi thrust a bundle toward her. "David will do whatever you ask him to do. Here are their things. These children don't belong with me. They belong with you." Naomi took hold of her arm and her voice softened. "For their sakes, Marah, please. You need to take them. Obed…well, Obed doesn't care anything about raising a passel of children."

Benjamin, now ten, stepped forward and took the bundle from Naomi. "We won't be much trouble, will we?" Asher and Noah shook their heads. "We'll help with the chores, won't we?" They switched from shaking their heads to vigorous nodding. Phoebe clung to Marah's neck and buried her head in her shoulder.

"Very well, but I'll need to confer with my husband."

Her husband. She had not become accustomed to the term. It felt foreign on her tongue and to her ears, but David was truly her husband. She loved him more each day that passed.

Naomi turned abruptly and left. Marah had seen her or Obed very seldomly—only at community gatherings. Honestly, Marah was so happy and content, she did not miss them, especially Jonathan.

When David came home from the village that day, he found a much fuller household than he left earlier. "Shalom! What have we here?"

Marah walked to him carrying Phoebe and waited for him to gather her in his arms as he always did upon coming home. He put his arms around both of them and kissed them on the cheeks, Marah first, then Phoebe. "I saw the boys outside. Looks like we have company." ~*33*

She set Phoebe down on the floor and reached for the wine. "I think you'd better have a seat. It's more than company."

David sat at the place where she'd set his cup. "This sounds serious."

"I suppose it is, but…but it…it doesn't have to be a burdensome thing—I don't think…." Her voice trailed off as she realized that all of a sudden they now had four children. She sat across from him and looked down at her hands. "Obed and Naomi don't want the children. Naomi said they would be better off with us." Marah looked up at David as tears sprang to her eyes, surprising her. "Obed's terribly mean sometimes, David."

"And all of those are his children." He shook his head.

"All except Benjamin, but he doesn't care about

any of them. And Naomi doesn't want to have to raise them." She grabbed David's hand. "He's not a nice man, David. And Jonathan…please, we have to take them in. I know how…"

David's eyes grew dark, and he frowned at her. "What about Jonathan?"

Marah shook her head and turned her face away from him, still holding his hand.

He leaned across the table toward her, his voice growing more intense. "What about Jonathan?"

"I don't trust him. He's vulgar."

His jaw moved back and forth as he clenched his teeth. "Did he ever do anything to you?"

"No, not really. I mean one time he pushed me up against the wall and threatened me, but nothing happened, except…"

David stood. "Except what?"

"He rubbed up against me, but Naomi and Obed came around the corner, and he stopped. That's all. He never did anything else. He did threaten me, but it was soon after that we were married."

David smacked his fist into his palm. "I ought to teach him a lesson or two." Phoebe jumped at the sudden noise and began to whimper.

Marah ran to Phoebe and picked her up. "No, David. Just let it be. He's simply a stupid young man." She swallowed, shook her head, and clung to Phoebe. She didn't dream that David wouldn't agree to take the children. Now she wondered. "Please, David, I beg of you. We must take these children as our own." Her chin began to quiver, and tears filled her eyes. What would happen to them if David refused? And she could not go against her husband's wishes.

He took her in his arms again, with Phoebe between them. He caressed Marah's cheek. "My love, why didn't you tell me before?"

"I was embarrassed." Marah wiped a tear away and

shifted Phoebe to the other hip. "Can we please take them in?"

"Won't it be too much for you? My concern is for you."

Marah laughed. "I've taken care of them as long as I can remember. And Benjamin is really very mature. He'll be a big help." She tweaked Phoebe's nose. "It's this one who is my shadow and takes most of the attention."

David sighed and sat down. "We have about six months left of my year to be with and get to know my bride before I have to go back to work. I can help with the boys. After that though, it will be your responsibility to take care of four children."

"Actually, it will soon be five."

David's eyes widened, and he laughed. "You're… you're with child already?"

She nodded. "I think so."

"That certainly didn't take us long, did it?"

Marah blushed and shook her head.

David shook his finger at her. "We will try this until six months after our own child is born. That will give us the total of a year. If it proves to be too much for you, we will have to send them back to Obed and Naomi."

"I can handle it. I know I can." She had never known David to be so stern. She made a vow that she would make it work. It had to work. Marah couldn't bear to send the children back into Obed and Naomi's troubled household.

Chapter 5

She was determined not to scream, but as the labor progressed, the cries squeezed unbidden from her throat. The midwife arrived and immediately began to massage Marah's legs and abdomen. Leah and Naomi bustled in and out, busying themselves preparing warm olive oil and strips of cloth for the baby. They took turns with the midwife massaging her body.

The hours wore on from daylight to early evening, then into the night, the pain escalating in intensity. Marah lapsed into unconsciousness between the unbearable tightening of the muscles of her abdomen. Johana sat beside her and bathed her forehead with a cool, wet cloth. Marah grabbed her mother-in-law's hand and clutched it until her fingers turned white.

Marah thought she was going to surely die. Finally the midwife nodded to the other women. "It's time to place her over the birthing stool." Leah and Naomi supported her underneath her arms, and Johana supported her back.

Marah insides twisted as if turned wrong side out. She could not control the urge to bear down, then the women took up the chant to push. She pushed with all her might, but the baby still did not come. Moments passed with nothing but searing pain.

The midwife looked at Johana and shook her head. She watched between Marah's legs as the next contraction contorted her body. "Naomi, put her back on the bed. Bring the lantern here and hold it up so I can see what's happening."

She held the lantern up and then, sighing, straightened. "She's tearing. Get me more towels."

"God have mercy." Johana turned and ran from the bedside.

The comments from the women swirled in Marah's mind. Their faces faded in and out of her vision. She didn't comprehend fully what was happening to her body except that the pain was unbearable, and she wanted the baby to come out.

"Push, Marah. You have to push through the pain if this baby is going to be born."

She pushed with all the strength she could muster and felt as if her very life was being expelled with this babe ramming its way into existence.

Fighting to stay conscious, she forced her eyes open through the fog and saw Johana standing beside the bed with David holding the child.

So weak she could hardly lift her head, Marah reached out for her baby. "L…let me see. What did we have?"

Beaming with pride, David smiled and laid their babe in her arms. "It's a boy, Marah. We have a son."

Our son.

They would call him Matthew, after David's father, and he came into the world on a cold morning when flurries of lacy snowflakes danced in the air, but scampered back into the sky or melted once they hit the ground. The painful contractions were a shock to Marah. She remembered her mother screaming in childbirth, but couldn't imagine that anything so painful could result in something as precious as this beautiful baby. Now she knew that the greatest pain produced the greatest joy.

The baby turned his head hungrily, searching to nurse. Marah touched his tiny fingers and toes and marveled at God's creation—how delicate and perfectly formed. He suckled hungrily.

Something inside of her billowed and cramped. "Oh! Something's happening, Johana!"

She patted Marah's shoulder. "Be calm, my dear. That's just the afterbirth. Your body needs to expel it. You'll have some mild contractions—"

"More contractions?" Marah shifted and started to panic. The baby whimpered as her jostling about caused him to lose hold.

"Very mild. Nothing like labor. It may already be over. I'll clean this up. You tend to feeding our little Matthew."

The cramping did indeed lessen, but she could feel the rhythmic pulsations as Matthew nursed. Johana efficiently cleaned the bed clothing and gave her a fresh robe to wear.

David's father poked his bald head in the door. "Is everything taken care of in here? Is my namesake well?"

"He's just fine, dear. You wait for David." Johana closed the door.

As much as Marah loved David, Phoebe, and the boys, she thought the love vibrating in her heart for their son might burst forth at any moment and spill onto everything and everyone about her. She didn't know one could love a helpless little baby so much. Her world was good. Her world was complete. She had a family, and she belonged. Nothing would ever change that.

Marah thought they would have another baby soon after. When she didn't, doubt constantly battled the hope. Had the damage done to her body during their son's birth had destroyed her ability to conceive again?

She was happy, though, with her husband and their son. Her world revolved around them. They would have to be enough.

David came in for the evening meal. They had been experiencing a drought, and the vineyards were dusty and dry. He was unusually quiet that evening.

Marah placed his plate on the table, and he muttered his thanks.

"You are worried, aren't you?" She put bowls of fruit, cheese, and fish out. Benjamin and the two younger boys joined David. "Here's bread." She touched his shoulder as she put a round loaf of hot bread at each end of the long table.

"If we don't get rain soon, I fear we'll lose this harvest of grapes. And the olives too." He looked up and spread out his arms. "God in heaven. Have mercy on us and send rain so that your people may live."

They didn't talk much that evening. David sat outside on the roof and watched the sun set. The older children's voices rang through the dusk as they played tag and hide-and-seek, bringing the day to a close. Matthew, now two and a half, sat at David's feet and played with a cup in the dirt. David reached down and tickled his toes. Matthew responded with gales of laughter and kicked his feet in the dust. David stood and scooped the chubby toddler up in his arms. "Let's go for a walk in the vineyard."

Marah fanned herself with a towel. "Oh, David, not tonight. It's so hot. And I need to get Matthew in bed."

"It's cooling off. Come, walk with me. I just want to be with you."

Thunder rumbled in the distance.

"But the children—"

"Listen, Marah. Thunder. Perhaps we'll get some rain tonight." He held out his hand. "The children will be fine. We can take Matthew with us."

"You go on, and I'll put Matthew down. I'll wait out here for you." But by the time he got back she was busy getting Phoebe and the boys settled in for the evening. She barely spoke to David before they all went to bed.

David held her in his arms until she fell asleep, but she was aware of his restlessness. He tossed and turned throughout the night. Lightning crackled from nearby, followed by the loudest clap of thunder she'd ever heard. She sat up in bed and covered her ears, which rang from the boom. Lord, please send rain.

Sometime during the early morning hours, shouts of "Fire!" jolted them awake.

Marah jerked up, her heart racing, and shook David's shoulder. He leapt from their bed.

Workers ran through the courtyard shouting, "Fire! Lightning strike! The vineyard is on fire!"

Clothed only in his tunic, David dashed from their house to his parents' house calling over his shoulder as he ran. "Buckets! Get buckets of water and form a line. Come! Hurry!"

As the word spread, men from the village thronged to their house. Marah saw Obed and Jonathan in the crowd. Even Benjamin, Noah, and Asher stood in line passing buckets of water from the well to the vineyard, terror mirrored in their eyes. Matthew slept, even through all the shouting. She stood on the roof of their house peering through the smoky haze until she could no longer see David and his father.

The night sky reflected the angry orange glow of the fire and echoed with tense calls of "Hurry!" or "Don't spill all the water." Smoke rolled and curled through the rows of vines. The whole community, men, women and children, fought the fire for hours. But as the eastern sky began to lighten, they walked away from the vineyard blazing out of control, their buckets hanging from limp hands, their shoulders sagging and heads bowed.

Marah ran down the stairs, frantic to find David. Johana met her at the bottom of the steps, tears streaming down her smoke-streaked face. "Marah, they're gone. Both of them are gone. Oh, God help us!" Her mother-in-law fell on her knees in the dust, hiding her face in her hands as if her anguish could be contained by her fingers.

"What do you mean?" Marah's hysterical voice rose above Johana's sobs. "Gone? No! How can they be gone? David!" She ran in the opposite direction of the returning friends and relatives, against hands trying to restrain her, tugging on her robe. Smoke stung her eyes and nose as she ran. Finally, someone grabbed her by the shoulders and held her back. She struggled and pulled away from the strong hands that gripped her as in a vise. Gasping for air, she tried to bury the creeping dread that threatened to overtake her.

Obed turned her around to face him and shook her by the shoulders. "Marah, you cannot go into the vineyard. It's burning out of control. David and his father went too far in and got caught. It's too late. There was nothing we could do."

The earth spun beneath her, and she fell to the ground, swallowed into a black hole of nothingness.

Months later, the next spring, Marah sat outside in the evening just as she and David had that dreadful night. Come, walk with me. His voice haunted her,

41

and guilt tore at the memory that she had refused to take a simple walk in the cool of the evening with her husband.

Marah and the children moved in with Johana. They tended to the children as best they could in spite of their raw emotions. Johana had lost her husband and her son. Marah, just her husband, but he was the only person who had ever truly loved her. And now here she was, a widow, only seventeen years old, with five children to care for. What was she to do?

Cinders from the fire filled the air with the scent of smoke for months. The house smelled of smoke. Their clothing did as well, especially in the evenings when the cooler air and humidity descended.

She called to her mother-in-law. "Would you mind if I take a walk?"

Johana poked her head out of the door, wiping her hands on a towel. "Of course not, dear. It would do you good. Take your time." She picked Matthew up and stepped out on the roof as Marah went down the stairs.

She walked toward the vineyard where the charred remains of gnarled roots lay scattered over the ground. She stopped in the middle of the vineyard where they had found David and his father's bodies, huddled together, trying to protect each other from the inferno.

A stratus of glowing pink colored the horizon and spread to create a shimmering canopy over the sky. She looked into the heavens and opened her arms. "I've come to walk with you, David. Why was I too busy to spend a small bit of time together? All you asked of me that evening was that I walk with you. I–I'm so sorry." A sob gripped her throat, and she couldn't continue. She whirled around and stared at the burned vines, ugly and twisted—broken, like her life. The branches would never be green again, bursting with the abundance of life. They would simply exist in the dust until they decayed and returned to the earth. Or perhaps be gathered and burned up to serve mankind. She crumpled to the ground and wept—wept for herself, her children, her husband. It was dark by the time Marah returned to the house.

Obed arranged another marriage for her with a much older man whose wife had borne him no children and had died barren. He provided well enough for Marah and her family, but he demanded strict obedience from them. She was his wife to serve him in whatever needs he had. He deemed it beneath him to converse on any level with a woman except when it came to meeting his needs. When he came to her to serve him physically, his touch repulsed her. He was not clean in his personal care, and she could not stand to lie next to him. Marah usually slept with the children. She was ashamed to admit it, but she was glad when he died in his sleep only a year after they married. Strange…she could hardly remember his face.

Early one hot, still summer morning Marah went out to gather eggs with Asher tagging along. "Look, son. A fox or something has gotten into our chickens again." Tufts of feathers lay scattered all over the ground, and the gate leaned crazily on its hinges.

Marah was still a young woman at only nineteen, but she had no desire to remarry. Simon, the overseer, a single man about five years older than she, seemed to know what he was doing in getting the vineyard replanted. A hard taskmaster, he worked the boys and the crew far into the night at times, but the fields were springing back to life.

When Marah remarried, Johana had come with them, but the older woman became ill shortly afterward and passed away. It seemed death's curse surrounded her family.

But then there were the children. Although she was grateful for them, she didn't know how she was going to care for them. She and Matthew had inherited the vineyard, but it would be three years before the grapes matured after the fire. Three years before they could earn any income. Benjamin, now almost sixteen, worked hard in the vineyard—too young to run it himself, and the overseer did not pay him fairly. Thirteen-year-old Noah went with Benjamin and worked when the overseer needed him. Asher and Phoebe, now eleven and ten, helped with the chickens and small garden plot that they managed to maintain. Matthew, five, still seemed like a baby, but he tried so to be grown and help out the family. He had David's heart of tenderness and compassion. His gray eyes, surrounded by thick black eyelashes, looked just like his father's and tugged at Marah's heart every time he looked at her.

Simon approached and looked into the chicken pen with an axe in his hand. "I'll set a trap and catch that fox."

"Thank you, Simon. That would be very helpful."

Marah jiggled the gate and attempted to set it aright.

"You don't need to worry about that either. I'll take care of it."

She looked at the overseer of the vineyards whom she had not paid that much attention to except as a hired hand and saw him in a new light. "I would be most grateful, sir."

Of only medium height, he was muscular and strong. He wore his dark, straight hair long, pulled back and tied with a leather band most of the time. A smile hardly ever brightened his countenance. Instead a serious and somber expression seemed to be most at home on the face of dark, swarthy, leathery skin. But today he grinned and nodded his head. "A simple task. Glad to do it."

Little did she know one of the worst chapters of her life was about to begin.

Chapter 6

The slap across her face sent Marah stumbling back into the table, dishes and food crashing to the floor. Her husband of only six months stood over her shaking the headdress that David had given her as a wedding gift. The jangle of the coins that she had always loved before now sounded a warning in her ears. Simon's face reddened and his eyes bulged as he threw the headdress into the flames in the fireplace. "Didn't I forbid you to wear this ever again? I want nothing to remind you of your first 'boy husband.'" He whirled around and swept the rest of the dishes from the table.

She stood on wobbly legs she feared would not hold her up. Benjamin burst through the door and stepped between her and Simon. He stuck out his sixteen-year-old chest and bravely challenged the drunken man. "You'll not hit my sister again."

Simon grabbed his arm and slung him aside as easily as he had swept the dishes from the table. "I'll not take disrespect from you either."

Benjamin bounced off the side of the fireplace and slid to the floor, stunned. Flashes of her brother as a little boy exploded in her memory, and, as she had always done, she tried to protect him. Marah lunged for Simon and caught the brunt of his kick in her stomach. Gasping for breath, she fell facedown on the floor. He swung his leg at her again, but she caught it with her hands. Simon stumbled and fell on top of her. A roar that sounded more like an animal than a human erupted from his throat. He scrambled to his feet and, taking hold of Marah's sleeve, threw her against the wall. Bright yellow spots danced in front of her eyes. The room spun as he picked her up and carried her to their bed.

He threw her down and jabbed his finger in front of her face, punctuating each word as he spoke. "Don't—you—ever—defy—me—again." His low and menacing tone was worse than if he'd been yelling at the top of his voice. Demons danced in the glint of his eyes as he hovered above her. She attempted to rise and get to Matthew, who was wailing in the middle of the room. Simon's fingers locked around her shoulder and held her on the bed.

"M…Matthew. Let me ta…take care of Matthew."

"Matthew? I'll take care of Matthew." He stalked to the child, picked him up by his arm and threw him toward Benjamin, who was struggling to his feet. "Take this screaming brat outside and don't come back in until I give you permission."

Benjamin took Matthew and stared at Simon, then at Marah, a worried expression wrinkling his forehead. A trickle of blood oozed down his temple. She nodded and waved her hand toward the door. "Go on. I'll be fine."

He sheltered Matthew in his arms and scurried out the door, glancing back over his shoulder at her. Volumes spoke through his eyes—he didn't want to leave her inside with Simon, but fortunately he must have realized he needed to protect the children.

Simon pinned her on the bed with his knee and tore at her robe, ripping the cloth. Her heart shredded like the tearing of the fabric. She lay naked and ashamed before him as he ravaged and tore her body. She fought against him until he beat her about the head into near unconsciousness. Fearful of further inciting his rage, she ceased her struggle and kept silent, biting the inside of her cheek to keep from crying out.

When he finished, he sat in a chair next to the bed refusing to allow her to dress or cover herself. He simply stared at her bare, quivering body and derided her. He mocked her tears and ran his fingers up and down her body, laughing at the involuntary responses he evoked. Then he took her again. This time after he was through, he allowed her to dress. As he walked away, he reached down and touched her swollen cheek.

Rage and fear consumed her, but she would not allow him the pleasure of seeing that he had defeated her. Marah pulled her robe around her and stood to face him, clenched her jaw, and looked directly in his eyes.

"You're a feisty little thing, aren't you? Just remember what awaits you if you ever disobey me again." He turned to leave the room. "Now, go fix dinner and get ready for evening prayer."

Prayer. How can you pray to our God after what you did to me today?

Marah watched her husband walk down the stairs and past the children huddled in the front of the house. Smoke drifted out the window from the smoldering fire. Clutching her robe, she knelt on the hearth and, with a small piece of pottery, scooped the coins from the embers. The band from which the coins had hung was gone, but the coins remained. She gathered them, burning her fingers as she did, but she didn't care. She placed them in a cup and hid it beneath a stack of blankets, vowing to make a new headdress when she could. Simon would not obliterate David's memory from her no matter how hard he tried.

Benjamin ran up the stairs. Marah spun away from him and pulled her veil over her face to hide the bruises and swelling. He gently turned her around to face him. He took hold of the edge of the veil and slowly pulled it aside. His look of horror spoke more than any words he could have said. She sat down on a wooden bench, her knees wobbling beneath her. "Don't fret, Benjamin. I'll recover."

Her kind and gentle little brother dipped a cloth into the water basin on the table beside the bench and, with trembling fingers, attempted to wipe the blood from her cheek. "I vow to you—he will never do this to you again. I will kill him first."

"Benjamin! Do not make such a vow. I just need not to anger him. He is a good, hard worker. He simply loses his head when he's had too much wine."

Benjamin wrung out the cloth, and his eyebrows knitted together. "Mark my words, I will not allow him to ever do this to you again." He handed her the cloth and walked out the door where Asher, Noah, Phoebe, and Matthew stood, their eyes wide.

~49

"The bread is too brown on the outside and doughy on the inside." Simon shoved the loaf down the table at her. "Will you never learn to get it right, wife?"

The months and then years had crept by, Marah's emotions and perceptions dulled by being always on the precipice of triggering Simon's anger. It seemed no matter how hard she tried, she could not please him. Her cooking did not please him; she didn't keep the house clean enough; she didn't obey his wishes quickly enough. And then there were the children. They were always in his way or too loud or took too much of her time. She considered it an answer to prayer that she never conceived. Much as she may want another child, this was not a home to bring one into.

Benjamin continued to labor long hours in the vineyard alongside Simon. Thankfully, the vineyards had recovered from the fire and produced a good income for them. Benjamin never complained, but his eyes grew cold and hard whenever Simon was around or his name was mentioned in conversation. He made a wide swath around the man.

Now Benjamin put his bowl of soup down and stared straight ahead. "She has a name."

"What did you say?" Simon glowered at Benjamin from beneath his heavy eyebrows.

Benjamin continued to stare ahead. "I said, 'She has a name.'"

Simon stood, turning his chair over as he rose. He raised his hand to slap Benjamin, but the younger man was too quick for him. Benjamin leapt to his feet and grabbed Simon's wrists, pinning him against the wall. Through clenched teeth Benjamin snarled. "You have tormented us for the last time."

Simon twisted and kicked Benjamin in the groin. The blow sent him to the floor, gasping, coughing, and retching. Simon bent over him, shaking his fist in Benjamin's face. "You sniveling fool. What makes you think you can successfully oppose me? This is my house. You will act according to my rules or you will find another place to live." He straightened up and tucked his robe back into his sash, kicking Benjamin aside. "Get out of my sight. You'll sleep in the stable tonight."

Asher and Noah kept their heads down, staring at their bowls as if the soupy contents held some kind of hypnotic power. Marah started after Benjamin.

"Sit down!" Simon sat back down at the head of the table and pointed to a chair in the corner of the room beside the oven. "You're not going anywhere."

She knew to oppose this man only served to escalate his rage, so she did as he bade her to do.

After he went to sleep and Marah got the children bedded down, she crept downstairs to the stable with a blanket for Benjamin. The night air was cold. Her breath formed smoke as she called out to him.

No answer.

Her heart flipped. "Benjamin. Are you here?" She scurried from stall to stall searching for him, but he was nowhere to be found. She left the blanket for him and went back upstairs. He probably went into the village to seek out his friends. She spent a sleepless night, her ears alert for any sound from the barn.

The next morning Benjamin came to breakfast and barely spoke to anyone except Matthew. He tweaked the boy on the cheek and looked at Marah with a barely discernible nod. Simon ignored him, and Benjamin returned the favor. After the meal of awkward silence, they left for the vineyards.

At dusk Benjamin came home alone. He avoided Marah's eyes and busied himself washing up.

"Where's Simon?"

"He didn't show up when it was time to quit. I dismissed the laborers and came on home."

Marah and the children ate supper—still no Simon. Benjamin went outside into the gathering darkness and walked toward the vineyard. He stopped with his fists on his hips and gazed toward the horizon. He paced back and forth.

Marah approached him and touched him on the shoulder. He turned and hung his head.

"Look at me."

Benjamin met her request with the saddest eyes she'd ever seen.

"Do you really not know where Simon is?"

He shook his head. "He simply didn't show up. He

went to work in the far north field and—"

"Benjamin." She paused. "Are you telling me the truth?"

He nodded. His mouth flattened into a grim line, and he turned away from her.

They never found out what happened to Simon. They found no body. Either he simply decided to leave, or he was involved in some terrible accident and animals carried his body off or…Marah couldn't bear to think about it, but she wondered. She always wondered.

Benjamin was never the bright, playful young man he had been after that. Marah was ashamed to say she was glad Simon disappeared from their lives. Deep down, she believed eventually he would have killed her. And then what would have become of the children?

For months after the night he didn't come home, she startled at every shadow that fell across the entrance to their house. Every rustling in the wind, every voice from the village set her heart banging against her chest. But with each passing month she began to accept the fact that Simon would never return to torment them again. She shoved the probable truth of what happened to him into the recesses of her mind. She could not bring herself to speak of what was unspeakable. It was never mentioned.

Every now and then Marah would catch Benjamin staring into the vineyard at night as if he were expecting someone. On occasion he would awaken from a deep sleep, sweating, shaking, and shouting Simon's name. However, as the years passed, those occasions became more rare and finally stopped.

One evening six years later Benjamin came in a

bit later than usual, and his eyes had the sparkle in them reminiscent of the boy Marah had known. He washed up and sat down for the evening meal.

He tousled eleven-year-old Matthew's hair. "Quit it, Ben! I'm too old for that."

Marah had refashioned another headdress from the coins she retrieved from the fire. The jangle of the coins reminded her of David. Benjamin had taken on the full responsibility of the vineyard and helped with his siblings. He had a good sense of business, and the vineyards did well. Asher and Noah, now nineteen and seventeen, young robust men, worked alongside him.

"You're in a good mood tonight." She touched Benjamin's shoulder as she lit the candles.

He grinned and prepared for evening prayers. After he finished eating he shoved back from the table. Asher and Noah started out the door to take care of the animals. "Wait a moment, my distinguished brothers."

"Distinguished? Something's amiss." Asher slapped Noah on the shoulder.

"I have some good news to share, and I want everybody to hear it at once." The corners of Benjamin's mouth lifted slightly. "Dinah's father and I had a talk earlier today."

Butterflies tickled Marah's stomach, and her heart leapt. "Go on." It was past time for him to be married, but now that it was here, her protective nurturing toward him pulled in the opposite direction. *My Benjamin? What will I do without him?*

Benjamin ducked his head and cleared his throat. "He asked me what had taken me so long." Looking up, his grin turned into a wide smile revealing the broken tooth he had received as a child when he got too close to a stubborn donkey's kick. He wouldn't look normal without it. It didn't detract from his handsome face.

"Oh, Benjamin, I am so delighted." Marah held out her arms to embrace the one person left in the world who had known her from her childhood. She blinked, fighting the tears that filled her eyes and the gulp in her throat.

Benjamin drew back and brushed the tears with the tip of his rough finger. "Tears?"

"Only of joy, my dear brother."

"I will still be here. You will simply have another one to add to our household."

"You must build your own house. Dinah doesn't need to take on the responsibility of an already established family." Benjamin, in practice, was the head of their household, but he needed to have his own family. He must have his own children, not simply care for hers.

Benjamin put his arm around her shoulders, and he ushered her out onto the roof. "Yes, I will build us a house, but it will be right over there." He pointed to a clearing overlooking the vineyard. "I've always planned for that plot to be where I would build. There's already a path where the children will run back and forth—yours and mine."

The house rang that evening with chatter concerning the upcoming wedding.

The rest of the children grew up and did the same. Asher and Noah. Phoebe married her Mark, and they lived in the village.

Marah had been surrounded by children from the time she was a child herself. Now she was alone, except for Matthew.

Chapter 7

Marah was outside feeding the chickens when Benjamin approached her that day. The little chicks always reminded her of Phoebe when she was a child, and how she loved to make pets out of them.

"Marah, Ezra, the priest, came to me as head of our household this morning, to ask permission to... make you his wife."

She couldn't believe what she was hearing. She stared blankly at him. Ezra was not retired yet from the priesthood, which meant he was under fifty, but he had to be close. And she was still a young woman, just twenty-five, although she had to admit she felt much older.

A kind man with a long, gray beard and sparkling blue eyes, Ezra's wife had passed away the year before. Marah didn't know quite what to say. "Ben, why would Ezra be interested in marrying me?"

"Why wouldn't he be? You're a good woman—and a very beautiful one."

She ducked her head. Her brother's compliment felt strange to her, like an ill-fitting garment. "But I'm so much younger, and I've had three husbands already, and—"

"Why wouldn't he desire and value a young wife to be a companion to him in his increasing years? And it is a respected position. You would be well taken care of."

"Give me some time to think about it. This has

caught me off-guard."

"Don't take too long. Ezra is eager to move ahead with the marriage." Benjamin smiled. "He's been watching you."

She turned and went into the house. A jumble of thoughts spun in her head. *I don't want to get married again—and yet I do. No, what I want is someone to feel safe with, someone to make me feel secure. Benjamin and the other children care. They love me. Somehow, however, it doesn't seem to be enough.* She busied herself kneading the sticky dough she'd left to rise on the table earlier. *Why wasn't it enough? Benjamin did all he could to support them.* She added more flour. *His wife, Dinah, was thoughtful and caring. Asher and Noah and their families checked on her regularly, and Phoebe came by nearly every day.*

But I still feel alone. *The mornings are lonely as I rise to ready the day. The late evenings are lonely when no husband comes home to me. The nights are lonely as I sleep by myself on my bed. Of course, I still have Matthew at home.* She looked out the window at her son, on the verge of manhood, splitting wood. *But not for long. He will leave home eventually. And I will probably live with him and his betrothed, Mary. Let's say that's eight or ten years in the future. I will still only be in my mid-thirties.* She turned the bread over and dug the base of her palm into it.

Matthew came through the door with an armload of wood. He dumped it in the basket beside the oven. Sweat beaded on her forehead as she pummeled the bread.

"Mother, are you angry at the bread dough?" He grinned as he brushed bits of bark off his sleeves.

Marah laughed and covered the dough with a cloth. She loved Matthew's sense of humor. "I suppose I was thinking about something else." Wiping her hands on her apron, she walked over to her son and gathered him in her arms. "You are getting almost too big to hug—almost."

He kissed her on the forehead. "I'll never get too big for hugs from you, Mother." He touched one of the coins on her headdress. "You wear this nearly every day."

She covered his hand with hers. "Your father's wedding gift. It is precious to me."

Matthew smiled and brought her hand to his lips. "I wish I could remember him. He must have been a good man." Matthew had David's sweet disposition—and David's penchant for the romantic. He was always ready to take a walk instead of splitting wood or linger to talk after dinner instead of doing the chores. She prayed that sensitivity wouldn't change as he matured.

"Sit down, son. I want to ask you something." Marah poured him a cup of wine and sat beside him. "What would you think about... How would you feel if..." She couldn't say the words "marry" or "marriage."

His eyes darkened. "What is it, Mother? Is there something wrong?"

She patted his hand, his fingers, long and slender, so like her David's. "No, no. Nothing at all is wrong." She turned to face him. "Perhaps something very right. Benjamin has brought me an offer of marriage from Ezra, the priest. I...I honestly don't know how to feel about it." Tears filled her eyes, and she turned away from her son. "What do you think?"

"What do I think? What do you think? Do you want to get married again? Would he be a suitable match? Does that sound favorable to you?"

Marah shook her head. "I don't know. I've not had any desire to remarry, but I do get lonely. And you will soon marry and have your own family."

"You will always have a place in my home. You

know that, Mother."

"I know." She stood and turned to look at her young son who had assumed the too-early responsibility of taking care of his mother nearly all of his life. Of course, Benjamin took the official role as head of the household, but Matthew bore the day-to-day responsibilities. If she remarried, he could be relieved of some of that burden. She had reached a conclusion. "I think I shall tell Benjamin to proceed with the arrangements."

The delighted expression on Matthew's face told her she'd made the right decision. She motioned toward the door. "Would you please go tell Benjamin that my answer is yes?"

Matthew drew her into a tight embrace. "This is wonderful, Mother. Perhaps now we can be a proper family." He let go and patted her shoulder. "Benjamin is right outside. I saw him as I came in."

Marah leaned against the table and fingered the cloth over the dough.

Matthew laughed and called over his shoulder as he ran out the door. "By the way, Mother, I think you've kneaded that dough enough."

She startled, lifted her hand, and shooed him on.

"Ezra, why do we Samaritans worship at Mount Gerizim, but the Jews say Jerusalem is the holy place? Do we not worship the same God?"

Ezra, unlike many men in their culture, believed that women could learn. Many evenings after the meal, they sat around the fireplace and he willingly answered Marah's questions. His face came alive, and he looked years younger when he talked about Jehovah God. At first she was cautious in asking questions about their faith, not certain of his opinion about speaking to a woman concerning those things that were sacred. Then little by little she sensed his eagerness to expound, and she became more daring.

His eyebrows quirked, and he touched Marah on the shoulder. "How is it that you do not know these things, my dear?"

"Nobody ever taught me. I was so young when I married, and I had the responsibility of all those children. Of course, I know about Jehovah God and understand somewhat, but I want to know more. Do you mind answering my questions?" She looked down at her hands, embarrassed at her ignorance. Her hands no longer looked like the hands of a young woman, but were red and chafed—beginning to take on the wrinkly texture of an old woman's hands, with brown spots sprinkled here and there. She clasped them in her lap.

Ezra touched her folded hands. "Certainly not, my dear one. This is our privilege as husband and wife."

Ezra treated them kindly and provided well for them. She had to admit she enjoyed the status that came from being the wife of a priest, and he was surprisingly attentive to her. Their home was peaceful. She settled her heart to be content with this good man. And he taught her much about the God whom they served. To her, God was some high entity, impersonal and far removed from them. To Ezra, God was real and present. Ezra tried to convince her that their God cared for them and provided what they needed. That he was a merciful God.

But when he came home from the Temple, after having slaughtered innocent animals all day to atone for the sins of the people, she was repulsed. However, she was curious too.

He began and explained how their people became separated during the Babylonian exile and how they believed that they were the true keepers of the law.

But the teaching that quickened their heart and spirit was when he talked about a Messiah who would come and make all things new and right.

"When will this one appear?"

"In Jehovah's time."

"Will it be in our lifetime? Where will he come—to Mount Gerizim or to Jerusalem? Will he descend from the sky, or will he ride in as a mighty king?" She paused to try to picture it. "I think as a king—on a white horse and angels all around him."

Ezra slapped his knee and chuckled. "So many questions that I cannot answer. I do not know how or exactly when or where. Although I do know that our God is faithful and that the Messiah will come when it is time."

"Oh, Ezra, I do want so to meet this Messiah."

Ezra rose, shaking his head and smiling. He put his arm around her shoulders as she rose with him. "Time for bed. I am weary of questions, and the morning will come early."

They retired, but she could not stop thinking about this Messiah. Her dreams were filled with a mighty warrior king coming to rescue her and carry her away to a paradise forever with him.

"Marah, my dear, stop pacing. Your worry and concern will not bring Matthew home any sooner." Ezra's deep voice was filled with disquiet as well.

"But what if he's hurt and needs help? What if someone has killed him and taken his money? What if he fell ill, and we know nothing about it?"

"Is the fretting and worry going to help? Trust in God. He will keep Matthew safe." Ezra's reassurance did not serve to calm Marah this time.

Matthew had matured into a fine business

man. He persuaded Benjamin to let him develop a signature wine from their vineyard and began selling it to a merchant in Jericho, which meant he had to travel once a month into Judea. It was dangerous to travel through Judea as a Samaritan, but necessary for business. As long as one simply did what they needed to do and didn't cross or confront a Jew, the trips could pass without incident.

But had something gone wrong this time? Frantic with worry, her mind raced with horrible possibilities.

He was to return midmorning of the fourth day of his trip, but midmorning came and went; midafternoon came and went; then darkness fell. Marah spent one of the most sleepless nights of her life.

The next day shortly after the noon hour she heard him. "Mother! I'm home." He called out before even dismounting from Lazy, his donkey he'd named for the animal's disposition. He might have been lazy, but he was dependable. She ran down the outside stairs to see Matthew tying him to a tree and hoisting the bulging saddlebags to his shoulder.

"Matthew! Where…where have you…" Marah ran into his arms, tears of anxiety and laughter mingling with a choked sob. "I was afraid something had happened to you."

"Something did, but I'm fine. Come, let us go inside, and I'll tell you about it." They went into the house, and he dumped the saddlebags on the table. Hundreds of coins tumbled out of them. "The Lord our God has blessed us with abundant sales."

"Why—why so much more this time?"

He laughed and threw up his hands. "I'm not sure, but it may have something to do with what happened on my way to Jericho." He removed his robe and sat down. "Could I have some of our wonderful wine?" He grinned as Marah poured him a goblet of the deep purple liquid. He drank deeply. "Now that's a good vintage."

Ezra sat down beside him, and she poured another goblet full.

"You, too, Mother. I have a tale to tell. You know the large curve in the road on the way up to Jerusalem from Jericho? The one where if you meet someone coming the opposite direction, one of you will have to dismount and wait for the other to pass—where the rocks overhang?"

Ezra nodded. "I know it well. A dangerous curve not only to maneuver, but where marauders lie in wait."

Marah's knees weakened, and she sat down. "Why did you go to Jerusalem? Those were not your plans, were they? If I'd known that—"

"Yes, my contact in Jericho told me of another merchant north of Jerusalem who he thought might be interested in our wine. So I decided to investigate that possibility. However, as I approached the curve from above, a priest passed by me, muttering to himself and shaking his head." Matthew scoffed. "Of course, he avoided me, but I caught a word here and there: shame, probably dead, thieves. His words caused me to slow my pace. I tried to see what he was mumbling about, but the sharp curve prevented me from seeing what was ahead. I remounted and started up the hill. As I rounded the bend in the road I saw what had upset the priest. A man lay on the side of the road, naked and bloody. A Levite was bending over him, but as he saw me approaching he gathered his robe around him and hurried on."

Matthew took a deep breath. "Mother, I didn't know whether he was Jewish or Samaritan, dead or alive, but I couldn't just leave him there. I got off Lazy and led him to the spot where the man lay and found that he was alive—barely. He half-opened his eyes through swollen and bruised eyelids—they pleaded wordlessly with me to help him. I don't know how long he had been there." Matthew shook his head and wrinkled his nose. "He smelled terrible. He had no clothes, no pack or belongings of any kind. The thieves had taken everything. I wrapped my cloak around him, put him on old Lazy, and took him to the inn where I was planning to stay. I gave the innkeeper two silver coins and asked him to look after him. I promised that if his care exceeds the two coins, I'll pay him upon my return."

Matthew leaned back and chuckled. "The innkeeper eyed me suspiciously. I know at first he must have suspected that I was the one who had taken advantage of the poor fellow. But after I offered him the money, he was willing to help. The man was only half-conscious when I left, so I still don't know anything about him, except he did manage to tell me that his name was Zacchaeus."

~63

Marah had never been so proud of her son in her life. That he would risk his life to care for a wounded man spoke volumes for his character. And for the first time, she perceived perhaps God might really care about her and her family.

He continued. "Then the contact in Jerusalem proved to be a good one. He ordered an abundance of wine with a superfluous down payment." He quirked his eyebrows and looked at her. "God's blessings perhaps?"

Ezra folded his hands and nodded. "That is most assuredly what it is. God blesses abundantly when we give of ourselves to others."

Ezra fell ill the next winter and passed quickly and peacefully. Marah was filled with grief at the loss of this benevolent man. He had been good to them, and she had learned to love him. Matthew and Mary wed in the spring. And although they built an addition on the back of Marah's home and basically lived in her house, she once again felt alone.

She determined never to marry again. She thought often of David, the one of her four husbands she had truly been in love with. She longed for that kind of marriage once more, but that would never happen. Not for her. Not again. Marah would content herself with being surrounded by her children and grandchildren.

Chapter 8

The stranger shielded his eyes from the sun with his hand as he looked up at Marah. An awkward silence hung in the pulsating heat of the midday. He waited.

"I have no husband."

"That's honestly put." He stood, facing her. "You've had five husbands...and the man you're living with now isn't even your husband. You spoke the truth."

Gradually, almost imperceptibly, bitterness had become her dominant emotion. Her comments became cynical and cutting. She didn't laugh often. She didn't play as much with her grandchildren. If God cares about us and we are his people, as Ezra tried to convince me, why have I been condemned to widowhood four times over before I am thirty-five years old? She'd always tried to do the right thing—be a good wife and mother, take care of those entrusted to her. And what had it brought her? Matthew and Mary took over the house, but even though the home was full and busy, in the midst of all the activity, she felt isolated and alone. Benjamin and Matthew tried to encourage her, but she sank deeper into her own whirlpool of self-pity.

Bitter. That was what her parents had called her from birth. Perhaps it was what she was destined to be. Why fight it?

Marah finished removing the last loaf of bread from the outside oven and, upon hearing voices, pulled her veil over her face. But not before she caught a glimpse of the dashing merchant who walked into the courtyard with Matthew. Eyes the color of copper, set in an angular face of flawless olive skin that any woman would envy, lingered a bit too long as he looked her way. His beard was thick but neatly trimmed—his appearance impeccable. Unlike most men who ignored the presence of a woman, he nodded his head slightly to acknowledge Marah's presence. A deep dimple creased his countenance.

She piled the loaves of warm bread in a basket and scurried up the stairs. The aroma from the bread wrapped itself around her as she ascended to the living quarters. She smiled to herself as she set the basket on the table. Why is my heart beating so fast? Surely not because of one glance from a random merchant. I must have run up the stairs too fast. I'm not as young as I used to be.

She unfastened her veil and peered out the window past the entrance in the courtyard wall. The gutteral growls of dusty camels amidst the jangle of metal finery on their harnesses signaled the large animals' impatience. A dozen or so servants held the caravan in check. Well, I hope Matthew strikes a bargain with this man. It appears he can purchase whatever he desires—and pay for it on time.

Matthew bid the merchant farewell and came upstairs. He pinched a piece of crust off the end of one of the loaves in the basket as he had done since he was a little boy. He loved the crunchy crust.

"Matthew! Stop it. You know how I dislike you to

do that." Marah shooed him away with her hand. "Sit down, and I'll get you some." She set a plate of cheese before him. "The gentleman you were talking to had quite an impressive caravan."

"Yes, he did." Her son cut a hunk of cheese from the block.

She set a loaf of bread beside the cheese—the loaf from which he'd already torn the end. Matthew bit off a bigger piece. "He's a government official from Sychar. He'd heard about our wine." Matthew grinned and motioned toward the wine holder. "Speaking of, could I have a goblet of the finest wine in the country?" He took another bite of bread as she handed him a goblet and poured the purple liquid. Marah paused and watched the beverage slosh into the cup, almost as if it were alive, as it danced around the lip.

"To go along with the finest tasting bread in the country." He lifted his goblet in a mock toast. "What are you staring at?"

"Oh, nothing out of the ordinary. I've just always considered wine beautiful, especially when it is being poured." She shook her head. "Silly, I know."

Matthew covered her hand, still holding the pitcher, with his. "I don't think it's silly. I think it shows…well, shows strength…or perhaps courage in how you find beauty in little things."

"My mother said that to me one time—that it takes strength to see beauty in the ordinary. Weak people complain, but strong people see beauty where there appears to be none." Marah busied herself putting the bread on the mantle. "What's his name?"

"Who?"

"The merchant."

"His name is Nabal—and he has a wife."

His mother kept her back to him. "Oh, I care not about that. I was just curious. I don't believe I've ever seen him before."

Matthew arose from the table. "I saw him looking at you. You are still a fine-looking woman, Mother, and perhaps you might want to remarry someday, but this one is not for you. This one can have any woman he wants…and he wants often. Like I said, he already has one wife."

"And I already said, 'I care not.' Now, I have work to do. And you need to get home to your little family. Take some of the bread and give Mary my love."

Nabal returned in a few weeks, wooed Marah, and won her over with his charm and flamboyant manner…and his wealth and fortune. She held him at arm's length at first, trying to convince herself she could not possibly consider marrying again. But in spite of her back-and-forth internal logical arguments, her heart was drawn to him.

Matthew had misgivings about the marriage from the beginning. "Are you sure you want to do this? Move away from your family, your children and grandchildren? We want and need you here."

She looked into the dark eyes of her only son whom she loved more than life itself. He looked more and more like his father as he matured into a man. She was so proud of him. "I know you love me and want me to stay. But I still have desires as a woman—to feel loved and to love in return. To be secure within my husband's care. I only had all of that with your father—and Ezra, to some degree. Perhaps I can find it again."

So Marah left her home and family to move to Sychar with her fifth husband. His first wife was older and had born him no children. Nabal deduced that since Marah was younger, she would be more than willing to have lots of babies. With all the children around their compound it was a natural assumption they were her offspring. She never told him any different. She too hoped that perhaps God would be gracious enough to grant her another child.

But it was not to be. Her lingering fear through the years that her body had been so damaged in Matthew's birth that she would not be able to bear more children became a cruel reality. She supposed it should have been obvious to her with all the men she had known, but she had continued to hope. With Nabal, she accepted the truth of it.

Nabal's house was large, with many rooms and a multitude of servants. He came to her quarters often at night. He was pleasant enough at first and wooed her with his charms. He was an experienced and skillful lover. His caresses sent her heart aflutter, and she willingly acquiesced to his sexual demands. Marah tried so hard to please him, but as the months passed and no child was conceived, he came to her chamber less and less and became cruel and insistent when he did. The awful realization that it was not she he cared for at all finally dawned upon her. It was his desire to have children that motivated him to marry her.

Finally after two years of no pregnancy, he sent a servant to bring her to his quarters. "Marah, you are a good woman, but evidently I have chosen two barren women, and I would like to have an heir." He steepled his fingers as he sat in his chair and gazed at her with those magnificent eyes. "I have decided to divorce you. I am willing to send you back to your home with an escort." He stood. His voice softened. "I'm sorry, Marah. You need to go back to your family."

She knew that was what she should do, but she was too embarrassed. She ran to her quarters, her lavish quarters, dismissed her servant and lay across her bed with the tapestry pillows and coverings and wept.

-69

alone

The silky hangings around her barren bed floated in the gentle afternoon breeze. What am I to do? Where am I to go?

She felt useless, helpless, and once again completely alone. Matthew had warned her about Nabal. And his warnings proved to be correct. She couldn't bear going home to her children with another failed marriage trailing behind her. She felt certain they would welcome her and forgive her, but she was too disgraced. She would not burden them with her failures.

Marah waited for Nabal to retire for the night. When all was quiet she packed a few things, some fruit and bread, laid her coin headdress on top, and slipped out under cover of darkness. She made her way to the marketplace and found an alcove, pulled her robe around her shoulders and spent a fitful night, tensing at every sound. What was I thinking? This is not a safe place to be by myself.

A small urchin approached Marah early one morning after she had been on the streets a week or so, as she folded her thin blanket and stuffed it into her bag. The filthy little girl stared at her with eyes as black as coal. Her matted hair fell over her forehead. Marah knelt down and brushed her hair out of her eyes.

The child stuck her index finger in her mouth and whispered. "I'm hungry." She couldn't have been any more than three or four years old. She held out a grimy hand. "Bread?"

Marah encircled her arms around the child. "Oh, sweet thing, I don't have any bread." She stood and looked into the street for her mother or someone who might have been with her. "What's your name?"

The child simply stared at her.

"Don't you know your name? How old are you?"

She held up four fingers.

"Where's your mother, dear one?"

She stared at Marah. "Mommy sick."

"Where is she?"

The child pointed across the street. Marah saw someone huddled in the shadowed archway of a building. She took the child's grubby hand and followed her to the emaciated form lying on the stones. Marah leaned over and touched the woman's shoulder. "Hello?" No response. "Hello?"

The woman stirred and looked up at them. "Tabitha?" She reached for the child and pulled her down to her level and spoke words hardly discernible. "Water. I need some water." She turned milky eyes toward Marah. "Do you have water?"

"No, but I'll find some." Marah looked down the street where the village merchants were just setting up their booths. She reached in her bag and found her cup. She picked up the little girl in her arms. She was so light, too light for her age. "Tabitha? Is that your name? Sit down here and stay with your mother. I'll find us some water."

A merchant was setting up his tent for the day in the next block. Marah took a deep breath and approached him. "A cup of water?"

He shooed her away with a wave of his hand like she was a pesky fly. "Filthy beggar! Get away. Go on!"

She looked down at her clothing and touched her face. It was true. She was filthy…and a beggar. She'd been the wife of a priest and a government official, and now was a beggar.

"Please, sir, can you just spare a cup of water?"

The merchant shook his head and waved her away again. She went to the next vendor and the next with the same response. Finally she came to one of the larger shops in the marketplace, but after suffering one rejection after another she simply started to pass by. However, she lingered on the side as a woman swept the stones in front of the booth. Their eyes locked in a glance, and Marah recognized pity in the woman's eyes. She looked away and continued to sweep and then began to straighten their wares on the shelves at the rear of the shop. Rickety carts rolled down the street pulled by small gray donkeys. The clip-clop of their hooves and the clatter of the wheels on the stones filled the morning air.

Marah turned to leave, but something halted her. She had detected compassion in the woman's eyes. At least she didn't chase Marah away. Clutching her headdress underneath her chin, she decided to approach the shopkeeper. But as she turned, the woman retreated into the large living quarters built on to the back of the shop. A man emerged and came into the street. He looked both ways and then spotted Marah. He walked directly toward her.

"What is it you want? I'm told you were loitering beside our shop."

"Please, sir. I simply want a cup of water." Marah held out her cup. Her hand was shaking. "A woman down the way is ill and needs water."

"Wait here." The man spun on his heel and went to the back of his shop. He came back with a basket holding two flasks—one of water and one of wine, a loaf of bread, and some dates and figs.

"Thank you, sir. You are very kind. Thank you."

He stared. "Don't I know you? You look very familiar to me."

A warm flush spread from her belly up to her cheeks. She pulled her veil over her face and shook her head, then turned and rushed out of the booth. As the gentleman spoke to her she recognized him as one of the men Nabal had done business with—a man as wealthy as Nabal, well respected in the village. She should have recognized the shop. Humiliated, she hurried back to Tabitha and her mother.

Marah lifted the woman's head and urged her to drink. Her headpiece fell around her shoulders, revealing a head full of lice and sores. The woman managed a few gulps.

Marah sat on the ground with her and Tabitha and gave a chunk of bread to the child. She gobbled it down and held out her hand for more. Marah gave her another piece and a few dates which she also bolted down.

"Thirsty."

She poured water from the flask into her cup and handed it to her. The little girl finished it straightaway, the water dribbling down her chin. Marah filled the cup about half full again and gave her more. As she was drinking, suddenly the cup flew out of her hands. Marah looked up at a large man holding a switch. Tabitha's chin began to quiver, and her mouth dropped open in a noiseless cry.

He slapped the switch in rhythm into the palm of his hand. "Get out of here! You're trespassing on my property."

Marah turned to face the man. "Please, sir. Can you not tell? This woman is ill. Have mercy."

The man scowled and grumbled. "That's no concern of mine. If I give shelter to one of your kind, then I'd be overcome with beggars. Go outside the city wall with all the others like you. Go!" He raised the switch and brought it down on her back. It sent her to her knees. Stunned to the point she couldn't react, she shielded her face from the switch as he brought it down another time. "Now, let this be a warning to you. Leave and don't clutter up my entrance again." He raised the switch again.

"No, no. We are leaving. Please…please. Give us just a minute." Marah turned to help Tabitha's mother to her feet. "Can you walk?"

A barely discernible, "I think so," escaped her

lips. Marah picked up her bundle with one hand and managed to get the woman's arm around her shoulders. She leaned her bony frame against Marah's. How long had it been since the woman had eaten a meal—or cleaned herself? She clenched her teeth together to keep from gagging at the stench.

"We need to get you away from here."

Tabitha hung on to her mother's robe, whimpering.

"Tabitha, you too. Can you help—carry my bag?"

The girl nodded and took the bag, trying to lift it onto her shoulder, but ended up simply dragging it on the ground. The woman shuffled alongside Marah, doing her best to walk.

"Not…not much farther." Marah struggled to catch her breath. The gates of the village lay just ahead. "What's your name?"

"Ra…a…chel." Her name exhaled in a puff of foul air.

The city elders gathered at the gate in their daily clusters of complaints and judgments. Marah spotted Nabal off to the side, but his back was turned, and he didn't see them. Two beggars and a dirty little girl who staggered past them that morning barely caused a glance from a one of them.

A congregation of miserable beggars languished in a shallow ravine outside the city wall. Marah found a rock against which she could lean Rachel and eased her onto the ground as gently as she could. Tabitha dropped the bag at her feet, sat down against her mother and stuck her thumb in her mouth.

Rachel raised a frail hand and pushed her veil away from her forehead. "Thank you. You are very kind."

Marah shook her head. "Not at all. I couldn't leave you there to be abused by that horrible man." She sat down beside her, dug in her bag, and gave her a piece of bread. The woman nibbled on it and took the wine Marah offered her. "Rachel, why are you on the street? And this precious child…how…?" The words would not come. To speak the misery she saw in this woman seemed simply to heap further humiliation on her.

Tears gathered in the woman's eyes.

"I'm sorry." Marah sighed and tried to wipe the dust from her own clothing. "I guess I'm in the same position, aren't I?"

Tears spilled down onto Rachel's cheeks and wet the face that was probably a very attractive one in her younger years. But now missing teeth and wrinkled skin gave her the look of an old woman. "My husband died, and we were poor. We had no family to take us in. What were we to do, where were we to go? A woman alone? I had no option but to beg…or sell myself." She looked down. "I never thought I would… do…do that." She leaned back against the rock as if that little bit of conversation had exhausted her. Her forehead creased into a frown, and she began to moan and rock back and forth. "When your child is crying because her belly is empty and bloated, and then she becomes silent because she doesn't have the strength to cry, a mother will do anything." Rachel put her head down and covered her face with her hands. "I'm so ashamed…so ashamed. A mother will…do… anything." She paused. "I…I managed to feed us until I got sick. Now, I don't know what I'm going to do."

"You'll get better. I'll help you."

"I don't mean to be unkind, but how can you help?" Rachel stared at her with eyes weary from illness and seeing the cruel side of life. "It doesn't appear you are much better off than I, except you're not sick—yet."

"I…I don't know. I'll figure something out." Marah had no plan. She didn't know what she could do— for either of them. But she had to do something. God wouldn't just let them die, simply because they were alone? Would he?

Marah carefully unfolded the soft fabric wrapped around the coin headdress. She glanced about at the beggars and downtrodden, sleeping wherever they had found a flat spot to lay their vermin-infested heads, whether it be a rock or a mound of sand. The sun barely peeked over the horizon, and no one seemed to be stirring yet. Lifting the treasured piece as the coins glinted in the gentle sunlight, she smiled through her tears at the faint jangle that always brought memories of her David flooding through her mind.

Eight...nine...ten. All ten of the coins were still attached to the new band she had to make after Simon's tirade.

It would look fine with a coin missing, wouldn't it? With an uneven number she could center one coin in the middle of her forehead with four on either side. And David would understand. I am alone. I have to do something. But when Marah wore the headdress, she didn't feel so alone. She could feel David's presence beside her. She tugged on one of the coins and pulled it loose. Then she brushed her hair, put the headdress on, and pulled her veil over her head. Tiptoeing around sleeping bodies, she made her way to the small stream that ran alongside the city wall and washed her face.

She returned and found Tabitha sitting up, rubbing her eyes. Rachel yawned, stretched, and smiled up at her. "You are awake early." She wrapped her blanket around Tabitha and pulled the child to her. She shivered. "The nights are turning cool."

Marah nodded. "How are you feeling?"

"Better, I think." She scratched her scalp, and her cheeks flushed. "The lice are still troublesome, but it's not as bad."

Marah was embarrassed for her. "Don't be concerned, dear. I'll try to get more vinegar today. If only we had a nit comb." She picked up the wine flask from the flat rock they had commandeered as a table and poured the last of it in their one cup.

She left Rachel and Tabitha and slipped through the city gates carrying the now-empty basket the kind man had filled previously with bread and fruit and hurried to his stall. Several weeks had passed since that day. Marah had been avoiding going back for fear he would recognize her again and remember who she was, but her options were exhausted. She had begged from every other vendor in the market and none of them had been as compassionate as he. She needed to find food. In addition, cold weather was on its way, and she didn't know what to do about shelter.

The early shoppers turned their backs on her as she made her way through the growing crowds. The mordant whispers, spoken too loudly, scorched her ears, but she acted as if she did not hear them. She ducked her head, brushed the unwelcome tears away, and skirted through the early morning shadows of the shops. Occasionally she would see Nabal in the marketplace. Once she thought perhaps he caught her eye, but he acted as if he did not recognize her.

The man who had given them food previously was arranging fruit and vegetables this morning instead of the woman. As the sign above his store indicated, Marah supposed his name was Dan. She waited until he went inside before she started toward the produce.

She began stuffing melons, eggplant, and cucumbers into the basket.

A hand clenched her arm and turned her around. "This is how you repay my kindness?" Dan searched her eyes as the question died on his lips. He was not what one would necessarily call handsome, but his eyes were mesmerizing—hazel, greenish hazel. He had a rather large nose and a sharp jawline. His black hair was curly, and he wore a headband around his forehead to keep it out of his eyes. A dark beard with sprinkles of gray curled around a sensitive mouth. He tilted his head, shook his head, and let go of her arm.

"No…no. I can pay you." She reached in her pocket and pulled out the coin. "See, here. I have money."

He took the coin and bit down on it. He smiled at her, and his eyes crinkled shut. It was a nice smile. "It is indeed authentic, but I'm not sure it's negotiable."

"Oh, please, sir. It's all I have, and we need food."

"We?"

"The woman I told you about the last time I came here—and her little girl. She's recovering—slowly. But we need supplies."

"Is she a relative?"

She shook her head. "No. She simply was alone and needed someone. And I was alone as well. I suppose you could say we found each other."

He pointed to her headdress. "That coin wouldn't have come off of your headdress, would it?"

Marah ignored his question and turned away.

"Take what you need. I'll accept your coin as payment. Do you need a blanket or anything else— pots, pans, eating utensils?" He put his hands on his hips. "By the way, I figured out where I have seen you. You were Nabal's second wife, weren't you? And he put you away?" He paused. "The town gossips are all too eager to fill one in on the details."

"I'm sure." Marah busied herself filling the basket.

"Do you have any hard vinegar?"

"For your drinking water?" He looked at her veil that had slipped back on her head. "Or lice?"

"Both." She pulled the veil back over her hair. "I'm fine, but Rachel and Tabitha both had lice from the deplorable conditions they'd been living in. We are attending to that."

"Which? Your living conditions or the lice?"

"The lice." She looked at the shelves in the interior portion of the store. "Could I please purchase a nit comb, sir?"

He grumbled. "Humph!" He turned and muttered something as he reached into a box and brought out the comb.

"Excuse me, sir?"

"Dan, my name is Dan."

"I know."

"You know?"

She pointed to the sign above the store.

He grinned again. "And yours?"

"My name is Marah."

"A severe name for such a lovely woman." His face grew solemn. "Do you have shelter, a place to stay?"

"I need to go. Thank you, kind sir."

He arched his eyebrows and smiled again.

"Uh…Dan, sir."

"You didn't answer my question. Do you have a place to stay?"

"We will manage."

He pointed toward the stairs on the outside of the building. "I have an extra room on the roof. You are welcome to it. Cold weather will be here in a few weeks. You cannot survive sleeping outside."

"What about your wife?"

"My wife?" He chuckled. "Oh, you mean Priscilla. She is my sister. I am a widower. My wife died the first year of our marriage, and I've never remarried."

Her heart pounded. She wanted nothing more to do with any man—ever again. And an offer of free lodging carried a suggestion of being beholden to this man. She shook her head. "Thank you for your kind offer, but we will find something."

Dan shook his head. "Very well. Do as you like."

Marah gathered her goods together. "Again, I thank you for your kindness and all the supplies."

"It's not kindness." He held up the coin. "You paid for the goods this time."

Marah worried about Tabitha as the nights grew cooler. Her hands and cheeks stayed red and chapped. And Rachel was so frail she trembled like a leaf.

Each day's dawn brought the uncertainty of how the trio would survive. As she opened her eyes every morning, she was disappointed that she hadn't died during the night. Stumbling through day after day with barely enough to eat to stay alive was no way to live. The sight of Tabitha holding her tiny hand up for a coin to gruff men who brushed her aside like she was a pesky fly broke Marah's heart. They found little compassion on the streets with the exception of Dan and his sister. Perhaps everyone is insensitive to the poor until one finds oneself in that very position. Have I ever been the insensitive one who hurried by a hungry little girl begging a coin? She vowed never to do so again as long as she lived.

As the days crawled by, she pulled one coin after another off the headdress for food until they were all gone. What were they going to do now? They were running out of options. I could return home to Matthew and Benjamin and my family. I know they would take me back. I would be warm and loved, and no longer hungry. They would take Rachel and

Tabitha in too, she knew they would. Nabal said he would send her to them—with an escort even. But she couldn't go to him now, after having been on the streets—begging. And she couldn't admit to her family the depths to which she had descended. She had failed them. They thought she was living the rich life of a government official's wife. I can't face them. I can see the disappointment and hurt in Matthew's eyes now. I cannot bear that. I'll probably have to face that eventually, but not now. Not yet…

She found herself avoiding Dan's store. She didn't want to have to deal with his offer again to occupy their extra room. However, to go around the shop in the middle of Sychar's marketplace was awkward. He watched her as she went from vendor to vendor. She would walk around a corner, and he would be there speaking with a neighbor. His scrutiny made her uncomfortable.

One day as the clouds hung gray and heavy with threatening snow, Dan confronted Marah in the street behind his shop as she tried to circumvent it. She carried Tabitha in her arms and tried to go around him, but he would not let them pass. "Marah, why have you been avoiding me? Why do you work so hard to garner food at the other shops, when I will gladly help you?" He chucked Tabitha under her chin and made her smile.

"I do not wish to presume upon your benevolence." Even at that moment her resolve began to crumble at the insistence of a hungry stomach and a child shivering in her arms from the cold. She looked at him as tears burned in her eyes.

He put his hands on his hips. "Where is your headdress? Have you spent all of your coins?"

She nodded. "I have no more, and, I must admit, we are bereft."

"Release your pride, and let us help you."

Marah looked into the face of this man whose offer to help them defied reason. "Why are you willing to help us?"

"You. I am willing to help you. Your 'friends' would have to make other arrangements." He cleared his throat and looked away.

"Then the answer is no. I won't abandon them."

Dan frowned and searched her eyes. "Why? They are not even family to you."

"They have no one. And neither do I. I cannot…I simply cannot…" A sob erupted, and she could not continue.

Tabitha reached out and brushed Marah's tears with her fingers. "Don't cry."

She set her down and clutched her hand. "Thank you, sir, for your offer, but I must refuse."

He cleared his throat and rolled his eyes. "Dan, the name is Dan." He shifted his weight. "Very well. All of you may come."

She fell to her knees and wept. She grabbed Dan's hand. "Thank you, sir. Thank you."

He blew a sigh through pursed lips. "Dan, the name is Dan."

Shortly after Priscilla moved to the country with their mother and sisters, Marah was cutting up vegetables for a cool supper when Dan walked up behind her. Rachel was cooking fish over the fire in the outside oven. They were alone in the house. He eased close to her, encircled her waist and spoke softly into her ear. A shiver raced down her spine. "Marah, I need to talk to you."

She kept her back to him and ceased peeling the vegetables. "What is it?" Her heart thudded. She had not been able to admit to herself that she had begun to develop an affection for this man who had been so kind to them. And the more she was around him, the more attractive he became to her. She could not look at him.

"Put the knife down and look at me." Dan turned her around to face him. He removed the knife and cucumber from her hand and set them on the table. "We cannot continue to deny what we feel for each other." He brushed her cheek with the back of his fingers. "From the first time I saw you begging in the marketplace, I loved you." He held a package in his hand.

"What is this?"

"Open it."

Marah sat down and untied the twine. She heard the familiar jangle before she saw the headpiece. On a beautiful new braided band hung her treasured coins—the coins she had spent for food. The coins her beloved David had given to her as a wedding gift all those years ago. "How...? How did you get these? Where...?" Then she recalled seeing Dan speaking to the various store owners as she scurried from stall to stall trying to avoid him. She could not contain the tears. She laughed, and she cried. She hugged him, and they laughed together. She counted the coins— nine. One was missing. This wonderful man had bought back all but one coin that she had spent for food. She put it on and adjusted it.

He touched her forehead. "I...I'm sorry. There is one coin missing. I couldn't find the tenth one."

"Oh my sweet, sensitive Dan. No matter. This is such a lovely gesture. I am overwhelmed. I...I don't know what to say." She covered his hand with her own. "The headdress of coins was a wedding gift from my first husband. Somehow I didn't feel so alone as long as I had it."

"You need never be alone again. Say you will

marry me."

She shook her head. She did not answer him immediately. Moments passed. He cleared his throat and shuffled his feet. She touched him on his arm and looked up at him. "I cannot. I will not. I have been married five times—a widow four times and divorced once. I determined never to marry again. I cannot bear children. I am a shame and a disgrace. I will not place that burden on you."

Dan took her face in his hands. "You are the most beautiful woman I have ever known. And your beauty is not only external, but internal as well. You are kind, caring, and compassionate."

"No, I'm not. I'm selfish and bitter and of no good to anyone. I am a disgrace."

"Look at Rachel and Tabitha. They would have died if you had not taken care of them."

"Perhaps, but I still cannot marry you."

Dan bent toward her and lightly touched her lips with his. His kiss made her feel like a young bride again, not like the used-up woman that she was. Her heart pounded wildly, and she felt heat rising to her cheeks. She had not experienced emotions like this since David and she married. She allowed herself be swept away. What difference did it make anymore? This felt good. This felt right. She threw her arms around Dan's neck, dug her fingers into his thick hair, and returned his increasingly insistent kisses.

He pulled her against his body and caressed her shoulders. Groaning, he pushed her away. "Will you? Will you marry me?" His voice was hoarse and raspy with emotion.

She stepped back and shook her head again. "I will not." She locked her gaze with his. "But I will agree to be your concubine if you will take me that way. You deserve a respectable wife, not someone who has already been married five times. Dan, I cannot have children. I am a shunned woman. If we can find a small bit of happiness together this way, I would consent to that, but I will not marry you. If you are willing to listen to the whispers and scorn and…" She turned her back on him, picked up the knife, and returned to slicing the vegetables.

Dan caught hold of her sleeve. "If you will not marry me, I will take you any way I can get you. I will treat you well. You will never regret staying with me."

Dan and Marah were reasonably happy with their arrangement. However, some nights she could not sleep with this good man resting beside her. She felt guilty because of the scathing gossip that followed them wherever they went—the whispers and sidelong glances. Business had even declined. He brushed it off, saying his customers would eventually return. But Marah had her doubts.

What kind of woman am I, that I could do this to him? Live as a concubine? I can never return to see my son now. Not living in sin like this. I have become a harlot, forever rejected by God and men. How could she have done this?

One day, she stared at her reflection in the water of her washbowl and saw a stranger looking back at her. She touched the water with the tip of her finger, disturbing the image. "Who are you? I don't even know who I am anymore."

The troubling thoughts nipped at the heels of her soul constantly, but she shoved them away, not allowing herself to dwell on them. But at night…at night they came out to haunt her, robbing her of sleep and peace of mind. *I want to turn to God, but where is he? And can I even reach out to him now…or am I doomed forever?* She didn't know, and she was afraid to think about it. She wished someone like Ezra were around to sort it out for her.

Rachel's health improved some, but she still was so fragile. Marah was concerned for her. She had very little stamina. Tabitha gained weight and grew taller. They almost felt like a legitimate family. Marah was totally spurned by the other women in the village, all except Rachel, of course. She simply avoided them the best she could and tried to ignore the whispers and gossip. And she made a habit of going to fetch water when the other women were not there.

"I'm going to Jacob's well to fill the water jar. Be back soon."

Dan looked up from his ledger and smiled at her. "Don't be too long. It's hot outside."

"I won't. Just out and back," she said. "There's never anybody else there this time of day."

Chapter 10

"Oh, so you're a prophet?"

The stranger didn't offer his knowledge of all Marah's husbands in an accusatory manner, nor did she detect cruelty in his voice. But he called it accurately. How did he know her history? Who was he?

Perhaps she could change the subject and direct the conversation away from her multiple marriages. "Our ancestors worshiped God at this mountain." She pointed to Gerizim. "But you Jews insist that Jerusalem is the only place for worship, right?"

The man stood and faced her. "Believe me, woman, the time is coming when you Samaritans will worship the Father neither here at this mountain nor there in Jerusalem." He gestured toward Mount Gerizim with his hand. "You worship guessing in the dark; we Jews worship in the clear light of day. God's way of salvation is made available through the Jews. But the time is coming—it has, in fact, come—when what you're called will not matter and where you worship will not matter. It's who you are and the way you live that count before God. Your worship must engage your spirit in the pursuit of truth. That's the kind of people the Father is out looking for—those who are simply and honestly themselves before him in their worship."

The words of this man seared her heart and her spirit. "I'm not proud of my life. I didn't plan to have all these husbands. I've simply struggled to stay alive. I have tried to worship God, but I don't understand how to do that. I get so confused." She sat down on the edge of the well.

He joined her and turned to face her. "God is sheer being itself—Spirit. Those who worship him do so out of their very being, their spirits, their true selves, in adoration."

"I don't know about all of that. I do know that the Messiah is coming. When he arrives, we'll get the whole story. My husband, Ezra, who was a priest, taught me about the coming Messiah. Ever since he told me about him I've looked for him to rescue me from the terrible mess I've made of my life. I really don't think he would care about a soiled woman such as me, would he? Would he waste his time on someone like me? Can you tell me when he will come?"

The stranger paused and deliberately captured her gaze with his. The moment grew long and silent between them. She looked down. Finally words came from his mouth that were so incredibly unbelievable she didn't know if she heard him correctly. Words her people had been waiting to hear for thousands of years, and he was speaking them to her? "I who speak to you am he. You don't have to wait any longer or look any further."

Marah gasped and coughed. She frowned and stared at the stranger as she caught her breath. Did he say what I think I heard him say? Did he just say that he's the Messiah? This rather ordinary-looking man—who has...has told me everything I've ever done. Everything I ever...

"Are you truly he? I...I thought you would come on a white horse."

The stranger threw back his head and laughed. Then he leaned forward and whispered, as if it were their secret, "Not yet."

The man pointed to her coin headdress. "That is a very handsome piece."

She touched the coins, her fingers trembling. "My first husband's wedding gift to me. It's my dearest treasure."

"There's a coin missing."

"Yes, how…how did you know?"

"Have you searched for it?"

"When I was reduced to begging for food I began to sell the coins one by one. A…uh…a friend, unbeknownst to me, followed after me and retrieved them—he found all but one coin."

"You need to know that the heavenly Father has followed you—like your friend followed you and retrieved your treasure. You thought you were alone, but you weren't—you never have been. Someone was watching out for you. Your heavenly Father loves you and treasures you just as you have treasured the headdress. The coin will be found—and you will be found."

Marah swiveled around at the sound of footsteps. The young man with the stranger arose and greeted the group who approached with baskets of food. She recognized the expressions on their faces, which reflected their disdain. They obviously were shocked and disapproved of their friend carrying on a conversation with a woman, and a Samaritan woman at that.

Marah took the hint and left. In fact, she was eager to return home and tell Dan and Rachel about her encounter with this man. The Messiah. *Did I just have a conversation with the Messiah?*

She hurried from the well, confirmation growing with each step she took that the stranger was who he said he was. She looked back at the man. He raised his hand in a farewell wave and a nod of his head. Marah gathered her robe around her and started to run. Her heart banged against her chest as she gasped for breath. *My heavenly Father loves me. He treasures me. A fallen woman like me.* She stopped to catch her breath and smiled at the jangle of the coins on her headdress. *The Messiah has come, and he told me that the heavenly Father has followed me throughout my life. I've never really been alone.* She started to run again. Never had the trip from the well seemed this long. *No, he did not look like what she thought the Messiah would look like, nor did he come like she thought he would come.* She chuckled to herself. *How silly and juvenile of me to think that the Messiah would come on a white horse.*

By the time Marah approached the city gate, the heat of midday had passed. The slanted, late-afternoon rays of the sun offered a bit of relief, and people began to come out of their residences to resume the business of the day. But it was still warm, and perspiration trickled down her forehead. She had forgotten her water pot at the well, but she was not going to return and retrieve it until she talked to Dan. She must take him out to meet this amazing man before darkness fell.

The elders sat in their usual official places around the gate pontificating. Nabal was seated with three other officials to her right. Her first thought was to rush past them as she usually did and ignore their haughty expressions, but her encounter with the stranger had filled her with a new confidence. Breathless, she stopped in front of the group with whom Nabal was conversing. He looked up at her, his eyes flashing a warning.

"I...I would have a word with you, Nabal." Speaking to a woman in public was forbidden, but if the Messiah could speak to her, certainly she could address her ex-husband. He rose and ushered her away from the hearing of his colleagues.

"What is the meaning of this?" His tone was clipped and curt.

"I encountered a stranger out at Jacob's well today I thought you might be interested to meet."

"Why would I be interested in meeting a man you were conversing with in public? You harlot!" His words slithered out through clenched teeth, oozing with contempt.

"Because he claims to be the Messiah. You and your fellows might want to interrogate him."

"You fool. Why would the Messiah reveal himself to a woman? The Messiah would not break the law."

"Perhaps, but you need to know that he knew everything about my past."

"Everything?" Nabal cleared his throat and rubbed the back of his neck.

She nodded, enjoying his discomfort.

"He knew about us, our marriage and divorce?"

"He did."

He shifted his weight. "Humph. I'll discuss it with the elders."

"I thought you might like to do that. I feel like a new person since meeting him. He told me…" She hesitated, not wanting to further antagonize Nabal.

"What? What else did he tell you?"

Marah straightened her headdress. "Nothing about you. He just spoke on the issue of worshiping in Jerusalem or Mount Gerizim."

"What did he tell you about that?"

"Go see for yourself. He has a group of followers with him." She turned on her heel. "I need to get home." She left her ex-husband fuming and sputtering.

Marah couldn't wait to tell Dan and Rachel about the stranger. The stranger. She hadn't even ask his name. A multitude of questions flooded through her mind. Where was he from? If he knew everything about her, did he plan their meeting? Of all people, why would he seek her out? Would people believe her? She wanted to know more about him and from him. Perhaps they could invite him to stay with them for a few days.

Marah ran into the shop where Dan stood in front of a vegetable bin assisting a customer. She motioned to him to come into the house. "One moment, please." He excused himself and paused in the doorway. "What is it? Is something wrong? You seem agitated." He looked around. "Did you get water? Where's your water jar?"

"I left it at the well. Come with me. We…we have to go back. I met a stranger…" Her words came in short spurts. She paused to catch her breath.

"Calm down, my dear. Let me take care of this, and I'll go with you." He completed his transaction, and they left Rachel with the shop and took Tabitha with them.

Marah filled Dan in as they half-walked, half-ran back out to Jacob's well. Tabitha ran alongside but could not keep up, so Dan lifted her in his arms. By the time they got to the well, a crowd had gathered around the stranger, and he was talking about reaping the harvest, a harvest of souls. He spotted her and motioned them to come to him. The three moved through the crowd. The stares and whispers of "slut" and "harlot" didn't faze Marah this time as the crowd parted for them to come through. He smiled and pointed to her water pot beside him. "You forgot your water jar."

"I did indeed." She picked up the jar and grinned. "I must have been distracted." She motioned to Dan. "This is Dan and Tabitha."

"Marah told me about you. I am pleased you took the time to come out to meet me."

"The pleasure is mine." Dan acknowledged the man with a slight nod of his head.

Tabitha held out her arms, and the stranger took her and tossed her into the air. She squealed. "Do it again!" He laughed and hugged her. "Do you know what your name means?"

She shook her head.

"It means 'beauty.' You are beautiful, a precious treasure."

Marah cringed and hoped he would not call attention to her name. He didn't, but the way he looked at her, she knew he was aware of her uneasiness.

"Sir, speaking of names, I realized when I got home that I didn't ask you for yours. You revealed to me who you are, but I don't even know your name—or where you are from."

A smile seemed to always be ready to spread across his face. "That's true. My name is Jesus, son of Joseph, and I am from Galilee."

The people pressed around them straining to hear the nuggets of truth that seemed to so easily flow from his lips. Nabal was uncharacteristically silent. Simply listening. The sun began to dip beneath the horizon. But the people did not want to leave.

Marah stood on tiptoe to whisper in Dan's ear. "Could we invite Jesus and his disciples to stay with us? We have ample room. It's warm—they can sleep on the roof."

"Of course. If he would agree to. It's not every day we get to host the Messiah in our home." He smiled at her. "Shall I ask him, or would you like to?"

"You ask him, Dan. It's your house."

"It's our home."

"I know, but…"

"I will ask him."

Dan shouldered his way back through the crowd to where Jesus stood. "It's getting late, and we would be honored to invite you and your disciples to spend the night in our home."

Jesus turned and put his hand on Dan's shoulder. "The honor would be mine. We happily accept."

Marah took Tabitha and ran ahead to ready the house. She burst through the door almost incoherent in her haste. "Rachel! They are coming to spend the night!"

"Who's spending the night?"

"The Messiah! The Messiah is coming to our house!"

Rachel's response of a wide-eyed gape turned into a mad dash to gather up things lying about and to freshen up. How does one get one's house ready to greet the Messiah? Just the sound of it was ludicrous. They gathered food from the shop. Within the hour Jesus and his followers arrived.

Dan met them at the front of the shop. A crowd followed Jesus, clamoring for his attention. "Sir, we are most honored to have you in our home. Please come in." Dan greeted the men with the customary kiss and proceeded to instruct the servants to wash the guests' feet.

Hearing the men come in, Marah hurried to Rachel, who was bustling from one task to another in preparation for the meal. "Come, Rachel. Come meet Jesus."

Rachel pulled her hand from Marah's and backed up, her eyes wide. "No! Not I. I am not worthy."

"If anyone is not worthy, it is I. He will want to meet you."

"B...but a woman cannot mingle with the company of houseguests—with the men."

"He doesn't care about that. He cares about people—men and women. Come, you'll see." Marah took her wrist and gently tugged her into the room.

Jesus turned and greeted Rachel. He took her hand and simply held it for a moment.

She stepped back and gasped and looked at Marah.

"I—I—something…is different." Her cheeks flushed. Marah stared at Rachel and watched the woman's countenance change before her eyes from gaunt and sallow to healthy, glowing cheeks and bright eyes. She was healed. Healed, in just an instant.

Then he looked between her and Dan, to the house beyond them. She knew in that moment that he saw more about their relationship than he ought… perhaps more than she did. He said nothing about their living arrangement, nothing about their sin.

He didn't have to.

Many lives in the village were changed before Jesus left. As they bid him good-bye, Jesus took her aside. "Marah, you will not understand what I am about to say, but your life will be an encouragement to women for centuries to come. As long as you walk in this life, things will not necessarily be easy, but I will be with you. Trust the words I have spoken. You will be with me in the kingdom." And then he walked out the door and was gone.

Marah's family, her home, and her community were never the same.

Chapter 11

"Marah" fit her no longer. She was not bitter anymore. She was full of joy, so when she and Dan married, she changed her name to Abigail, which meant "joy." It took Dan only a little while to get used to it. He said it settled well on her, although he did call her "Abby" rather than the more formal Abigail. She remembered her mother's words telling her that one day she would understand her name. Did she have a premonition—and would she approve of her choice of a new name?

Although many of the villagers found the same new birth in Jesus, not all did. Nabal was among the nay-sayers. Abigail didn't think she would have ever been able to say it, but now she was grateful that Nabal had divorced her. If he had not, she would not have met Jesus, and her home would not have been transformed. Even the months of living as a beggar served to make her who she had become.

One evening as Dan was closing the store, Rachel came into the house holding something in her hand. She opened her fingers and looked up at Abigail, smiling. "I saw this in Bartholomew's store. Doesn't it belong on your headdress?"

Abigail squealed and hugged Rachel. Both of them jumped up and down like excited little girls. "Ah! The lost coin! Jesus was right. He said we would find it. I thought it was lost forever. Thank you, thank you, thank you!"

Once it was lost and alone, but God knew where it was all the time. It was simply waiting to be found.

Abigail sensed a stirring in her heart to return to her family—her Matthew and her grandchildren, Benjamin and Phoebe, Noah and Asher and their families. She was no longer an embarrassment or disgrace. She was a woman affirmed and set free. She wanted to tell them about Jesus. She wanted them to know Messiah had come.

Dan closed the shop and came in for the evening. Rachel and Tabitha had already gone up to their rooms. She needed to speak to Dan, but a cough that had been plaguing her for weeks interrupted. She poured a cup of wine, stirred some honey and vinegar in it, and took a sip.

"I don't like the sound of that cough. It's lasted far too long." Dan hugged her, and she leaned into his embrace. His arms spelled security. She loved to linger there.

She tucked a curly lock of his hair back into his ever-present headband. "I'm fine. It's getting better, I think."

He released her and sat down. "Hmm. Maybe." He waited for Abigail to speak. She poured him a goblet of wine.

"I would love to be able to serve you some of the fine wine my Matthew produces."

Dan grinned as he lifted the cup to his lips. "Is that what this is about?"

"Excuse me?"

"Did you want to talk to me again about going to see your family?"

She sat down with him and touched his arm. "Yes, Dan, please. I feel an urgency to go home and tell them about Jesus. I want you to meet my Matthew, Benjamin, and Phoebe and the boys. Goodness knows how many children have been added by now.

alone

You know, Matthew and Benjamin did not want me to move here to Sychar. I want them to be assured that I am doing well. I want them to see what good care you give me and how much you love me. I know they have been concerned." She folded her hands on top of the table. "Dan, I want not only to go see my children, I want to move back home."

"I see." He remained silent for a few moments staring into the wine goblet. "I'm not surprised. I've been expecting this. What about my business here?"

"Would Priscilla and her new husband be interested in buying it?"

"I don't know—perhaps." He rotated his cup, swirling the wine. "I must admit that I wouldn't mind getting out from under the constant stress of 'Dan's Fine Foods.' Do you think Matthew would be willing to hire me to help with his wine business?" He lifted his goblet and grinned. "I do know something about fine wines."

"I'm sure he would. I…" A bout of coughing interrupted, and Abigail had trouble catching her breath.

Dan knelt in front of her as she struggled. "This is not getting better. I'm going to call the village physician."

She patted his hand. "I think I'll go lie down for a bit. Will you promise me you will take me to see my family—when I feel better?"

"I promise." Dan helped her to their bed and sat with her while she fell asleep.

She remembered Rachel placing a cool cloth on her forehead. She remembered Dan sitting beside her bed. She remembered the village physician shaking his head and speaking in hushed tones to Dan. Then blackness with flashes of brief consciousness; tossing on her bed in sweat-drenched blankets; chilled and shivering the next time she fought her way to a waking moment.

She dreamed of David and her Matthew when he was a little boy. In one of her dreams David was calling to her from the vineyard fire, and Matthew was a toddler running to her with his arms outstretched. But he never got to her. She called and called to him as he faded into the mist. Abigail dreamed of sitting with Jesus at the well, then the vision ebbed and flowed into one of Jesus riding toward her on a white horse. He rode to her bedside and dismounted. He bent over where she lay on her bed and placed his hand on her head. She took it and pressed it against her cheek.

The fever left. "You did come on your white horse. You came." Then he mounted the magnificent steed and rode away. As he rose into the clouds he held a sword in his hand and pointed toward the earth where Matthew stood with his family, with Benjamin and Phoebe, Noah and Asher.

Abigail opened her eyes and looked at Dan asleep in the chair next to her. She could not tell what time it was. She looked out the window. It seemed to be early morning. Had she slept all night? She sat up and swung her legs around. "Dan?"

He stirred and opened his eyes. "Abby! My dear, you are awake." He grabbed her hand and kissed it over and over. He moved onto the bed, gathered her in his arms, and rocked her back and forth. "I was so scared. I thought I had lost you." He brushed her hair away from her eyes and kissed her cheeks, her eyes, her nose, her mouth.

"My goodness. What a greeting!" Abigail looked around. "I am really thirsty. Did I sleep all night? What time is it?"

"My sweet Abby. It is dawn of the third day since I put you to bed. You have been in and out of consciousness for three days."

She lay back on her pillows. "I…I don't remember anything except being hot, then cold. And the physician being here."

"He did not believe you would make it."

"What…what was wrong with me?"

"Some kind of fever."

She stood up, her legs wobbling beneath her. Dan took hold of her arm and steadied her. "Take it easy. You are quite weak."

She sat back down on the bed. "We need to get ready to go home."

"We will, but you need to gain your strength first." Dan handed her a cup of water. She gulped it down.

"That tastes so good. It's sweet."

"It has honey in it. It will give you energy."

"Dan, Jesus showed me that we are to take his message home to Matthew. We must go." She slumped back onto the pillow and closed her eyes.

"We will, Abby, dear. We will." Dan took her hand. "I promise."

Dan steered the donkey around Jacob's well. What a pivotal piece of property in their lives. If Marah—or Abigail—had not come out to draw water at precisely that particular time to avoid the gossiping women of the village on that particular day, she would have missed him. But then Jesus knew that, didn't he? He had to have planned it exactly as it happened. Thoughts that occupied him during the long journey through Samaria.

Approaching the vineyards and the road that led to Matthew's compound, Dan stared at the expansiveness of the operation. He'd had no idea how large the family business was. And to think Abigail was a beggar when he met her.

A young man emerged from the archway of the large courtyard and hurried toward him holding his arms open. "You must be Dan."

"And you are Matthew. I see your mother's smile."

The two men embraced as women and children surrounded them. Another man who looked like Abigail, but older than Matthew, approached. "And you have to be Benjamin."

The man nodded and embraced Dan as well.

"I am overwhelmed at last to meet Abby's—uh, Marah's—family. You know, she changed her name after she met the Messiah."

Matthew spoke up. "She never liked her name. I'm glad she changed it." He looked at the extra donkey Dan had with him. "May I help you with your things?"

"Yes, of course."

Matthew and Benjamin started unloading Dan's saddlebags, amid introductions to Phoebe, Noah and Asher, and a multitude of children running and squealing.

"You have quite a family." Dan pointed to a heavy tapestry bag. "Pass that one to me, please." Matthew pulled it off Dan's donkey and handed it to him. Dan set it on the ground and opened it. "I have gifts for everyone, but this one is extra special. It was your mother's wish that I bring this to you."

Matthew took the package from Dan and opened it carefully. The soft jangle of coins greeted him, and he shook his head as he held it up and fought tears.

Dan placed his hand on Matthew's shoulder. "She instructed me to tell you that the headdress which was your father's wedding gift to her was to be given to your wife and then handed down to your son's wife in the future. To her it represented everything that was good, beautiful, and lovely in her life." A tear trickled down the side of Dan's cheek into his beard. "She wanted you to have it and to rejoice every time you hear it jangle that her life did not end unhappily." Dan looked toward the vineyard that burst with so much life. "Her last wish was to come home…and… tell you about her encounter with the Messiah… and…"

Dan paused and swallowed before he went on. "I promised her I would complete her journey. She wanted you to know that she did not leave this earth alone. In her last moments as I sat by her bedside, she raised her hand as if she were greeting someone. 'He's come for me,' she said. Then she closed her eyes and was gone. Her Messiah had come for her—and I choose to believe he came on a white horse."

DISCUSSION QUESTIONS

1. A victim of her culture and expectations—and perhaps a poor choice here and there—Marah found herself in marriage after marriage. Do you think she was a weak woman or a strong woman? Explain your answer.

2. I'm sure you had heard many sermons on the woman at the well, as had I, but there was never much information about her, her background, who she was—only that she was a Samaritan. Have you ever wondered why Jesus chose to reveal Himself as the Messiah to her when a Jew was not supposed to have any contact with a Samaritan and a Jewish man certainly would not ever speak to a Samaritan woman? Did it have more to do with who Jesus was or who the woman was?

3. Would you have chosen her to spread such an important revelation as this? Why do you think He chose her?

4. I was intrigued with the fact that the people of the village even listened to her. Why do you think they sought Jesus out after hearing her testimony?

5. Do you think she probably married the man she was living with after meeting Jesus, as Marah did? Shouldn't an encounter with Jesus change the way we live?

6.   Marah was embarrassed to let her family know what a mess she had made of her life. Secrets greatly hinder relationships. What about you? Are there any secrets that need to be revealed, perhaps with the help of a counselor or pastor, to your spouse or family? The Scripture tells us: "Therefore confess your sins to one another, and pray for one another *that you may be healed.*" (James 5:16). There is a sense in which the healing comes as we confess. An encounter with Jesus enables us to be transparent in our relationships and seek reconciliation.

7.   Marah felt isolated and alone her whole life until she met Jesus. All of us have an empty void inside of us until we allow Jesus to fill it with his Spirit. The invitation is always open, and Jesus waits for you. He offers living water to your parched soul. I pray you, like the woman at the well, will find refreshing and new hope for your life in Jesus.

Don't miss the other titles in the
Hidden Faces Series

Trapped: The Adulterous Woman
Available now!

*Broken: The Woman Who Anointed
Jesus's Feet*

*Hopeless: The Woman with the Issue
of Blood*

And the compilation
of all 4 novellas
*Hidden Faces: Portraits of Namelss
Women in the Gospels*

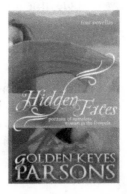

If you enjoyed *Trapped*, you may also enjoy these other titles from WhiteFire Publishing.

Shadowed in Silk
by Christine Lindsay

She was invisible to those who should have loved her.

Dance of the Dandelion
by Dina L. Sleiman

Love's quest leads her the world over.

Jewel of Persia
by Roseanna M. White

How can she love the king of kings without forsaking her Lord of lord?

A Stray Drop of Blood
by Roseanna M. White

One little drop to soil her garment.
One little drop to cleanse her soul.

Walks Alone
by Sandi Rog

A Cheyenne warrior bent on vengeance.
A pioneer woman bent on fulfilling a dream.
UNTIL THEIR PATHS COLLIDE.